# The New
# Corporate Cultures

# The New Corporate Cultures

*Revitalizing the Workplace
After Downsizing, Mergers,
and Reengineering*

Terrence E. Deal and
Allan A. Kennedy

PERSEUS PUBLISHING
*Cambridge, Massachusetts*

Many of the designations used by manufacturers and sellers to distinguish their products are claimed as trademarks. Where those designations appear in this book and Perseus Publishing was aware of a trademark claim, the designations have been printed in initial capital letters.

A CIP record for this book is available from the Library of Congress

Copyright © 1999 by Terrence E. Deal and Allan A. Kennedy

Perseus Publishing is a member of the Perseus Books Group
Text design by Heather Hutchison
Set in 11-point Sabon

  2 3 4 5 6 7 8 9 10–02
First paperback printing, October 2000

Perseus Publishing titles are available at special discounts for bulk purchases in the U.S. by corporations, institutions, and other organizations. For more information, please contact the Special Markets Department at HarperCollins Publishers, 10 East 53rd Street, New York, NY 10022, or call 212–207–7528.

Find us on the World Wide Web at
http://www.perseuspublishing.com

# Contents

# Acknowledgments

We are grateful to a number of people for their help in writing this book. First and foremost, our gratitude must be extended to John Kotter, James Heskett, James Collins, and Jerry Porras, who believed enough in the ideas we expressed in 1982 to undertake major projects that have added immeasurably to our and everyone's understanding of the importance of corporate cultures. We are indebted to their additions to the literature.

Many others helped us in the preparation of this book. They include the incomparable Homa Aminmadani, Terry's indefatigable associate, without whose initiative this book would not have been written. Intrepid researchers Brian Jensen and Chris Kane put up with a lot to help us support our arguments. Michael Kennedy, a renowned scholar of culture in his own right, offered invaluable editorial comments. Ken Kalb, Dennis Powers, Suki Mudan, and Parker Llewellyn all made useful suggestions, as did our editor at Perseus, Nick Philipson. Sandy Deal and Alison Kennedy were pillars of support and inside critics who contributed immensely to the effort.

We have also benefited enormously from the writings of other observers of the business scene, whose efforts are annotated in the text. Any errors or misinterpretations are the fault of the authors alone.

*Terry Deal*
*Allan Kennedy*
December 1998

# Introduction

In 1982 we published *Corporate Cultures: The Rites and Rituals of Corporate Life*. We were motivated to write the book because of a nagging feeling that something was missing in our ability to understand organizations. The missing link was obviously very subtle—but also extremely powerful. Along with other pioneers, we ventured an idea about what lay underneath the rational-technical veneer of business. We tagged the phantom force "corporate culture."

The launching of our book, and others with a similar theme, produced a firestorm of controversy. Some reviewers thought we had put our fingers on something important. Others thought we had trashed the fields of both management and anthropology. Some business leaders offered kudos for providing a language that allowed them access to the deeper inner workings of their enterprise. Others scoffed at the ideas, predicting corporate culture would be the hula hoop of the 1980s.

It is now nearly the beginning of a new millennium, and "corporate culture" has become a widely accepted term in mainstream business. Many executives pay as much attention to culture as strategy in shaping a business plan. Some mergers are shunned because of cultural differences; others proceed because the cultures of the merging partners line up. The symbolic side of leadership has been given special attention by, among others, Edgar Schein of MIT, author of *Organizational Culture and Leadership,* who offered the bold insight, "There is a possibility, under-emphasized in leadership research, that the only thing of real importance that leaders do is to create and manage culture and that the unique talent of leaders is to work with culture." Other books, most notably, John Kotter and James Heskett's *Corporate Culture and Performance* and James Collins and Jerry Porras's

*Built to Last,* offered solid quantitative evidence to demonstrate that companies with strong cultures outperform run-of-the-mill companies by a massive margin. Corporate culture has come of age in the fifteen years since we wrote our original book.

## What's Happened to Corporate Cultures Since 1982?

With all the hoopla and attention corporate culture has received, it would follow that business cultures would have become even stronger and more cohesive since our first book was written. Unfortunately, nothing could be further from the truth. Because of events in intervening years, corporate cultures have come under assault across the board. Some developments, such as the increasing sophistication and use of computer technology, have been inevitable. Others, like the widespread adoption of shareholder value as the driving ethic of business, have emerged to cast a pall on robust corporate cultures everywhere.

Some of the most destructive trends have been imposed by management as it strove to come to grips with the new ethic of shareholder value. Downsizing has cut the core out of many companies. Outsourcing has helped companies focus on core capabilities often at the expense of internal cultural cohesion. Mergers have thrown diverse groups of strangers together with little or no thought for how well they will relate one to another. The list goes on.

Proponents would argue that these changes were essential to recapture the edge needed to survive and thrive in increasingly competitive global markets. Critics of the changes, and we include ourselves in their number, would counter that the often near mindless pursuit of such business tactics has cut the heart out of businesses. In many cases, management actions have destroyed the social fabric of life at work for employees. The truth probably lies somewhere between these optimistic and pessimistic extremes.

In this, our new book, we plan to chronicle changes that have occurred—where they came from, why they happened, and their effect on business cultures. We also offer suggestions for how corporations can be revitalized in the wake of the grueling assaults since the early 1980s. Our hope is that modern managers can use our book to find a balance between the management actions needed to stay competitive and the human needs of workers to belong to meaningful institutions. In our most optimistic moments, we aspire to guide managers on the restoration of work as a mainstay of modern life. In our more pessimistic moments, we hope only to arrest the slide toward corporate anonymity occasioned by thoughtless management actions in pursuit of short-term goals. If we accomplish a bit of both with this book, we will have exceeded our expectations for it.

## Refocusing on the Elements of Culture

The key to effective leadership in corporations is reading and responding to cultural clues. Throughout human history and across national boundaries, culture articulates a distinctive way of life. As recently as 1995, *Fortune* magazine reported the results of its corporate reputation survey. The report highlighted a conclusion we reached in 1982: "There is growing concern that companies cannot live by numbers alone. The one thing that set the top-ranking companies in the survey apart is their robust cultures." A robust culture in a cohesive enterprise is committed to a deep and abiding shared purpose. Its robustness is highly dependent on a unifying cultural tapestry woven over time as people cooperate and learn together. It is woven from the interplay of a set of interlocking cultural elements: History yields values. Values create focus and shape behavior. Heroic figures exemplify core values and beliefs. Ritual and ceremony dramatize values and summon the collective spirit. Stories broadcast heroic exploits, reinforce core values, and provide delightful material for company events. We described such a framework in our 1982 book and briefly review it again as background for our new book on what has happened to culture in the intervening years. In the words of Lee Walton, a former managing director of the consulting firm McKinsey & Company, culture is what "keeps the herd [of employees] moving roughly west."

## History: The Power of Corporate Roots

Today's companies are obsessed with short-term performance. Because of this near singular focus on the present, companies often neglect where they've come from as a way of understanding better where they are and where they're going. Collins and Porras's book *Built to Last* points out that corporate visions are rooted in the lessons of the past:

How could we possibly understand Merck today without examining the origins of its underlying philosophy laid down by George Merck in the 1920's? ("Medicine is for the patient, not for the profits. The profits follow.") How could we possibly understand General Electric under the stewardship of Jack Welch without examining GE's systematic leadership and development processes that trace back to the early 1900's? How could we possibly understand Johnson & Johnson's response to the Tylenol poisoning crisis without examining the historical roots of the J & J Credo (penned in 1943) that guided the company's response to the crisis?

Good companies go to great efforts to make sure that new arrivals learn their historical roots. They understand that it is from history that the symbolic glue congeals to hold a group of people together and bond them to their shared mythology and enabling purpose. Disney's "Traditions Program" is required of all new employees; Arthur Andersen's cultural orientation program is held at St. Charles (where a corporate museum captures the early history of the firm); the Hershey Corporation issues new arrivals a book about its founding years. These are representative of the various ways that companies try to convey their past to new recruits and reinforce their cultural roots for seasoned veterans.

A shared narrative of the past lays the foundation for culture. Too often today's companies casually cast aside their historical roots in favor of what is in vogue. In doing so, they often forsake the core values and beliefs that have contributed to their success. They become rootless, sterile enterprises stalking whatever fashionable economic opportunity comes along. How do we balance the tradition that keeps us anchored and the innovation that keeps us current? That is one of the many dilemmas today's corporate leaders wrestle with. The trick is to maintain core values while altering peripheral practices to deal with contemporary issues.

## Values and Beliefs: The Bedrock of Culture

Beliefs and values form the bedrock of a company's cultural identity. Beliefs are shared convictions, widely accepted notions, of what's important. Values are what we stand for as a group, what we're all about, what we rally around even when things get tough. Johnson

& Johnson's aforementioned reaction to the Tylenol crisis (when it ordered a massive and expensive product recall in response to the discovery of bottles on retailer shelves that had been injected with poison) was a direct result of its credo: "We believe that our first responsibility is to the doctors, nurses, hospitals, mothers, and all others who use our products."

The link between values, beliefs, and profitability has spawned a deluge of recent efforts to create a vision or mission statement. Although the intentions are almost always meritorious, the results often fall well short of expectations. These statements of purpose are typically wordy, flowery, and posted conspicuously. The problem is that they tend to hang on the wall rather than being lodged in the minds and hearts of employees. In a recent interview with the vice president of a large bank, we asked, "What does this place stand for?" His answer: "It's all in the mission statement." In response to our next query, "What does it say?" he fell silent for a minute, grimaced, and then admitted, "I can't tell you, and I helped write it."

How well do the words and deeds of today's corporations match up? Many laudable value commitments have fallen victim to an emphasis on short-term results and shareholder return. There are, of course, notable exceptions. Minnesota's adhesive manufacturer H. B. Fuller is widely recognized as a highly ethical enterprise. Some years ago, TV's *60 Minutes* aired a highly critical program condemning the company. It presented evidence that one of the company's products was being used extensively by children in Central America to get high. Although product distribution was well outside its control, H. B. Fuller launched an extensive R&D effort to produce an adhesive without hallucinatory properties. Last year, with millions invested, its efforts paid off. How many companies today would stand so solidly behind their values?

## Ritual and Ceremony: Culture in Action

However important, values and beliefs remain intangible and often difficult to pin down. When anthropologists study primitive cultures, they look at repetitious activity—which they call ritual—for clues about the group's beliefs and values. They study ceremonial occasions to find out what a group deems worthy of celebrating. In our modern world, routine activities (ritual) and special celebrations (ceremony) also tell us a lot about how people in groups think and what they value.

Think about how large a portion of our personal lives is devoted to ritual and ceremony. We have our personal rituals: the morning cup of coffee, shaving or putting on makeup, walking the dog in the evening. These are more than habits because they give us time to reflect. When we engage in rituals with others, it's time for mutual reflection and connections: handshakes or hugs as greeting or parting rituals, the chat around the coffeepot or watercooler, lunch breaks at noon, happy hour after work. Rituals are bonding times; they build ties that hold people together—even when times are tough.

Work rituals have important functions. The cockpit checklist is a ritual that ensures that pilots don't overlook a detail that would jeopardize a safe flight. Going through your e-mail before starting the day ensures that you will not overlook a message that commands a prompt response. Making a "to do" list before leaving work helps you shape the next day's agenda when things are fresh in your mind. But work rituals have a deeper symbolic meaning as well. Just below the surface, they are physical enactments of important values. In acting out a ritual, we reinforce intangibles that are difficult to convey in spoken language. In ritual, behavior speaks and helps us feel and connect with things below the conscious level. It helps groups to prepare themselves for cultural duties.

Although rituals are a regular part of everyday life, ceremonies offer periodic opportunities to celebrate who we are, recognize key events, and help mark the passage of time. Most companies—good ones at least—convene periodic recognition ceremonies to honor employees and gather people together at seasonal festivities such as the company picnic or holiday party. Like rituals, these events have a symbolic subtext. They provide opportunities for connections, memories, and learning that the regular workday cannot always provide.

But ceremonial occasions cost money and in the face of cost cutting and downsizing can be seen as frivolous—the first things to go. As a result, the bonding and energy that authentic ritual and ceremony provide are lost. People become isolated in their individual cubicles or group silos with little collective glue to hold things together. Technology offers e-mail as an alternative communication tool. Although it works to accelerate the flow of information, it cannot provide the intangible benefits of face-to-face encounters. As times get tough and technology gets even more sophisticated, how can companies encourage ritual and ceremony to draw people together under the same corporate tent? How can we achieve a balance between getting on with the task at hand and getting to know our colleagues better?

## Stories: Cultural Oral History

In today's world, television, technology, and rapid pace have undermined storytelling as a vital human activity. Stories carry cultural values and are a part of everyday life. As Richard Stone observes in *The Healing Art of Storytelling,*

> It's our nature to tell stories and to collect them. In fact, it's hard to conceive of life without story. After a hard day compounded by fighting traffic, one of the first things we do is tell our spouse or a friend about everything that happened—how the jerk in the yellow Camaro cut us off, nearly causing an accident, and how our employer just instituted a new policy at work for vacation time so that all the days we've been accumulating for an anticipation are gone. This is not just passing the time of day. It's the mechanism through which we explain our world and come to understand who we are.

What are corporate stories about? Many times they focus on cultural heroes. Stories also exemplify core values. Stories capture dramatic exploits of employees. Stories sometimes focus on mistakes. The magic of stories in creating cultural focus, direction, and cohesion is well known among enlightened managers. It is a prize highly sought by top performing companies. But to a CEO riveted on costs and short-term results, stories don't seem to make much sense. A spreadsheet tells all the tales that need to be told. In such a busy world, how can time be set aside to recount the dramatic episodes that capture the essence of what work is really about? Where are the occasions where we can learn about people and situations that reflect what an enterprise stands for? How can merging companies combine their tribal legends effectively to create a new corporate oral history?

## Heroic Figures

Cultural tales, as illustrated above, highlight the exploits of special people. In doing so, stories elevate individual employees, managers, or bosses to a special symbolic designation in the culture as heroes and heroines. These gallant characters embody cultural values. In their day-to-day comings and goings, they serve as role models or living logos, signaling through their words and deeds the ideals to which a company aspires.

Take Herb Kelleher, CEO of Southwest Airlines. He's an outrageous character who has been known to dress as "the High Priest of Ha-Ha" for the company's Halloween party or to arm wrestle another CEO in a Dallas arena to decide who would have the rights to a disputed marketing slogan. Kelleher's behavior reinforces his oft-repeated words that "fun is not a four-letter word. Fear is." He tells employees publicly that he loves them, reinforcing the company's reputation as "the airline that love built." His caring and compassion is heartfelt and well received by employees.

Not all heroic figures cluster at a company's apex. They are scattered everywhere—across functions, divisions, and stations. Recognizing their contributions offers another opportunity to solidify and reinforce cultural values. Here again Southwest shines as an example of a company that regularly anoints ordinary people who accomplish extraordinary feats. Winning Spirit Awards are given to folks who radiate the Southwest spirit. The Founder Award is given to someone who consistently goes beyond the call of duty. The President's Award is given to individuals who demonstrate Southwest's virtues and values, among others compassion for customers and co-workers, willingness to learn, embracing change, and spreading a sense of humor and fun. A Special Leadership Award is bestowed on someone who exemplifies the principles of the company's mission. Other awards include Community Relations Awards, a Good Neighbor Award, a Sense of Humor Award, and a Positively Outrageous Customer Service Award. A "top wrench" program is used to recognize mechanics, a "top cleaner" program to recognize plane cleaners. Kelleher calls all this "a daily celebration of employees." In conducting these celebrations, the company assures that its everyday cultural icons are highly rewarded and widely recognized.

But how often is someone's cultural value factored into the most recent downsizing decisions? Do executives ever consider what someone means to others in the company before deciding to make him or her redundant? Or do they simply consider the job that people being downsized actually do? Do executives ever consider what others in the company think when someone with years of meritorious service is suddenly let go? The costs of whacking off people others look up to don't show up on a balance sheet. But reducing the head count takes its toll on individual morale and company spirit. It lets people know that everyone is expendable—even those whose daily exploits are a tangible reflection of what the company supposedly stands for.

## The Cultural Network

Ever wonder why nothing remains a secret for long? Or why some individuals seem almost a veritable storehouse of company lore? Although people have an official job, they often are assigned or take on other duties that won't ever appear on their business cards. Welcome to the inner workings of the informal network, a communication hub that almost always outperforms the official channels or the formal chain of command. The informal players include storytellers, priests and priestesses, gossips, whisperers, and spies. People with shared interests may form cabals to advance a shared agenda or plot a common purpose. The real business of a business gets done by the cultural network. In robust cultures, this informal group of players can reinforce the basic beliefs of the organization, enhance the symbolic value of heroic exploits by passing on stories of their deeds and accomplishments, set a new climate for change, and provide a tight structure of influence for the CEO. In toxic cultures, the network becomes a formidable barrier to change.

Storytellers capture a dimension of the workplace that others usually overlook or ignore. They interpret what goes on and package reality to reveal its subtle secrets. The tales storytellers tell, like myths in a tribal setting, give meaning to the workaday world. For the corporation, storytellers maintain cohesion and provide guidelines for people to follow. Storytelling is one of the most powerful ways to convey information and shape behavior. Storytellers preserve institutions and their values by reporting company legends to new employees. They carry stories about heroic figures. Through their tales, storytellers reveal much about what it takes to get ahead. The best storytellers are typically found in positions central to the flow of information and in the epicenter of activity. Storytellers need imagination, insight, a good sense of detail, and a flair for drama. Through their stories they wield a powerful influence on corporate culture.

Priests and priestesses exist as surely in companies as they do in churches or tribes. They are the designated corporate worriers who fret over cultural details. They are the primary guardians of the culture's values. They worry about keeping the flock together and headed in the right direction. They always have time to listen to a confession and always have a response to a moral or ethical dilemma. Most priestly figures are encyclopedias of the company's history. They preside over and protect cultural traditions. The duty they are most often called on to perform is the recitation of historical precedent for planned action. "Back in 1977 . . . ," they say as they interpret the company's beliefs and values. They also come to the aid of people in the event of defeat, frustration, or disaster.

Gossips are the company troubadours. Priests talk in analogues and tell you the scripture. Storytellers put their interpretative spin on key events. But gossips are the prime sources of names, dates, salaries, and other juicy details taking place now. People come to rely on the gossip for the latest stuff—even as they remain wary of the gossip's tongue. Without a steady diet of interesting trivia, life in most companies would be grim—and pretty dull.

Whisperers are the powers behind the throne with ready access to the ears of top management. They are powerful movers and shakers who shape policy and strategy without formal portfolios. Their source of power is the boss's ear. Anyone who wants to get a message to the top without going through formal channels will head for the local whisperer. Whisperers have a symbiotic relationship with the boss and are intensely loyal. They also have a vast system of contacts across layers and levels and work hard to maintain sources for keeping current and keeping the boss up-to-date. In his reign as the CEO of Nissan America, Marvin Runyan enlisted an army of whisperers. Any employee had his ear. A company vice president once remarked, "If you want to get a message to Marvin, tell an employee."

Spies are invaluable sources of information for almost every good senior manager. These agents are planted in key places to watch out for daily happenings that upper levels need to know about. A spy is generally a well-oiled, longtime friend—someone loyal enough to keep you informed about what is going on behind the scenes in other functions or at lower levels. Occasionally, trusted spies become double agents carrying out espionage for other managers as well. Their cloak-and-dagger efforts help keep senior managers from being caught off guard, unaware of other people's tactics and intentions. Some companies create counterespionage units who try to stanch the extralegal activity that creates unwanted leaks or jeopardizes proprietary company secrets.

Cabals are groups of two or more people who secretly join together to plot a common purpose—either to advance themselves or champion a shared interest. Cabals exist everywhere in organizations. They can be very large or limited to a two-party conspiracy. Trust and loyalty to the informal group is crucial; whatever the cabal's size, it must have a clear identification with common goals. A cabal is by definition focused on a clear mission. Members of the cabal can borrow reputations or ideas from other members to further a personal agenda as long as it's a fair trade and the core purpose of the cabal is not undermined. A strong company culture will deliberately encourage and tolerate cabals because when the cabals' interests intersect with those of the company the result is a strong management lever. It's one of the best ways to get things done.

In times past the characters of the informal network had the best interests of the company at heart. Even the titillating tongues of gossips were constrained from passing on tidbits that would betray company secrets. But in today's corporate environment dedicated to shareholder value and short-term results, efforts of the cultural network turn sour and become toxic. Priestly figures oppose departures from traditional values. As a result, they are often terminated. With them goes the corporate memory. Tales told by storytellers champion resisters and saboteurs. Gossips leak inside information to outsiders. Spies become whistle-blowers, selling secret intelligence to the highest bidder. Cabals turn on senior executives. In short, an informal group of cultural players that once contributed to cultural cohesion now becomes a key force in cultural decline.

## Cultural Types

Our earlier work also developed a typology of corporate cultures, not as patterns for people to copy but to help managers and executives think more creatively about their own situations in terms of the kind of business environment they faced. We hoped their reflections could pinpoint the degree to which culture was helping or hindering their ability to compete and succeed. To simplify things, we identified two marketplace factors that influence cultural patterns and practices: (1) the degree of risk associated with a company's key activities and (2) the speed at which companies—and their employees—get feedback on whether decisions or strategies are successful. In some environments, the stakes are high. In others the risks are fairly minuscule. The amount of time it takes to establish whether something flies or flops varies a great deal across industries. Some companies learn almost overnight whether something works or not. In other environments, it may take years to determine whether a strategy or product paid off. From these market realities dichotomized into high/low risk, quick/slow feedback, we distilled four generic cultural types, each of which is discussed briefly below.

The tough-guy, macho culture is a world of individualists who regularly take high risks and get fast feedback on whether their actions are right or wrong. The commercial world provides a variety of organizations that fall into this category: construction, management consulting, investment banking, advertising, television, movies, publishing, sports (in fact the entire entertainment industry). Their financial stakes are high—big advertising campaigns, expensive construction projects, the fall television season, a $32-million movie, the World Series—and the feedback is quick: A year is probably the longest it takes to determine success or failure; more likely, companies will know whether their products will make it or not in a single season. In extreme cases—like a Broadway show or a movie opening—feedback is virtually immediate.

The all-or-nothing nature of this environment encourages values of risk-taking and the belief that "we can pull off the big deal, the best campaign"—whatever. Persons who survive this culture best are excitement junkies who need to gamble and crave instant feedback. This is a world of individualists. There is no reward in being part of a team; the goal is to become a star. Chance plays a major part in tough-guy cultures. What worked once may not work again, so employees devise rituals that tend to "protect" them from the vagaries of the environment. Bonding is often exclusive and exclusionary. Stars in some cultures bond together so that their "magic" won't be diluted. The tough-guy culture is one that rewards individuals who are temperamental, shortsighted, and superstitious and devastates people whose careers take longer to blossom. Because of the high turnover created by people who fail in the short term, building a strong, cohesive culture can be quite difficult in the tough-guy climate.

The work hard/play hard culture is the world of sales, where fun and action are the rule. Individual employees take few risks but receive quick feedback on whether they were successful or not. Most of the sales-driven companies in the economy fall into this work hard/play hard category. These include computer companies, office equipment suppliers, most high-tech start-ups, and a whole raft of support industries like automobile retailing, telemarketing, and stockbroking. To succeed in such a culture, people are required to maintain a high, almost frenetic level of activity and stay upbeat all or most of the time. Success comes with persistence. The heroes of this culture are the super salespeople. If anyone who succeeds in a tough-guy culture becomes a star, here the team beats the world because no individual really makes a difference. The team produces the volume. That's why salespeople's clubs and contests are so important to companies whose core business places them in the center of this cultural type.

The bet-your-company culture is one where big-stakes decisions are taken and years pass before employees know whether the decision was right. Industries in this culture include capital-goods companies, mining and smelting companies, large-systems businesses, oil companies, and service businesses like architectural firms. Instead of putting their careers on the line, as tough guys would, corporate bettors may risk the future of the entire company. These corporate giants may not founder on one bad investment decision, but it's possible for two bad decisions to sink the whole enterprise.

The importance of making the right decisions fosters a collective sense of deliberateness. The world of bet-your-company cultures moves in months and years, not days and weeks. Values focus on the future and the importance of investing in it, as is best symbolized by the slogans of some of the major players in this sector of the economy: "Progress is our most important product" (GE); "Better living through chemistry" (DuPont); "Alcoa can't wait . . . for tomorrow."

The process culture is a world of little or no feedback, where employees find it hard to measure what they do; instead they concentrate on how it's done. This low-risk, slow-feedback corner of the world is populated by banks, insurance companies, financial-service organizations, most retailers, large chunks of the government, utilities, and heavily regulated industries like pharmaceutical companies. As in the work/play culture, the financial stakes here are low: No one transaction will make or break the company—or anyone in it. But unlike worker-players, the employees here get virtually no feedback. The memos and reports they write seem to disappear into a void. As a result, they have no idea how effective they are until someone blames them for something. This lack of feedback forces employees to focus on how they do something, not what they do. To compensate, they start developing artificial ties to small events. A certain telephone call, that snippet of paper, or the section head's latest memo takes on major importance.

The values in this culture center on technical perfection—figuring out the risks and solutions and getting the process and the details right. "Underwriting Excellence," the Chubb Insurance slogan, is a good example. So is "Strive for Technical Perfection" (Price Waterhouse & Company). Rituals highlight work patterns and procedures, and there is a great deal of discussion about these small details.

## How the Corporate Landscape Has Shifted

This division of the world of business into four discrete categories is not only simple but fairly simplistic. No company we know today, or knew then, precisely fits into any one of these categories. In fact, within any single real-world company, a mix of all four types of cultures will be found. Marketing departments are tough-guy cultures. Sales departments work hard and play hard. Research and development is a world of high risk and slow feedback. Manufacturing and accounting, if they are to be successful in most companies, follow a process model of the world. Moreover, companies with very strong cultures—the companies that most intrigue us—fit this simple mold hardly at all.

These companies have cultures that artfully blend the best elements of all four types—and configure them in ways that assure top performance even when the environment around them changes, as it inevitably does. However, we thought then and still think now that this framework can be useful in helping managers begin to identify more specifically their own companies' cultural profiles.

What has happened to the prevailing cultural typologies since 1982? The long-term vision of the bet-your-company profile has been eroded. When orders for its aircraft slowed down, Boeing laid off scores of workers. Now, when demand has accelerated, Boeing is struggling to find the talent it needs. In days gone by, Boeing might have gambled. The high-energy level of work hard/play hard companies has undoubtedly shifted more toward working harder, playing little. Even well-known process cultures such as Aetna Insurance or NationsBank now hold people accountable for short-term, measurable performance objectives. In short, the rich diversity of cultural forms has declined. Is this a problem? It is when people at the top are misreading environmental signals and trying to impose cultural values and ways that may not capture long-term success.

How have individual companies adapted in response to the changes in the business environment? The answer is complicated because there are probably as many answers as there are companies. We have been privileged to observe many companies' inner workings, but we have not had universal, firsthand encounters. Nor did we have the time or opportunity to conduct detailed research across the board. Nevertheless, our exposure is broad enough to offer the following speculation about the state of culture in a wide spectrum of companies.

In some corporations, *traditional* cultural patterns have been seriously eroded. General Motors, Sears Roebuck, General Electric, Woolworth, and Eastman Kodak are examples. As chronicled in *Big Blue: The Unmaking of IBM,* the extremely robust culture of IBM fell apart at the seams. Under new leadership, the company is now in search of a more cohesive, competitive identity. In the aftermath of Richard Scott's reign, Columbia/HCA is reassessing its commitment to traditional values that once gave the corporation an edge in the health care sector. For all these companies, the long-term prognosis is questionable. Letting go of long-standing traditions to compete successfully in a new economic game has not been easy.

In other companies, the struggle to compete under new conditions has created soul-searching. But the end result has been a recommitment to core values with a significant overhaul of patterns and practices on the periphery. We would include in this list Ford, United Parcel Service (UPS), Phillips Electronics, Asea Brown Boveri (ABB), Boeing, Marriott International, Motorola, American Airlines, Hewlett-Packard (HP), Procter & Gamble (P&G), Xerox, and Minnesota Mining and Manufacturing (3M). Delta Airlines, for example, is today trying to recapture the spirit that once made it the darling of the airline industry. Passengers once rated Delta as the top airline in the country. In 1988, in return for the company's commitment to full employment in the midst of recession, Delta employees pooled donations to buy the company a new 767 aircraft. Both passengers and employees are now waiting to see what the company that once set an industry standard will look like in the future.

Despite the turbulence since the early 1980s, a few companies have managed to maintain their traditional ways. These include Wal-Mart, Volkswagen and Daimler-Benz, Royal Dutch/Shell Group, HSBC Holdings, Exxon, Johnson & Johnson (J&J), Federal Express, Merck, and Intel. But even among these survivors the struggle is ongoing. Daimler-Benz and Chrysler have entered a risky merger. Whether a corporate shoot-out or a productive marriage ensues is unclear. Federal Express pilots threatened a slowdown or strike in the midst of the 1998 holiday season. Will their vaunted can-do culture survive the strains of a problematic labor situation?

Finally, some companies that appear to have survived with their traditional culture intact may have done so by default, not through conscious management. They have been so self-obsessed that in many ways the past fifteen years have just passed them by. We would count Microsoft and many of its sibling companies in the thriving high-tech arena in this category.

The evidence, however, is clear: It is not easy to maintain a cohesive culture in the face of external flux and economic ups and downs. It is difficult to balance the conflicting demands of customers, shareholders, and employees. It is hard to predict what will happen in the immediate future and impossible to predict long-term trends. Whether we like it or not, running a business in today's world is filled with problems, dilemmas, and paradoxes. Tomorrow will be shaped by those able to stay balanced on a moving tightrope without a safety net.

## Why This New Book, Now?

When we first approached a new version of *Corporate Cultures*, we realized the world had changed too much for a simple update. Everywhere we look corporate cultures are in disarray. Employees are frightened about their future job prospects. Loyalty to companies has flown out the window. Cynicism about management is rampant. Self interest rules the roost. Who in their right mind would try to make a strong and contributing culture out of the prevailing mess? Yet, deep down, people still yearn for the "good old days." They still want to identify with their companies' achievements. They still seek more meaning from their experiences at work. Is there a glimmer of hope that a positive workplace can be salvaged after all?

We decided, therefore, to review what has happened. As we did, it became apparent that changes in the 1980s and 1990s followed a logic and sense, however misguided. Even more interesting, the very factors that made this logic inevitable were changing. The shareholder value thinking that drove most of the changes is running out of steam as stock market valuations soar into the indefensible stratosphere. Managers everywhere seem bereft of ideas for where to turn next. Perhaps a new book could set a path forward that both managers and employees could share. We call the book, *The New Corporate Cultures*.

## Organization of the Book

This book is organized into three parts comprising thirteen chapters in all. The first part, made up of a single chapter, summarizes the evidence that has emerged since we first wrote about the importance of culture to superior performance over the long haul. We call this chapter "Culture Comes of Age" to underscore how a new idea in 1982 has entered the mainstream of business thinking over the years.

The second part, composed of seven chapters, is titled "Corporate Cultures in Crisis." This part chronicles, one by one, the forces that have chipped away at the culture of companies since the early 1980s. Chapter 2 discusses the shareholder value movement and the impact it has had on corporate decisionmaking. In Chapter 3, the focus is on downsizing, which has cut the soul out of many corporations. Chapter 4 shows how outsourcing has emerged as the new tool of cost cutters just when conventional cost-reduction approaches have begun to run out of steam. Chapter 5 then explores how merger mania has forced the most unlikely of combinations on workforces still reeling from the waves of cost cutting that decimated them in the early 1990s. With Chapter 6, we look at how computerization, potentially a tool for liberating workers from drudgery, has instead isolated workers from one another and made them servants to machines. We go on in Chapter 7 to see how the narrowing boundaries of the world have thrown peoples together to create a virtual Tower of Babel in the global workplace. Finally, in Chapter 8, we discuss how the combination of these factors has decimated traditional corporate cultures, replacing joy, commitment, and loyalty with fear, alienation, and self-interest.

In the third part, which comprises five chapters, we examine ways to salvage gold out of this witch's brew of noxious elements. We call this part "Rebuilding Cohesive Cultures." We begin in Chapter 9 by underscoring the importance of leadership in any effort to rebuild the cultural cohesion of business. Chapter 10 provides some basics about figuring out where you are now and beginning the journey forward, and Chapter 11 suggests ways to add momentum to a culture-rebuilding effort and have some fun in the process. In Chapter 12 we look at how even the most bottom-line-oriented managers can capitalize on the reemergence of strong cultural ties to induce high performance from their remotivated employees. We end the book with a chapter telling why and how the rebuilding of the social context of work is essential if people are to be motivated to give their best efforts on behalf of their employers. That is the crucial challenge of the decade, if not the millennium, ahead.

PART ONE

# Corporate Cultures and Performance

# Culture Comes of Age

We titled the first chapter of our earlier book, *Corporate Cultures*, "Strong Cultures: The New 'Old Rule' for Business Success." We argued there that companies that focus on their people and create a social environment—or culture—in which employees can thrive achieve superior, long-term business success. Then as now, the role culture plays in performance seems obvious since all businesses are people businesses. When people are vested in their work, they work harder, show up on time, stay late when needed, and take pride in the company's products or services. They are loyal, committed, and interested in the collective welfare as well as their individual careers. They speak up when things need to be changed rather than signing off or shipping out. Not only their hands but their heads and hearts are engaged in the enterprise's mission.

We also argued that the biggest single influence on a company's culture is the broader social and economic environment in which the company does business. A corporate culture embodies what it takes to succeed in a particular socioeconomic context. If hard selling is required for success, a culture will encourage people to sell and sell hard. If manufacturing precision is the requisite for success, a company will see that people employ strict standards to guide their work. How have these arguments stood the test of time?

We launched the initial version of *Corporate Cultures* with a certain degree of trepidation. Not too many voices then were championing the virtues of a cohesive company culture. Since that time, a large chorus of executives and academics has joined with us and other pioneers such as Edgar Schein, Stan Davis, Ralph Kilmann, and Tom Peters. Whether they call it culture or something else, the contemporary arguments fall under the same overall concept. Starbucks CEO Howard Schultz puts it this way: "If people relate to the company they work for, if they form an emotional tie to it and buy into its dreams, they will pour their hearts into making it better. . . . I pour my heart into every cup of coffee and so do my partners at Starbucks." Continental Airlines CEO, Gordon Bethune, says it a little differently: "Whatever problems you run into in running a business, they are all people problems. . . . Businesses are run by people. So at the root of whatever problems you have in your business you'll find people. . . . A lot of managers and executives miss the forest for the trees by forgetting to look at their people." Herb Kelleher and Colleen Barrett, Southwest Airlines CEO and chief operating officer, respectively, credit culture for shaping their unique enterprise: "Culture is one of the most precious things a company has, so you must work harder on it than anything else."

All four of these executives are solid businesspeople who through their firsthand experience have reached the conclusion that culture matters and needs to be taken seriously. Many of those who study organizations have reached the same conclusion. Kevin and Jackie Freiberg, whose chronicle of Southwest Airlines, *Nuts!,* has received a lot of attention, write, "The idea of corporate culture is too important to the effective functioning of today's corporations to be dismissed as a fleeting craze. Culture is the glue that holds an organization together." This also holds true of organizations outside the business arena. Thomas Ricks writes about the U.S. Marine Corps: "Culture—that is the values and assumptions that shape its members—is all the Marines have. It is what holds them together. They are the smallest of the U.S. military services, and in many ways the most interesting. Theirs is the richest culture: formalistic, insular, elitist, with a deep anchor in their core history and mythology."

In sum, if you look closely at any highly respected company, you're bound to find a distinctive culture. *Fortune* magazine reached this conclusion in its survey of businesses with stellar reputations: "The one thing that set the top-ranking companies in the survey apart is their robust cultures."

In 1999 we have a lot more people backing our assertions than we did in 1982. The support comes from both those on the firing line and those who take a more detached, analytical position. People do matter in business, and culture plays a dominant role in holding people together and giving their efforts focus and meaning. But the important bottom-line question remains: Do strong cultures pay off in financial performance? In 1982, opinions about this were strongly divided. How does the situation look now?

## Our 20/20 Financial Hindsight

In 1982 we cited a number of companies as exemplars of this emerging management philosophy, including Caterpillar, General Electric (GE), DuPont, Chubb Insurance, 3M, Jefferson-Smurfit, Digital Equipment, IBM, Dana Corporation, Procter & Gamble, Hewlett-Packard, Johnson & Johnson, Tandem Computer, and Continental Bank (as well as a number of privately held companies and one public-sector agency in the UK). Since then, not all these companies have fared well. Even as we penned our prose, IBM was in the process of selling off the huge installed base of computers it leased to its customers. This action in large part paved the way for the biggest one-year operating loss ever incurred in corporate history. Tandem and Digital, fellow travelers with IBM, did even worse: In 1997 and 1998 they were acquired by an upstart competitor, Compaq Computer, and ceased to exist as stand-alone entities. Continental Illinois Bank was gobbled up by BankAmerica in one of the first major mergers in the consolidation trend that hit U.S. banking.

Nevertheless, had we put our 1982 money where our mouths were and purchased one share of stock in each of the companies we so admired (which were then listed on the stock market), our initial stake would have increased by 987% through midyear 1998. In contrast, had we invested our money in the Standard & Poor's average, the most broadly based index of stock market performance, our stake would have increased by only 538%—around half what we could have gained by betting on our exemplary companies.

This simple arithmetic alone should be enough to substantiate that we weren't that far off base. A company's culture turns out to be a major determinant of its future economic success. Since 1982 other authors have entered the fray with even more compelling evidence to bolster our earlier claim. Not only have these more recent authors added verification, but they have also studied the subject of culture in sufficient depth to reveal nuances we may have overlooked.

## Culture and Long-Term Performance

The first serious book specifically evaluating the effects of culture on performance was written by two respected professors at the Harvard Business School, John Kotter and James Heskett. Their book, *Corporate Culture and Performance*, appeared ten years after the publication of our *Corporate Cultures*. They based their conclusions on a series of four empirical studies conducted between 1987 and 1992, exploring over 200 companies in considerable depth. Their major conclusions were:

1. Corporate cultures can have a significant impact on a firm's long-term economic performance.
2. Corporate cultures will probably be an even more important factor in determining the success or failure of firms in the next decade [meaning through the year 2002, we presume].
3. Corporate cultures that inhibit strong long-term financial performance are not rare; they develop easily, even in firms that are full of reasonable and intelligent people.
4. Although tough to change, corporate cultures can be made more performance enhancing.

Based on solid academic research, these conclusions are not to be dismissed lightly. Let's examine their evidence in a bit more detail.

Kotter and Heskett looked at financial performance over a ten-year period. They analyzed 207 companies—the largest nine or ten firms in twenty-two different U.S. industries. Using a survey questionnaire, the authors were able to construct an index measuring the relative cultural strengths of 202 of these companies. Then, as data permitted, they evaluated the companies' 1977–1988 financial performance using three different measures: (1) average yearly increase in net income, (2) average yearly return on investment, and (3) average yearly increase in stock price. Correlations tested the assertion that companies with strong cultures performed better than their weaker counterparts. The correlations, though positive, were not impressive demonstrations of proof. In their analyses, cultural strength itself did not seem to correlate significantly with financial performance.

Intrigued by their findings, we calculated the average performance of the top twenty culturally robust companies and compared these to ratings for the bottom twenty. We were concerned that with so many mediocre companies (in cultural terms) in their sample, the two Harvard academics might be overlooking something important. The results of this calculation are as follows:

- Culturally strong companies averaged 571% higher gains in operating earnings than those more culturally deprived over the eleven years.
- Companies with highly rated cultures averaged 417% higher returns on investment than their less culturally robust counterparts.
- Companies with strong cultures saw their stock prices increase 363% more than their culturally challenged peers over the time span of the study.

Sometimes analysis can obscure the forest while focusing too tightly on trees. The correlation analysis done by Kotter and Heskett appears a case in point: According to our reanalysis of their data, strong-culture companies massively outperformed weak ones between 1977 and 1988. Our 1982 assertion, emphasizing cultural robustness, seems vindicated.

## The Financial Success of Visionary Companies

The second major study of the link between culture and performance (although using slightly different language) was published in 1994. *Built to Last: Successful Habits of Visionary Companies*, by James Collins and Jerry Porras, examines the history and financial track records of thirty-six companies dating back to the 1920s. These companies are listed in Table 1.1.

Many of the "visionary" companies on Collins and Porras's list overlap with the companies studied by Kotter and Heskett, as well as examples cited in this and our previous work. Not surprisingly,

TABLE 1.1    Companies in the Collins-Porras Study

| Visionary Companies | Comparison Companies |
|---|---|
| Minnesota Mining & Manufacturing | Norton |
| American Express | Wells Fargo |
| Boeing | McDonnell Douglas |
| Citicorp | Chase |
| Ford | General Motors |
| General Electric | Westinghouse |
| Hewlett-Packard | Texas Instruments |
| IBM | Burroughs |
| Johnson and Johnson | Bristol-Myers |
| Marriott | Howard Johnson |
| Merck | Pfizer |
| Motorola | Zenith |
| Nordstrom | Melville |
| Philip Morris | R. J. Reynolds |
| Procter & Gamble | Colgate |
| Sony | Kenwood |
| Wal-Mart | Ames |
| Disney | Columbia |

SOURCE: From James Collins and Jerry Porras, *Built to Last* (HarperBusiness, 1994), p. 3.

there seems to be a remarkable consensus about what is virtuous among America's best-run companies.

Collins and Porras measured the performance of visionary companies versus comparison companies from the beginning of 1926 through the end of 1990—a much longer time frame than that of Kotter and Heskett. Their conclusions, however, were similar: One dollar invested in each of the visionary companies in 1926 would have been worth $6,356 by the end of 1990. In contrast, the same dollar invested in each of the comparison companies in 1926 would have yielded only $955. An investment in the general stock market average over the same time period would have been worth only $415. Vision pays, as Collins and Porras argue. But how does their notion of vision relate to culture as we define it?

The authors list ten characteristics of these companies that appear to explain their superior performance. Their first and perhaps most important finding is that building strong companies, rather than exploiting novel ideas or making great fortunes, was the driving rationale behind fabled business leaders of yesteryear. Consider the testimony from some legendary figures: "I have concentrated all along on building the finest retailing company that we possibly could. Creating a huge personal fortune was never particularly a goal of mine" (Sam Walton, as quoted in *Built to Last*) and "Our engineering staff [has] remained fairly stable. This was by design rather than by accident. Engineers are creative people, so before we hired an engineer we made sure he would be operating in a stable and secure climate. We also made sure that each of our engineers had a long range opportunity with the company and suitable projects on which to work" (Bill Hewlett, as quoted in *Built to Last*).

Other comparisons—GE and Westinghouse, Citicorp and Chase, Wal-Mart and Ames, Motorola and Zenith, Disney and Columbia Pictures—offer very similar leadership profiles. Founders' long-term visions rather than short-term efforts to exploit specific marketplace opportunities create great companies. Sustaining visions are also the driving force in strong-culture companies.

We find another point of similarity between visionary and culturally robust companies when we look at the relative importance of a shared set of core values compared to a narrow set of immediate objectives such as profit maximization. The history and evolution of a number of firms bear this out—HP versus Texas Instruments, J&J versus Bristol-Myers, Motorola versus Zenith, Boeing versus McDonnell Douglas (since absorbed by Boeing), Marriott versus Howard Johnson, and Philip Morris versus R. J. Reynolds. Core values appear central in both visionary companies and those we term culturally robust or cohesive.

Visionary companies are not content with minor achievements. They set huge goals and formidable tasks for themselves. People who are drawn to work in such companies relish challenge. Their willingness to take on and meet daunting challenges is one of the keys to long-term performance superiority. GE under Jack Welch insists on being number one or two in every one of its markets. Frank Vanderlip set Citicorp on a path to global dominance in 1915 when he said, "I am perfectly confident that it is open to us to become the most powerful, the most serviceable, the most far-reaching world financial institution that has ever been" (as quoted in *Built to Last*).

Collins and Porras also concluded that the truly great visionary companies have strong, insular, almost exclusionary cultures. Working for them is like being in the Marines: If you don't shape up quickly, you'll be out on your ear. They cite as examples Nordstrom,

IBM, Disney, and P&G—companies that consistently make our list of culturally sound firms.

The Collins and Porras book is crammed full of insights about what makes really good companies tick. Although couched in language different from ours, their message is fairly consistent with our views. The main point of convergence: the importance of culture in top performance. Details they cite expand and enrich our own perspective. In principle, we couldn't agree with them more when they state: "The essence of a visionary company comes in the translation of its core ideology into the very fabric of the organization, . . . into *everything* that the company does."

## Keeping Pace with the Business Environment

Cultural tensileness is important in achieving superior financial results, but there's more to it than that, as Kotter and Heskett documented in a more intense follow-up study. They focused on the performance of two companies in the same industry—those with "strategically aligned" cultures versus those where the culture is out of whack with the business environment. Their sample included twenty-one companies, listed in Table 1.2.

All the companies listed were reported as having strong cultures, but those in the left-hand column outperformed those on the right by a sizable margin: They increased net incomes by three times more, saw their stock prices increase between 400% and 500% (1977–1988) versus 100% average for the other companies, and returned 11.13% on invested capital as compared to 7.73% for the poorer-performing comparison companies. Industry analysts interviewed by the authors reported that distinctive cultures had helped the twelve higher-performing companies. In most cases, less robust cultural profiles detracted from the lower performers' ability to compete. The reason: The fit between the company's culture and its business environment was significantly better among the top performers. On a seven-point scale, with seven representing a perfect fit, industry analysts gave the top performers a mean score for the fit between culture and environment of 6.1; for the lower performers the mean was 3.7. Not one of the lower-performing companies received a higher culture-environment fit score than its higher-performing counterpart. What once worked for a low-performing

TABLE 1.2   Comparing Company Performance in Twelve Industries

| Industry | High Performers | Low Performers |
|---|---|---|
| Airlines | American | Northwest |
| Banking | Bankers Trust | Citicorp |
| Beverages | Anheuser-Busch | Coors |
| Computers | Hewlett-Packard | Xerox |
| Food | ConAgra | Archer Daniels Midland |
| Petroleum | Shell | Texaco |
| Retail (food, drugs) | Albertson | Winn-Dixie |
| Retail (nonfood) | Dayton Hudson Wal-Mart | J. C. Penney |
| Savings and Loan | Golden West | H. F. Ahmanson |
| Textiles | Spring Industries | Fieldcrest Cannon |

SOURCE: Adapted from John Kotter and James Heskett, *Corporate Culture and Performance* (Free Press, 1992), pp. 32–33.

company seemed to work against it when the business environment changed and the company did not or could not adapt.

According to Kotter and Heskett (and we certainly believe they're right), these results provided strong support for a theory linking culture and environment:

Its [the theory's] primary concept, that of fit, appears to be useful—particularly in explaining differences in short- to medium-term performance. That concept also has important implications for firms in multiple businesses. It says that one uniform culture won't work; some variations are needed to fit the specific requirements of those in different business.

In effect, Kotter and Heskett confirmed more systematically what we suspected and conjectured in 1982. To work its bottom-line magic, a company's culture must be aligned with the demands of the business environment.

## Leadership and Adapation

There's still another shoe to drop in the relationship between culture and performance: Adaptation. In a third set of studies, Kotter and

Heskett focused intensively on seventeen of the companies listed in Table 1.2 to pinpoint how these companies seemed so nimble in adapting to changes occurring in the business environment. Their approach consisted mostly of in-depth company interviews and surveys of experienced industry analysts. In their interviews, they tried to get a flavor for the nature of adaptive companies (open, risk-oriented, and entrepreneurial) in contrast to their less adaptive counterparts (reactive, risk-averse, and not very creative). Although some of the examples they cite as paragons are somewhat suspect, their primary conclusions are intriguing.

Their most interesting finding relates to the role of leadership in adaptive companies and demands the attention of senior managers who want to excel. Kotter and Heskett asked experienced industry analysts to rate seventeen companies in response to the question, "How much does the culture value excellent leadership from its managers?" (The scale went from one, doesn't value leadership, to seven, highly values leadership.) Not surprisingly, higher-performing companies averaged a rating of six on this leadership scale, whereas lower-performing companies averaged 3.9. This is a substantial difference, especially given the vagueness of the question.

These findings are certainly consistent with our own view of culture. Strong company cultures arise because of leadership displayed by senior managers at some point in their past. Such leadership has little to do with charisma. It has a lot to do with serving as a visible, living example of core values that become central to the culture. The core values are perpetuated from generation to generation. From time to time, leadership has to be willing to make hard decisions, but these must be consistent with a coherent set of values. Peripheral practices come and go. Core values remain constant. This provides the ability to adapt to changing conditions while still maintaining a strong corporate identity.

Leadership provides the key influence in successful adaptation. But leadership toward what ends? Some pundits, Tom Peters probably the best known, argue that leadership should focus on customers and their needs. Others whose claims are less well supported argue for entrepreneurship as the key to successful long-term adaptation. Kotter and Heskett once again offer a more balanced prescription.

Every business environment holds a number of diverse groups, each with its parochial interests. Shareholders want a high return on their investments. Customers demand high-quality products and services. Communities look to locally based businesses for funds to support schools and local charities. Employees ask for a good working environment, fair salaries, adequate training, and meaningful work. In a fast-shifting environment, it is easy for a business culture to get out of balance, favoring one constituency while overlooking the interests of others. In seeking to satisfy shareholders, for example, airlines sometimes add more seats to aircraft, reduce the quality of food, try to keep wages low, and cut down on charitable contributions. Although this keeps shareholders happy in the short term, it runs the risk of alienating customers, employees, and local communities over the longer term.

Kotter and Heskett found that successful companies constantly monitor key constituencies and make adjustments when any group is not being well served. Industry analysts familiar with each of the companies studied were asked how much value the culture placed on customers, shareholders, and employees. They ranked each company on the familiar seven-point scale (one = doesn't value; seven = highly values). The results are summarized in Table 1.3.

As is evident, business cultures that valued all three constituencies outperformed their competitors. In the eyes of business analysts, managers of less-productive firms often cared mostly about themselves. Follow-up visits to seventeen of the twenty-two firms added still more constituencies to the picture. Many of the top-performing firms also placed high value on contributing to the local community and society at large. For example, Albertson's cultural commitment to all five constituencies is part of its "cultural creed." ConAgra's cultural values embracing all five groups is written in tall letters on a wall next to its executive offices. Anheuser-Busch includes customers, shareholders, employees, community, and society as part of its mission statement.

In a business world where either shareholders or customers often receive high value, including employees, community, and society in some adaptive cultural balance seems to pay off over time. As Kotter and Heskett conclude,

> When managers do not care about all three constituencies and about leadership initiatives throughout the management hierarchy, the net result always seems to be less effective adaptation. This is perhaps

TABLE 1.3     Cultural Values Related to Serving Diverse Constituencies
(mean score)

| | Value | | |
| --- | --- | --- | --- |
| | Customers | Shareholders | Employees |
| Top performers | 6.0 (lowest score 5.8) | 5.7 (only two under 5.0) | 5.8 (lowest score 4.8) |
| Lesser Performers | 4.6 (only two above 5.0) | 3.9 (only one above 5.0) | 4.1 (only two above 4.8) |

SOURCE: Adapted from John Kotter and James Heskett, *Corporate Culture and Performance* (Free Press, 1992), p. 49.

most obvious when a high concern for customers and/or leadership is lacking. But it is also true in a firm with a strong customer orientation but without much concern for employees or stockholders. In such cases, managers try hard to meet customers' changing needs, even if that means significantly reducing margins and working employees very long hours. That strategy sometimes works well for awhile, but eventually capital becomes too scarce to invest much in needed new products or services. Furthermore, employees start to feel exploited and stop working hard for the customer. As a result, such firms find it harder and harder to meet changing customer requirements.

The same chain reaction would occur if any constituency were favored over others. Cultural values can provide the focus needed so that all significant links in the performance chain are maintained.

## Myths and Realities of Managing Culture

Amazon.com, the online bookseller, lists seventy-five titles that include the phrase "corporate culture." We suspect there are many other books about culture on the market that employ some other rubric. First Kotter and Heskett, soon followed by Porras and Collins, published books detailing how strong cultures well tuned to their environments produce superior financial performance for companies. These books together sell tens of thousands of copies to interested corporate and academic readers. A routine search of the Internet on one of the better search engines, nlsearch.com, returns almost 30,000 entries answering to that phrase. This chapter's opening assertion that corporate cultures have come of age seems well justified.

What's wrong with this picture, then? Despite the amazing exposure the concept of culture has received since the early 1980s, the world is full of myths about what culture is all about and how it really works. Although it seems ironic that myths would obscure a mythical concept, it happens a lot in the business world today. Along with acknowledging the robustness of the culture concept, we felt we should try to debunk some of these myths. As an idea, culture is established firmly enough to survive despite this unnecessary and misleading baggage.

*Myth: Culture is a (quick) fix for any problem.*   Shortly after our original book was published, the two of us were asked to give a talk to the top management team of a multibillion-dollar service firm. Our address was to be the capstone of a several-day, offsite meeting at a Midwest resort. We showed up, delivered our ideas about corporate cultures, and were pleased that our message seemed to be well received. Our pleasure evaporated when the company's CEO summarized our presentation with the words: "This is really good stuff. We need a culture in this place, too. Get me one in two weeks." At first we were taken aback by our apparent inability to communicate. Later we sensed that this was our first exposure to the idea that culture can be a fix for any problem a company faces—and, if this CEO was to be believed, a quick fix at that.

Culture is not a quick fix for anything. Strategy is. When Gordon Bethune took over the helm of a near-bankrupt Continental Airlines, he made a strategic decision. He stopped flights to cities where the load factor (the percentage of seats full of paying customers) did not justify the expense of the trip. This was a strategic shift in the direction of the company. And it paid off: Before long, Continental was again operating comfortably in the black. Strategic moves like this put the airline back on a path to success.

*Myth: Culture and strategy have nothing to do with one another.*
As an enlightened business leader, Bethune did not ignore culture; he gave it equal attention. At the same time he set out to redo the airline's route structure, he instituted a bonus scheme that applied to

all employees. Under the scheme, every employee got $50 extra in his or her monthly paycheck if the company ranked first, second, or third in on-time performance. This was culturally a signal that every employee could understand and most employees could do something about. Soon newly motivated employees were moving heaven and earth to ensure they would earn their bonus every month. Actions taken to guarantee on-time performance complemented the strategy of flying where people wanted to go. This became an irresistible lure to passengers. But the behavior of employees was cultural, not strategic. The strategic move was finding a way to channel the energy of employees into something that passengers really cared about.

In the combination of these strategic and cultural actions lies a great truth: In execution, culture (behavioral patterns deeply ingrained in people) and strategy (an idea about how to compete effectively) are inseparable. A culture changes very slowly. For a strategy to succeed quickly, it must take advantage of this cultural inertia. It must channel people's energies into actions they are comfortable taking. A strategy that asks people to do something unnatural or totally foreign is doomed to a slow death.

The link between strategy, where new ideas and quick fixes are possible, and culture, where change comes slowly, is intimate. A good strategist like Bethune of Continental knows this and chooses strategies that build on natural, cultural strengths. Many other strategists whose failures you are never likely to know ignore the symbiotic relationship between strategy and culture. They dream up superb strategic moves that fail in the real-world test. The strategies never work because they are incompatible with existing cultural realities. Our hope is that the soft side of organizations (concerned with intangible things like culture) will come together with the hard strategic side's concerns for numbers and financials. They will come together if each side realizes that one cannot exist without the other.

*Myth: Culture resists all change.*   Some years ago, we were consulting with a high-tech company. It was struggling to turn around a newly acquired division operating with a different technology in the company's core markets. The client was trying to instill a hard-driving sales culture in the division's more technologically driven atmosphere. We vividly remember one heated management meeting:

Decisions were made to change the division's entire top management team. The argument put forward was, "We'll never be able to get the culture of that division to change [without drastic changes at the top]." We resisted this action but were overruled. The mythology of the moment held sway.

The myth that culture resists change is deeply embedded in the psyche of many managers. Any time problems arise in implementing some new initiative, the knee-jerk reaction is to blame everything on the culture. Since the problem can't be the manager or the brilliant initiative, what better whipping boy than the culture?

Cultures in companies are the living, breathing manifestation of the most deeply held desires of people to do what's right and get ahead. Because of this, cultures thrive on change just as much as they champion tradition. New and better ways of doing things; new strategies in the marketplace; new offices, plants, and decorations: cultures love them as signs that all is right with the world. Cultures are always adapting to the changes around them. Failure to adapt would be threatening since it would be seen as a sign that the culture was falling behind. Where cultures resist is when long-standing core values or widely accepted rituals or practices are endangered. And they resist such changes because the force of history is behind them: Is this proposed change really what's needed to move on?

*Myth: Cultural change can be managed.*   There must be a million consultants promising to help "change the cultures" of companies. Many of these consultants are even making a reasonable living from the practice. What a lot of bollocks. Cultures change only when they need to and are damned well ready to change. They change when their collective intelligence recognizes that the world has changed and that the culture better adapt in order for the business to survive. When it comes right down to it, culture is all about surviving and thriving. But profound cultural change is a messy and painful process. It takes quite a while for individuals to get their heads and hearts attuned to the fact that the world has changed and they must change, too. People become highly attached to cultural ways and practices. When the attachments are broken, they experience a deep sense of loss. When a whole organization comes to the realization it has to move on, is it any wonder that the process is fraught with difficulty? People have to let go before they move on. Every human culture provides transition rituals to help individuals and collectives leave old things behind and move into a more promising future. Cultural change therefore requires a culturally sensitive process.

What role can a consultant play in easing this process? Not much of one. A consultant can facilitate meetings to help members of the culture think through what is going on. But isn't that what management is supposed to be doing anyway? And if the consultants are off facilitating while management has an entirely different agenda, aren't people smart enough to smell a rat? Of course they are.

Several years ago, we were asked to assist a major, newly deregulated company "manage its culture" while the company underwent a major reorganization and its first downsizing. Being naive at the time, we agreed. And with the help of a spirited and talented team of employees from the company, we did a number of magical things. We sponsored events where frontline personnel got to communicate directly with members of senior management. We instituted newsletters to keep all staff informed of the progress—and cultural significance—of the reorganization. We counseled the senior management team about the role they could play in managing the cultural transition.

We had a great deal of fun and took home some significant fees in the process. Thank God for these two rewards. There was little else of value that accrued from our "intervention." The reality was that the people we were trying to influence, with the full and willing backing of top management, were too busy figuring out their roles in the reorganized company. As a result, they gave little more than lip service to the hooey we had to offer. More power to them. People were struggling with what the changes meant and how they needed to respond. Our attempts to manage the process, though not really harmful, were at best a distraction from this central task.

So managers beware. The next time consultants offer to help you manage the culture of your enterprise, show them the door. Instead, spend your time managing and leading the process as well as you can. Given the right leadership and left to their own devices, people will understand and try to adapt as needed. If you think the process is moving along too slowly, look over your management agenda for what you might have missed. People are probably telling you they are not convinced. You should ignore this warning only at your own peril.

*Myth: Top-level leadership is the key to instilling a strong corporate culture.*   When authors like us tell tales of cultural derring-do, we invariably cite examples of some of the most famous and noteworthy corporate heroes. Our earlier book was full of stories about Tom Watson of IBM; Bill Patterson, his mentor at NCR; Dave Packard and Bill Hewlett; and Henry Ford. This book is also illustrated with such stories, now featuring the likes of Gordon Bethune of Continental Airlines and Herb Kelleher of Southwest. Does this mean that only corporate giants can influence the culture of their companies? If this is the case, what are the rest of us poor mortals to do?

We and other authors choose these larger-than-life heroic figures because they are names you are familiar with and companies you can immediately identify. The reality is that every company, large or small, has a cultural identity. These cultural patterns and practices are instilled and reinforced by the individuals who founded these companies and the people who manage them to this day. If a culture is strong, it is because the needs and aspirations of the mostly anonymous everyday heroes are closely attuned to the values and beliefs of the visionaries who launched the business. These visionaries sought to build companies that served the needs of their people while making a profit. They focused especially on shaping a business that would flourish over the long haul. Because hundreds, if not thousands, of employees bought into the founding vision and put out the extra effort to carry the dream forward, a strong culture emerged. Their effort adds fuel to the fire that makes the enterprise burn ever brighter in the minds and hearts of its employees. The corporation becomes a beloved institution.

Leadership, therefore, has a lot to do with building a cohesive culture. But it is not just the leadership that allows the company to carry out its economic mission successfully. It is leadership that seeks to shape a working environment that people at all levels can identify with. It is leadership that encourages leadership from everyone. It is leadership that is not afraid to stand for something. It is leadership that cares about a myriad of details that make the company work. It is leadership that strives to generate universal pride in what the company accomplishes, not just how people are enriched by its economic activities. It is leadership that all good managers should exercise if they take themselves and their responsibilities seriously.

There is nothing magic about such inspired leadership, except when it succeeds and others who admire its success try to emulate it. Leadership is the key to building strong cultures—but it is not necessarily leadership provided by extraordinary people on a mission to change the world. Ordinary, garden-variety leadership and good management up and down the company creates the real magic.

**Myth: People hang onto a culture they know even when it is no longer relevant.**    How many times have we all sat and listened to old-timers lamenting the passage of the good old days? How often have you been in a meeting when an emotional outburst occurs damning the current agenda and reaching back in history to recall with nostalgia something that once worked? People naturally hold onto the past as tightly as they can, and there is little anyone can do to sever their historical ties.

People hold onto the past because it made sense and gives their current work meaning. They cling to old ways because they worked and helped them progress to where they are today. If people reject the present and future and prefer to revel in more comfortable "good old days," it is usually because they cannot grasp new realities firmly enough to give them new confidence. This represents a failure in management's responsibility to communicate.

Good companies try to counteract this tendency to preserve the status quo by building a degree of planned anarchism into their ranks. Instead of always favoring the existing party line, these companies seek to reward risk-takers and entrepreneurs who question conventional wisdom. These corporate mavericks take glee in shaking up comfortable, traditional ways. Well-run businesses make challenging the status quo a cultural virtue and value, not grounds for persecution and ostracism. It takes inspired management to build into a company such a paradoxical ethic that in effect says, "Support things a little, but everything management is now doing is probably suspect. In short, be somewhat reverent about your continued disrespect." Such management encourages robust cultures able to adapt to continual changes in the business environment. Too much skepticism about change is a strong clue that something is wrong with the proposed course of action—not necessarily a sign of an ossified culture.

*Myth: Strong cultures are monolithic.*    It is certainly true that to outsiders some of the most notable corporate cultures appear monolithic in approach. Historical paragons of strong-culture companies such as IBM certainly fit this mold. But any thought that links a monolithic outlook with cultural strength is way off the mark. Monolithic cultures arise in industries where a particular, consistent pattern of behavior is the best guarantee of future success. Strong cultures arise anywhere. Where the environment demands diversity of thought and action, robust cultures will mirror the demand and foster diversity in the ranks.

One of the strongest cultures we know is that of Citicorp (but not necessarily Citigroup, the new incarnation of Citicorp after merging with Travelers, since it is far too early to tell how this culture will evolve). Banking is one of the most diverse industries in the world. The work of the banker extends from nurturing long-standing relationships with key customers, to selling new products aggressively, to operating efficiently in giant back-office factories. It takes all of these elements working together to maintain a well-run bank. Most banks fail on one or more dimensions and suffer the consequences. But a bank like Citicorp thrives. Why?

Citicorp's culture is an intriguing blend of optimism and hard work. The company was built by and is populated with people who can best be described as street-smart New Yorkers, whatever their particular origins might be. Street-smart New Yorkers get things done—and Citicorp is a veritable beehive of constant activity. Street-smart New Yorkers work hard—there is no such thing as a free ride in New York. Citicorp people, therefore, expect this ethic to apply to work as well. But street-smart New Yorkers also respect others. Life in the melting pot of New York is tough enough without alienating others and having to watch your backside. In Citicorp's cultural ways, it is expected that everyone will both fight his or her own corner and look out for fellow Citicorpers. The combination of these paradoxical traits and behaviors is a culture so diffuse as to confound most outsiders. It is not monolithic. Yet it is strong and resilient—a major factor in Citicorp's success. Different strokes for different folks, you might say, but only if the strokes make sense in the existing business environment.

*Myth: Culture is not for everyone.*    Whether you like it or not, you are immersed in a culture at work. Whether you think it is important or not, cultural mores and norms will dictate much of what you do on a day-to-day basis and determine how you think. Whether you conform or not is not a matter of choice—unless you want to leave. The culture of a company seeps into your pores and shapes your identity.

Managers uncomfortable with the idea of culture should beware. Culture, not official rules or policies, ultimately dictate what you can do and what you can't. Since culture may well be the key factor in influencing whether a company succeeds or fails, it needs to be high on the list of management priorities. Lack of comfort with the concept is no excuse: If you don't give cultural ways and practices the attention they demand, they will come back to bite you

•    •    •

We could probably fill another 300 pages elaborating on the multitude of myths that have arisen around the subject of corporate culture. But that is a task for others in another time and place. The bottom line is this: The idea of culture has been legitimized in the 1980s and 1990s. But during this time other events have occurred as well that have changed the face of corporate cultures around the world. In the rest of the book, we shift gears and examine some of the trends and their effects and what needs to be done in response.

# PART TWO

# Corporate Cultures in Crisis

## CHAPTER 2

# The Rise of Shareholder Value and Short-Termism

## The Gods Must Be Crazy

In 1981 a brilliant young film entrepreneur, Jamie Uys, released his first version of a new Afrikaans-language film in Botswana. It was titled *The Gods Must Be Crazy*. It proved so successful in South Africa that it was dubbed into English and re-released for the U.S. market in 1984. It soon became the highest-grossing foreign film in American history.

The film tells the charming story of an African Bushman whose serene and cooperative tribal life is torn apart. It all starts when a thoughtless pilot flying over the Kalahari Desert throws an empty Coke bottle out of his airplane window. Landing, quite literally, on top of the Bushman's head, the Coke bottle is mistaken by his family and tribe as a gift from the gods. Highly admired and quickly put to use, the foreign object soon threatens to destroy the very fiber of the tribal family as a harmonious functional unit. Family members grow jealous of one another and compete, for the first time ever, to hold sole possession of this unique treasure. The discord goes on until the hero, Xi, decides that the gods had been severely misguided. He then sets off on a trek to return their gift, thus launching the series of misadventures that compose the bulk of the movie.

At about the same time the Bushmen were contending with their godly gift in South Africa, Alfred Rappaport, an accounting professor at the Kellogg Graduate School of Management at Northwestern University, published a series of articles that pointed out that cash-flow analysis not only was a better predictor of the value of a business enterprise but also could forecast future stock market price levels more accurately. Thus, the notion of shareholder value was born. Like the introduction of the Coke bottle into the Kalahari tribe, it was to throw the world of management into a turmoil it has not yet recovered from. This chapter delves into the impact this innovation has had on the cultures of companies. Have the gods of academe tossed an attractive but ultimately destructive gift into our midst? And if so, what can we do to restore harmony and order in corporate life?

## Shareholder Value: The CEO's Coke Bottle

Until the early- to mid-1980s, most managers balanced the interests of the various "stakeholders" in their business *and* used accounting measures of performance to help them keep score. Ralph Cordiner, highly respected CEO of General Electric through the late 1950s, argued that senior executives were responsible for managing the enterprise "in the best-balanced interests of shareholders, customers, employees, suppliers, and plant community cities." David Packard commented in his 1995 book, *The HP Way,* about a business conference he attended in the late 1940s where he expressed the view that "business had responsibilities beyond making a profit for their shareholders. . . . We had important responsibilities to our employees, to our customers, to our suppliers and to the welfare of society at large." Packard, then a young executive in his fledgling company, expressed surprise that not everyone at the meeting agreed with him. The truth was that most did. Some, like Hewlett and Packard, believed in serving multiple constituencies so much that they enshrined it in the credo of their companies.

In this earlier era when companies were run to serve diverse needs of multiple constituents, virtually all companies and investors relied on commonly accepted accounting measures of performance, such as earnings per share (EPS), to keep track of how well they were doing. Sophisticated companies like General Electric used other accounting calculations, like return on investment (ROI) or return on capital employed (ROCE), to assist them in making capital investment decisions. Like the tribal world of the Bushmen, the world of management was held together by adherence to certain widely accepted traditions and practices.

Within the accounting world, however, voices were being raised in opposition to these traditional methods. Some academics suggested that accounting measures of performance did not always produce the right answer. For example, Ezra Solomon in 1966 published an article in *Research in Accounting Measurement* entitled "Return on Investment: The Relation of Book-Yield to True Yield" (initially ignored but subsequently reprinted in Rappaport's 1979 book *Information for Decision Making*). He argued that ROI was not a reliable indicator of the true "economic value" of an investment as calculated on the basis of discounted cash flow (DCF). Others, in particular Rappaport, argued that EPS was a very unreliable measure of the value of a corporation. His reasons: (1) EPS can be manipulated by using different but acceptable accounting assumptions (such as how to value inventory), (2) EPS does not measure the investment needed to run a business even routinely (such as working capital requirements), and (3) EPS does not take into account the time-value of money essential to determining an enterprise's true economic value. These revisionists had hard factual analysis to prove their case—especially in saying that future stock market prices could be forecast more accurately using DCF techniques. Since this pointed at potential ways to make more money, people naturally sat up and took notice.

It is indisputably true that discounted cash flows, properly constructed, offer a much more accurate way of valuing the worth of an enterprise. Even proponents of this approach to business valuation, however, admit that getting the calculations right is not a trivial exercise. Minor changes in assumptions about the "discount rate" appropriate to future cash flows can produce dramatically different valuations of the same business. Controversy still rages over how best to calculate (and then discount) the "terminal value" of a business. Even the simple exercise of estimating cash flows a scant few years down the road is fraught with difficulty. Proper shareholder value analysis requires a high degree of expertise in arcane analytic techniques and calculations. As a result, its application quickly spawned a new industry for numerate consultants. It just as quickly alienated a whole generation of managers who saw these complex exercises as a classic case of analysis paralysis.

In the early days of the shareholder value revolution, few managers took time to study the arguments carefully. Fewer still thought about the implication for changing the way they went about managing their companies. One message did get through loud and clear: Shareholder value meant dividends plus share price accumulation—not just smartly rising accounting profits. As a result, managers began to focus on stock price as a crucial measure of the value of their efforts. The die was cast. The most fundamental revolution in management thinking in at least one hundred years was about to occur.

## The Rise of the LBO Kings

In spite of management apathy in the early days of the shareholder value revolution, one group of observers saw the potential ramifications of this sea change in thinking. They moved quickly to take advantage of it. These were a new breed of investment bankers, the most notable being Jerome (Jerry) Kohlberg Jr. Kohlberg was the head of corporate finance at Bear Stearns, a unit that analyzed the financial conditions of companies and decided what kind of fiscal help they might need. In the summer of 1965, when a young associate, George Roberts, came to work for him, Kohlberg was already exploring a new concept that he then called a bootstrap. The world would soon come to know the concept by another name: leveraged buyouts, or LBOs.

A leveraged buyout consisted of buying a company, usually at an attractive price to the sellers. The deal was done with a mixture of a little bit of equity—supplied by the purchasers—and a lot of debt—supplied by banks and insurance companies. It was the debt that provided the transaction's decisive leverage. In the early days of the industry, managers who knew the company well were given an incentive to become part of the new management team. They were offered a stake in the equity of the recapitalized company (often around 20%, a substantial share in the future welfare of the company).

Management teams in LBOs, therefore, quickly confronted the problem of paying interest charges on the high level of debt needed to make the transaction work. Motivated to make their personal equity stakes realize value, management often undertook a series of restructuring activities. These involved making massive cost reductions to improve cash flow, selling off unprofitable divisions to raise cash and cut debt, changing approaches to distribution to improve the margins on surviving businesses (e.g., getting rid of direct company-paid sales forces and turning distribution over to agents), or often just raising prices to improve margins. After a few years of successful belt-tightening, they hoped debt could be retired, cash flows increased, and overall profitability and prospects improved. If so, the original investors could realize their gains by reselling the company to public investors through a stock offering or by selling the company to another business. Not all such deals succeeded, but many did. Overall returns in excess of 50% a year—sometimes even higher—quickly got the attention of more passive equity and bond investors.

For the next ten years, Kohlberg and Roberts, joined by Roberts's cousin, Henry Kravis, built this new style of business for Bear Stearns. *Money Machine,* a 1991 book by financial journalist Sarah Bartlett, reported that some of their deals were great successes, others relative flops. In spite of occasional setbacks, Kohlberg, Kravis, and Roberts were convinced they were onto a good thing. Their partners at Bear Stearns were not as enthusiastic. In May 1976, Kohlberg, Kravis, and Roberts struck out on their own and set up the firm of KKR. The rest, as people say, is history.

One of the company's first challenges was to obtain more capital. The three new partners, though hardly poor, needed more equity to purchase target companies. Besides using conventional sources like insurance companies, the three partners were the first to tap into the cash accumulating in pension funds. This source was especially lucrative in pension funds for public employees, the largest pools of investment money in the world. Their success in raising these funds (shown in Table 2.1) gave them the progressively larger war chests that allowed them to become major players in the business.

As the table shows, the war chest expanded so quickly that KKR's stake in its various funds declined rapidly from over 10% to under 3% within ten years. How, then, was the company to realize the

TABLE 2.1    Trends in KKR Fund-Raising

|       | Fund Size ($ millions) | KKR Contribution ($ millions) | KKR Contribution (% of fund) |
|-------|-----------------------|-------------------------------|------------------------------|
| 1978  | 32                    | 3.0                           | 10.6                         |
| 1980  | 75                    | 3.1                           | 4.1                          |
| 1982  | 316                   | 5.0                           | 1.5                          |
| 1984  | 1,000                 | 7.5                           | 0.8                          |
| 1986  | 1,800                 | 20.0                          | 1.1                          |
| 1987  | 5,600                 | 140.0                         | 2.5                          |

SOURCE: From Sarah Bartlett, *Money Machine* (Warner Books, 1991), appendix.

financial benefits of its successful investments? The answer was simple: Change the ground rules. KKR required that the first 20% of gains on any investments go directly to the company as a fee for carrying out the deal. Thus, KKR was ensured of making a substantial profit irrespective of its own small direct investment.

There was, however, another problem to be overcome. Deals took time to mature. Who was to subsidize the rent and overhead for the new firm while it waited for the fruition of its investments? Again, the answer was simple: Charge fees for all work done in relation to each investment—fees for structuring the deal, fees for overseeing each company in its portfolio, even fees for attending board meetings of the acquired companies. With these fees coming in regularly, KKR would be secure until it bagged the big money at the time investments were liquidated.

Why did investors put up with KKR's onerous terms? The answer, in a word, is profit. Even with the high charges imposed by KKR, investors made out very well. For example, investors in the 1978 fund achieved an annual return of 30.5% a year; the 1980 fund, 32.2%; the 1982 fund, 41.8%; the 1984 fund, 28.0%; the 1986 fund, 29.6%. Compared with single-digit returns from straightforward investments in stocks or bonds, these double-digit returns obviously caught the eyes of investors. And if KKR made a little money in the bargain, why not?

Especially as deal sizes got bigger, the LBO business was an attractive one. By mid-1985, each of the three founding KKR partners was estimated to have a net worth in excess of $500 million. And though KKR may have paved the way, a number of other firms soon joined them in this extremely lucrative pastime.

With all of this money and the variety of players chasing deals, the rules of the game began to shift. Originally, all deals were "friendly," and it was an accepted article of faith that retaining a committed management team was essential to the deal's success. Because of the increasingly crowded marketplace (there seemed to be no such crowd in terms of raising money for these deals), this golden rule was abandoned in 1985, when KKR launched a hostile takeover bid for publicly listed Beatrice Companies. From this time on, the by-word was "Managers, beware of takeover artists."

Both the deals themselves and the associated eye-popping fees were to have a major impact on management and the conduct of business in the years ahead. In a 1984 article, Michael Jensen argued:

> Scientific evidence indicates that activities in the market for corporate control almost uniformly increase efficiency and shareholders' wealth. Yet there is an almost continuous flow of unfavorable publicity and calls for regulation and restriction of unfriendly takeovers. *Many of these appeals arise from managers who want protection from competition for their jobs* [emphasis added] and others who desire more controls on corporations.

The aggressiveness of the takeover artists, combined with hefty profits, pushed the concept of shareholder value to center stage. Not surprisingly, the intense focus on improving shareholder value soon left management with little choice but to accept it as a key concern, just as it was for the raiders. Failure to take the new standard into account would make their own companies vulnerable to hostile takeover. Old methods for measuring progress would have to be jettisoned. When managerial pay practices changed to make sure managers heeded these new priorities, the future was determined.

## Bringing Home Management's Bacon

Managers in the 1970s were content to be compensated with salaries and, if they earned them, cash bonuses. Malcolm Salter's

1970 survey of executive compensation of the hundred largest industrial firms in the United States indicated that eighty-one used cash bonus systems as their primary incentives to executives. Although stock option plans were in existence, the laggard performance of the stock market in the 1970s, along with the preferences of executives, made cash-in-hand king.

Within a decade, proponents of shareholder value were arguing for more performance-based pay. For example, Alfred Rappaport, the guru of shareholder value, wrote a 1978 article in the *Harvard Business Review* arguing that executive pay should be more firmly tied to performance. His definition of performance was, of course, closely related to shareholder value. He advocated stock-based and longer-term executive compensation schemes. His arguments did not fall on deaf ears. By the mid-1980s, stock options had become the preferred form of incentive compensation for most senior managers.

Did stock-option-based incentive schemes for managers actually produce the intended results? Did they spur a massive increase in shareholder value—even if that one objective should not be the only one managers pursue, as the Kotter and Heskett analysis reported in Chapter 1 demonstrated? History would seem to say yes. The value of shares has escalated since the beginning of the 1980s. Between 1980 and 1997, the Dow Jones industrial average increased 533%, as shown on Figure 2.1.

The growth in executive pay levels in the 1980s and 1990s was therefore dramatic, as shown in Table 2.2 (see page 52), which tracks the top corporate pay packets year by year. As the table shows, the seven-digit level of executive pay was broached in the mid-1970s (still, seven figures generally represented the peak). By 1981, eight figures was becoming more common, although special circumstances surrounded the garnering of such high figures. For example, Boone Pickens (who appears twice) was really a corporate raider and part of the Wall Street gang. Similarly, Fred Smith at Federal Express was cashing in on his success as an entrepreneur. By the 1990s, however, eight-figure pay packets were the norm, not the exception. Although it would take a few more years before the gray suits would begin to score big points, thanks to these high-earning pioneers the goalposts had been moved and the playing field was open.

Michael Eisner and Tony O'Reilly, hired hands at their respective employers, Disney and Heinz, were the first "managers" (as distinguished from entrepreneurs) to benefit in a very big way. Eisner has

FIGURE 2.1    Dow Jones Closing Average

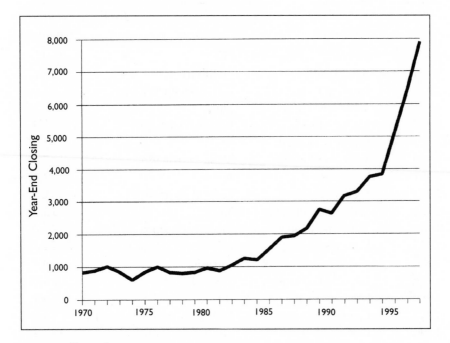

SOURCE: Dow Jones.

in fact hit paydirt more than once as Disney stock soared throughout the 1990s. But those who appeared on the top of the executive
pay bonanza list at the start of the decade were just the tip of the iceberg. The tenth-highest-paid executive by 1992 earned $22.8 mil-
lion—hardly a sum to be scoffed at but not even notable enough to
make a headline. In its 1992 survey of executive pay, *Business Week*
determined that 467 of the 730 executives included in the survey
earned more than $1 million a year; the average CEO in the survey
earned $3,842,247—an increase of 56% over the average wage in
1991. By 1997 even these figures looked puny. The *New York Times*
reported on a survey of half of the top 500 publicly held companies.
It showed that *average* CEO compensation in 1997 was $8.7 mil-
lion, a 37.8% increase over 1996. Fully one in ten of the CEOs sur-
veyed was taking home a pay packet worth in excess of $20 million.

Some individuals cashed in so much and so often that the compensation sums became staggering. For example, Steve Ross of Time
Warner made about $275 million for doing his job between 1973
and 1989. Lou Gerstner, a former management consultant called in

TABLE 2.2    Trend in Top Corporate Pay Packets

|  | Executive | Company | Total Pay That Year ($ millions) |
|---|---|---|---|
| 1974 | Harold Geneen | ITT | 0.8 |
| 1975 | John Halliburton | Halliburton | 1.6 |
| 1976 | Charles Lake | R. R. Donnelley | 1.0 |
| 1977 | J. Robert Fluor | Fluor | 1.1 |
| 1978 | Harry Merlo | Louisiana-Pacific | 3.4 |
| 1979 | Frank Rosenfelt | MGM | 5.2 |
| 1980 | T. Boone Pickens | Mesa Petroleum | 7.9 |
| 1981 | Steven Ross | Warner | 22.6 |
| 1982 | Frederick Smith | Federal Express | 51.5 |
| 1983 | William Anderson | NCR | 13.2 |
| 1984 | T. Boone Pickens | Mesa Petroleum | 23.0 |
| 1985 | Victor Posner | DWG | 12.7 |
| 1986 | Lee Iacocca | Chrysler | 20.5 |
| 1987 | Charles Lazarus | Toys "R" Us | 60.0 |
| 1988 | Michael Eisner | Disney | 40.1 |
| 1989 | Craig McCaw | McCaw Communications | 53.9 |
| 1990 | Donald A. Pels | Lin Broadcasting | 186.2 |
| 1991 | Tony O' Reilly | Heinz | 75.1 |
| 1992 | Thomas Frist | HCA | 127.0 |
| 1993 | Michael Eisner | Disney | 197.0 |
| 1994 | Charles Locke | Morton International | 25.9 |
| 1995 | Lawrence Coss | Green Tree Financial | 65.6 |
| 1996 | Lawrence Coss | Green Tree Financial | 102.4 |
| 1997 | Sandy Weill | Travelers | 230.7 |

SOURCE: Information through 1984 taken from Kevin J. Murphy, "Top Executives Are Worth Every Nickel They Get" *Harvard Business Review*, March-April 1986, based on various issues of *Forbes*; data after 1984 taken from various editions of *Business Week*.

to "turn around" IBM's dismal performance, was sitting on options worth $81 million in 1997. And that was before he negotiated a contract extension that granted him 2 million more share options.

What was wrong with everyone's making so much money by improving shareholder value? Potentially, quite a lot: Changes in the way the stock market works have driven extremely short-term thinking to the top of the management agenda. The ownership and management of equity has changed in recent years. In the United States as

FIGURE 2.2     Trend in Ownership of Large Companies

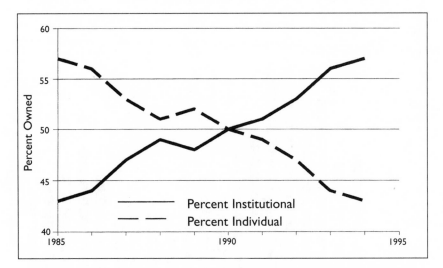

SOURCE: Michael Useem, *Investor Capitalism* (Basic Books, 1996), p. 26.

recently as 1965, 84% of equity was in the hands of private investors who were among the more wealthy in society. Now institutions control in excess of 60% of the major stock market equity around the world. This change in ownership of equity has had a massive influence on how companies are managed, especially in the United States.

The buildup of institutional equity ownership has been gradual but steady since the 1960s. It was fueled by a series of events. The first of these was the invention of the mutual fund, which gave individual investors instant portfolio diversification as well as access to professional fund management expertise. But mutual funds alone could not have spurred the institutional stake in the stock market. After World War II, pension funds became part of workers' standard compensation package. Recent changes in tax laws allowing individuals to fund their own tax-deferred pension schemes have added further fuel to the fire. These trends put even more investment funds in the hands of institutional investors. The combination of these factors has increased institutional equity in large companies, as shown in Figure 2.2. As early as 1976, management guru Peter Drucker predicted this coming shift in ownership of U.S. corporations in his book *The Unseen Revolution*. By the time the 1990s arrived, his prediction had come true.

FIGURE 2.3    Magellan Fund Churn

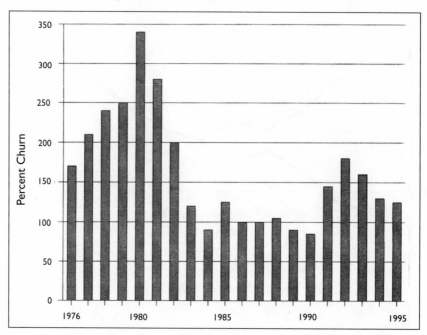

SOURCE: Michael Useem, *Investor Capitalism* (Basic Books, 1996), p. 33

Why should it matter so much? It matters because of who is doing the investing. Institutions are a collection of professional money managers—frequently but not always MBAs, mostly young, always concerned about the performance of funds under their control. Their livelihood depends on it. Money managers, unlike most private investors, oversee their investments full time. They buy and sell stocks at the drop of a hat in reaction to breaking news about a company. The most regular source is the company's quarterly report. Virtually every fund manager worth his or her salt watches quarterly financial performance like a hawk. The result is a great deal of churning. Stock portfolios turn over frequently as money managers react to every real or perceived change in future prospects of companies in which they have a stake. For example, as shown in Figure 2.3, Fidelity Magellan, the world's largest mutual fund, has turned over more than 100% of its portfolio every year since 1976 with three exceptions (1984, 1989, and 1990).

The effect of widespread churning is highly sensitized management attention to short-term detail. It is little wonder that certain management strategies (e.g., downsizing, outsourcing, globalization, and mergers and acquisitions) of the 1980s and 1990s have been so widely adopted across the business community. Managers who failed to get on the bandwagon would soon be left behind. With compensation tied heavily to stock options, managers' own pay comes under extreme pressure if their stock fails to perform. Stock-market-influenced, short-term thinking thus became the management norm.

There is another consequence of the explosion of executive pay: The enormous gains being realized by managers did not trickle far down the corporate ladder. In a recent research report, the AFL-CIO, not exactly a neutral observer, pointed out that from 1980 to 1995

- CEO pay increased 499%, whereas
- corporate profits rose 145%,
- inflation raised price levels 85%, and
- factory wages rose a paltry 70%.

As a result, the gap between the salary of the average worker and that of the CEO increased dramatically. Although there is some dispute about how to calculate the gap correctly, all attempts place the wage gap between 15–20 to 1 in the 1970s versus 150–350 to 1 in the mid-1990s. The widening pay gap between top managers and workers is a ticking time bomb. The first reaction to the pay gap has been cynicism: Why should I kill myself for a CEO who is the only one who will profit from my work? This initial reaction is likely only the tip of the iceberg. Increased employee militancy is almost inevitable as people decide they've had enough seeing their efforts feather mainly the nests of the top executives. The likely outcome of increased militancy is massive turnover for most large companies. Given that workers have learned not to be loyal to their employers any more, they are more willing to vote with their feet to achieve personal financial gain. The costs of this increased turnover, both direct costs of recruiting new employees and indirect costs of losing key capabilities, are likely to be enormous.

## The Upside: Making Money

The pressure imposed on managers by the threat of the takeover artists of the 1980s in some cases encouraged companies to act on their own behalf. Perhaps the most celebrated occasion of this occurred at Gillette, the razor blade manufacturer. In November 1986, Ronald Perelman, a raider who had previously taken over cosmetics giant Revlon for $2.7 billion, offered $65 a share in a $4.1-billion attempt to acquire Gillette. Gillette refused the offer but after a series of legal maneuvers ended up paying Perelman $43 million over and above the price of the stock he had bought in the company in return for his agreement not to attempt to acquire the company again for ten years. Although the company denied that the payment constituted "greenmail"—essentially blackmail payments to raiders to stand down—most of the public thought otherwise.

Despite his agreement, Perelman launched two further attempts to get the company to sell out (there was little honor among thieves or raiders in the dark days of the 1980s). The company repulsed both, but the attention Gillette received in the process eventually led to a proxy fight between the management of the company and a new group of investors called the Coniston Group, intent also on a dramatic restructuring of the company or its sale to the Perelman interests. Once again the company and its management prevailed by a razor-thin margin.

In reaction to the pressure from these raiders, the management team of Gillette decided to restructure its business. In a very short period for such an old and respected company, management ordered an 8% reduction in employment levels around the company. It sold its corporate jet and canceled an order for a new one. It also sold a luxury products company in France, a computer catalog business, a chain of skin care salons, a software venture, an eye care operation, and a group of luxury spas. The company closed factories and warehouses in Europe and other parts of the world, and cut back on advertising except for that needed to support the core of its profitable businesses. One immediate result of all of these cutbacks was a significant jump in both revenue and profit. A second immediate result was a substantial equity investment in the business by Warren Buffet, the "Sage of Omaha," one of the shrewdest investors in the world. This investment virtually insulated the company from further takeover threats and gave it the cash to pursue profitable new ventures. The most important result of the changes initiated by Gillette's management in response to pressure from Wall Street raiders was global competitiveness. After restructuring itself, Gillette went on to

FIGURE 2.4    Trend in Gillette Stock Price

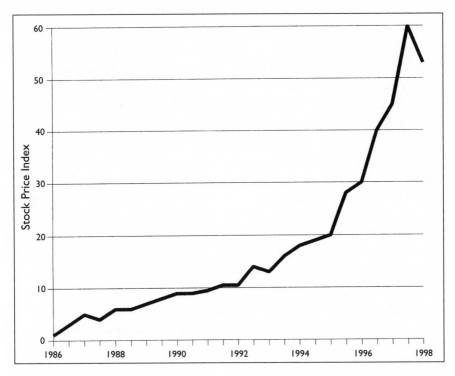

SOURCE: Dow Jones.

build a truly enviable position in the markets it served around the world. The company has barely looked back since, as shown in its stock track record (Figure 2.4).

## The Downside: Short-Term Management

Gillette was not alone in responding positively to the threat it faced from raiders. Many other managers began launching aggressive cost-reduction programs. They also began restructuring programs designed to hive off poorly performing parts of the business and build critical mass through acquisition in their core competencies. The combination of all these actions was a very short-termist view on the part of managers about what it would take to sustain and push their stock prices ever higher. The age of the short-term manager had arrived.

Arguments over short-termism versus long-range strategic views have been raging for some time. Boone Pickens, one of the high-profile raiders of the 1980s, defended the short-termist view in a *Harvard Business Review* article: "The short-term theory [meaning those who oppose short-termism] must be exposed for what it is, a weak argument advanced by weak managements." At around the same time, *Business Week*, hardly a bleeding-heart defender of the status quo, worried about the same phenomenon:

> Many factors have turned American industry into a high-stakes poker game. Pension fund managers, to cite one example, compete for more than $1 trillion in investments. One way they win business is to outpace each other in quarterly yields. And the importance that pension funds place on quarter-by-quarter performance is simply a reflection of the attitude the stock market in general holds toward quarterly earnings. Investors put pressure on portfolio managers and brokers who run funds to outperform the averages—and one another—in order to earn their bonuses and keep their clients. Moreover, companies themselves exacerbate this focus on the short-term performance by pressuring their own pension fund managers to generate high short-term rewards. . . . This forces management to put short-term earnings growth before such interests as market development, product quality, research and development, and customer and employee satisfaction. These are interests that help ensure the long-term success of a company.

By the 1990s, having lost the battle, *Business Week* turned mostly silent on the subject.

What exactly is wrong with short-termism? After all, some of the surge in stock market valuations can be attributed to management actions. And most people gain when the stock market goes up—especially since the majority of investors are acting on behalf of individual pension funds. That's the good news.

The bad news about short-termism is its influence on actions managers take—or, equally important, don't take. Managers firmly fixed on the company's share price are naturally motivated to take actions that will boost the stock price. One way to do this is by cutting costs. Managers of large corporations have been on a cost-cutting binge since the early 1980s. They do this because the stock market, peopled mainly by young money managers running institutional funds, responds positively to news of belt-tightening. Costs extracted from a company's expense base usually flow directly to the bottom line as increased earnings. Most cost cutters would argue that the proof of the pudding is in the eating: If costs can be reduced substantially without jeopardizing operations, it must have been unnecessary fat.

But often these costs were being incurred to build the company's long-term future. Since personnel costs are a large budget item, eliminating people has become a priority for modern managers. Yet some of the people terminated to shave costs are key figures in the informal network—important to maintaining the company's cultural identity and long-term performance.

Mergers and acquisitions (M&A) are other actions favored by short-term managers. The surge in M&A activity was initially fueled by LBOs and the actions of takeover artists. But with the level of stock prices so high in the late 1990s, LBO activity has slowed dramatically. And yet the level of M&A activity continues at record levels. Why? Because Wall Street loves a merger. Most managers with their eyes on their stock price know this. Moreover, mergers invariably open the door to an additional round of cost cutting. Overheads need to be consolidated; facilities need to be rationalized; "nonstrategic" assets need to be divested. Wall Street considers all this wonderful news, so merger mania goes on and on. The fact that it is difficult, if not downright impossible, to merge disparate cultures does not even enter into the debate.

Not all short-term-oriented actions are unjustified. Many companies faced with new competition or emerging technologies must cut costs to survive. And many mergers between large companies make good sense. The problem is the thoughtlessness with which these stock-enhancing actions are often pursued and the carnage they have wreaked among employees and therefore on the cultures of companies.

Also problematic is the absence of concern for the long-term futures of the companies in question. Too often the mentality of short-term-oriented managers precludes taking actions if the payback is too far away to influence current stock prices. These include needed investments in people, products, brands, customers, and suppliers. If these long-term investments are not made, promising future outcomes are foreclosed.

Consider one example: In the early 1980s, IBM legitimized and revolutionized the personal computer industry when it launched its PC. It also made several blunders that IBM's managers now readily concede. The biggest mistake occurred when IBM turned to Microsoft, then a relative upstart in the industry, to supply the operating system for the PC. To its credit, Microsoft capitalized on IBM's shortsightedness by building a company that now boasts the world's largest stock market capitalization. Once IBM recognized its bungle, what did managers do about it? They cut costs—more aggressively than almost any large company in the world.

What might they have done? They could have decided, as soon as they saw their error, to invest in developing a proprietary operating system of their own. That way they could compete with Microsoft. Instead, again working hand in glove with Microsoft, they invested a fortune trying to develop a new operating system standard (OS/2). Their intent was to smooth the transition between the company's traditional mainframe computer business and the new world of PCs. OS/2 never even came close to catching up with the basic Microsoft operating system. And with the release of Windows, OS/2 was doomed to the junk heap of failed software ventures. Would a more sensible investment in an operating system capable of competing with and ultimately supplanting Microsoft's product have been successful? There is no way to know. In fact, many have argued that IBM was simply incapable of producing the software needed for the emerging world of the PC. Whatever, the argument is now moot. IBM didn't make the investment necessary to compete in this new arena. We will never know what would have happened if IBM had wrested the PC operating system monopoly from Microsoft. One speculation is that it might have become more like the IBM of old, the most respected company in the world.

This example is not intended to knock IBM's management. At the time, the company had a lot of problems to overcome. And we were not privy to the internal debates that raged as the company settled on its ultimate course of action. We use the example only to illustrate the road not taken. No one can ever know what alternative futures might have been had another route been chosen. To his credit, one of the most significant decisions taken by Lou Gerstner after he was brought in from the outside to run IBM was to preserve the company's huge annual investment in R&D. One can only hope this was not another example of too little, too late.

## Cultural Implications of Short-Termism

The era from roughly the mid-1980s until the millennium will go down in business history as one dominated by short-term managerial actions. These actions have had consequences. Soaring stock market valuations in the 1990s have made many people rich. This "wealth effect" is widely cited by many pundits as a key influence on the prolonged expansion of the U.S. economy. Some such pundits even go so far as to argue that increased market valuations reflect the dramatically increased international competitiveness of American companies although more time will have to pass before these claims can be validated. While improved competitiveness and increased wealth are the positives of this era of management, there has been a downside, as well. Much of the downside can be seen in the wreckage of traditional corporate cultures that litters the business landscape.

To cut costs, companies have been repeatedly downsized, and the mindsets and attitudes of employees—both those who were victimized and those who survived—have been permanently scarred. Company loyalty as it used to be is a thing of the past. Employees have been forced to learn that their first loyalty must be to themselves. It will take some time for this fundamental attitude change to work its way through to tangible behavioral changes, but proof of the deterioration in people's willingness to work hard without question is near at hand. The next time a serious downturn occurs, and economic history suggests that it will, companies will have to look elsewhere than to employees for the extra efforts needed to weather the storm.

In the latter half of the 1990s, managers have resorted to stock-market-oriented mergers as last ditch efforts to shore up their companies' stock prices. Often as a result, people have been tossed together in the newly amalgamated companies, which have radically different beliefs and values as well as different ideas about the behaviors needed to achieve future success. At best these people will coexist in the newly blended entities (most people need a job). But they will find it hard to achieve any consistency in how they approach their work. It will be harder still to extract any real meaning from their employment. Again, traditional views of employee loyalty will suffer as a result. Of more immediate concern, productivity will suffer as people struggle to bridge the gap between the ways they once knew and the culture in which they now work. Managerial initiatives will fail or, more likely, bumble along, not because they were poorly conceived but their implementation will be hampered by perceptual differences among fragmented groups of employees. Confronted with these failures, management will be thrown back on even more short-term actions to cure the rot, and the vicious downward cycle will continue.

While long-term corporate performance and productivity are likely the immediate consequences of a long accumulation of short-term management thinking, employee disaffection is likely its most permanent legacy. Where earlier generations of workers around the world found meaning and value in their working lives, today's workers—at both junior and senior levels—are forced to look elsewhere. People will still work to earn a living, of course. The self actualization that once came from work will be missing, however. It will have to be found elsewhere. Instead of going to work to join in spirit with the doings of a great enterprise, workers will rush home to family, friends, communities and activities outside of work where their individual search for meaning will continue unabated. In due course, their disdain for life at work except as a necessary means to an end will manifest itself in a deterioration in the environment within which business hopes to thrive and a change in climate that few businesspeople today will have experienced.

Work without soul is spirit-destroying. Business without committed people is doomed to mediocrity and ultimately failure. This is the legacy shareholder value thinking and the short-termism it spawned have left for future generations. None of these consequences of shareholder-value-driven thinking is exactly a recipe for building strong and cohesive cultures. The gods (surely) must be crazy.

## CHAPTER 3

# Downsizing and Reengineering

## Corporate Lobotomy

Interest in cutting costs has been a preoccupation of managers for a long time—as it should have been. The increased focus on shareholder value and the short-term thinking associated with it, however, moved cost cutting to the very center of the management agenda. This shift in priorities eclipsed other strategies for improving financial performance. It turned what used to be a ripple on an organization's beach into a veritable tsunami. Some of the recent cost cutting has been a necessary means to recapture the competitive edge needed to survive in today's global marketplace. But much of the cost cutting was unsuccessful and, in hindsight, probably unnecessary. Virtually all the cost cutting undertaken by companies has seriously weakened their cultural cohesion. Since most cost cutting targets people as the way to bring costs into line, it wreaks havoc on the victims of downsizing. It also affects survivors, who wonder whether they will be next to receive the ax. Are the gains in corporate efficiency worth the human costs? Can the cultural fragmentation resulting from unprecedented assaults on corporate cost bases be undone? Can strong cultures emerge once again as powerful forces for superior financial performance?

## Moving from Operations Improvement to Reengineering

Attention to costs as a managerial priority is as old as modern management itself. "Scientific management," espoused by Frederick Taylor at the dawn of the twentieth century, focused heavily on measuring and understanding costs. The modern industry of management consulting took shape in the 1920s, when early Taylorites such as James O. McKinsey applied some of Taylor's ideas to create cost-accounting systems. As the world economy emerged from the ravages of World War II, cutting costs had become a featured management tool. Throughout the 1950s and 1960s, as shown in Figure 3.1, cost cutting in the United States and elsewhere focused mainly on production or production-related issues, since the vast majority of workers were still engaged in blue-collar occupations.

The practice or technology of cost cutting was labeled "operations improvement." It relied heavily on new advances in what was then called "operations research." The bible for practitioners of this ancient art was a book by Harvey M. Wagner published in 1969, *The Principles of Operations Research, with Applications to Managerial Decisions*. For most of the 1960s and 1970s, it served managers and consultants well as a template for cost-cutting initiatives.

As the percentage of white-collar workers increased, new tools were needed for addressing the cost-effectiveness of nonproduction staff functions. One of the first new tools was developed by a McKinsey consultant named John Neuman. His approach, known as "overhead value analysis" (OVA), advocated a disciplined process for deciding which staff functions should remain and which terminated in a company or department forced to downsize its operations. Neuman's *Harvard Business Review* article appeared in June 1975—just about the time that the workforce shifted from a blue-collar majority to one dominated by clerks and accountants. OVA claimed the ability to reduce costs by 40% by eliminating unneeded staff functions. In reality, it produced cuts in overhead manpower by 5–15%. But this was still enough to position it as a widely used management tool through the late 1970s and early 1980s. Its success got Neuman elected as a partner of McKinsey & Company. But it was not successful enough to satisfy managers' thirst for deeper cost reductions.

The mid- to late-1970s were a difficult time for many businesses in the United States and Europe. Starting with the 1973 oil embargo

FIGURE 3.1    Trend in the Composition of the U.S. Workforce

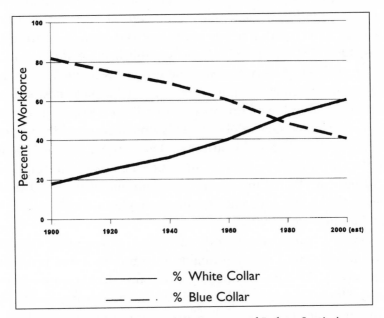

SOURCE: Monthly reports of the Bureau of Labor Statistics.

and the rampant inflation that followed, many companies faced extreme competitive pressure from newly emergent Japanese companies. Automobiles and office equipment (especially copiers) were two of many industries that struggled against this new offshore competition. It did not help that the Japanese products were typically cheaper and of higher quality than those offered by companies entrenched in their home markets.

Companies threatened by this competition responded—on both the cost and the quality fronts. For example, in early 1976 Xerox, then the dominant supplier of copiers worldwide, launched a multiyear cost-effectiveness program. It was the company's first major across-the-board assault on its cost base. Although the effort produced substantial cuts, it was only the beginning of a long and painful process. Automobile manufacturers responded in similar fashion, perhaps realizing more than most companies that they were just beginning a long and painful journey.

The response to perceived quality shortcomings was even more dramatic. It soon produced its own revolution in thinking about costs. It began quietly with the 1970 publication of a landmark book by Joe Juran and Frank Gryna: *Quality Planning and Analysis: From Product Development Through Usage.* But in 1970 the business world was not yet ready for the book's nontraditional ideas. By 1978, when Philip Crosby published *Quality Is Free: The Art of Making Quality Certain,* the ground was much more fertile. The book immediately shot to the top of business best-seller lists. McGraw-Hill followed this success in 1980 by issuing a second edition of Juran and Gryna's book. This time it received the response it deserved. With the publication in 1982 of W. Edward Deming's *Quality, Productivity and Competitive Position,* the total quality management (TQM) movement was truly under way. TQM was to dominate the management agenda throughout much of the 1980s and well into the 1990s.

TQM's greatest innovation was a focus on getting the process right. It advocated building quality into products and processes incrementally through an ongoing program of continuous improvement. These ideas derived directly from the gurus responsible for launching the movement. The major method they proposed for achieving quality objectives was to empower the workforce directly involved in the process. This empowerment, when it worked, also eliminated much of the need for middle-management oversight. This further fueled OVA-like initiatives to reduce overhead costs. TQM's focus on incremental steps, however, frustrated managers still concerned that costs were too high.

The emphasis on continuous improvement was not to last. A 1986 article by Wickham Skinner, "The Productivity Paradox," argued that more had to be done than simply fine-tuning a firm's production processes. Bob Tomasko's 1987 book, *Downsizing,* called for the overhaul of cost structures across the board. In early 1990, a method to cut costs dramatically came to the fore. Two articles that appeared in the summer changed the face of cost cutting forever. They were the first (to the best of our knowledge) to talk explicitly about business process redesign and reengineering. One, "The New Industrial Engineering: Information Technology and Business Process Redesign" by Thomas Davenport and James Short, appeared in the prestigious *Sloan Management Review.* Mike Hammer and James Champy published a similar article, "Re-engineer Work: Don't Automate, Obliterate," in the *Harvard Business Review.* Four years later, Hammer and Champy followed up with their landmark best-seller, *Reengineering the Corporation*, which sold over 2 million copies in a short period. It spawned a slew of imitators and created a fortune in business for every top-rate consulting firm. The reengineering revolution was under way. Large-scale cost cutting had come of age, and corporate life was never to be the same.

## Cost Cutting:
## The Beast That Roared

Just how large a corporate movement did downsizing and reengineering become? Headlines from the *Wall Street Journal* of the early 1990s tell the story:

- September 10, 1990    "Fast-Food Chain to Slash Corporate Staff by 25 Percent"
- November 16, 1990    "MCI to Revamp Units, May Cut 1500 Staffers"
- December 6, 1990    "Ford Motor Co's Australia Unit . . . Laying Off 22 Percent of Workers"
- December 14, 1990    "Thomson-CSF Intends to Cut 3,695 Jobs [in] Restructuring Program"
- January 28, 1991    "Avery Dennison to Reduce Employment by 700 to 900 Employees"
- February 7, 1991    "Service America Corp Unit Trimming Work Force by 1,000"
- February 14, 1991    "Occidental's Plan to Cut at Least 1,000"
- May 21, 1991    "Apple to Fire 10% of Staff in Restructuring"
- June 7, 1991    "General Tire Cuts 20% of Staff"
- September 19, 1991    "Cuts at Occidental Boosted to 8.8% of Staff"
- October 24, 1991    "Michelin to Cut 4,900 Jobs"
- December 12, 1991    "TRW Decides to Cut Staff" [by 10,000]

- January 22, 1992      "United Technologies Restructur-
                        ing Includes Elimination of
                        13,900 Jobs"
- May 6, 1992           "Petro-Canada to Cut Workforce
                        by 20%"
- July 9, 1992          "Amoco to Cut 8,500 Staff"
- January 26, 1993      "Sears Trims Operations—Laying
                        Off 50,000 People"
- April 26, 1993        "Heinz Plans Further 10% Cut—
                        3,600 Employees" [on top of an
                        earlier 10%]
- June 14, 1993         "GE Jet Engine Cutting 1,500
                        Jobs"
- August 19, 1993       "Procter & Gamble Slashing
                        13,000 Jobs"
- December 9, 1993      "Xerox [to] Cut 10,000 Jobs"

The list above is, of course, highly selective. It includes primarily names most readers will recognize immediately. It highlights only some downsizing or restructuring activities under way at most of these firms. And it covers only a fraction of the first three years of the 1990s. The list is, nevertheless, very revealing.

First, few industries or companies were exempt from the wave of job cuts of the late 1980s and 1990s. When highly successful and profitable companies like MCI and Heinz join the movement, no one can claim that downsizing is limited to industrial dinosaurs. Even involvement in high-growth and high-tech industries was no guarantee of job security in the 1990s. Arguably, Apple encountered other unique business problems that required it to take extraordinary measures to ensure survival. But the same can hardly be said for GE's Jet Engine Division. It is one of the top success stories of the recent business era. Moreover, downsizing and restructuring is global in scope, not just an American business fad. Names like Michelin, Thomson-CSF, and Petro-Canada just hint at the extent to which cost cutting had become an international preoccupation.

What became of the commitment to lifetime employment offered by strong-culture companies that dominated business life in the second half of the twentieth century? With names such as Sears, Procter & Gamble, GE, and Heinz on the list, it is clear that old assumptions about how to treat people no longer apply.

Finally, and what is perhaps saddest for employees in affected companies, a onetime reduction in force had been replaced by an ongoing campaign of slash and burn. Occidental announces cuts and shortly thereafter announces increased cuts. Heinz ups the ante after its first success in cutting 10% of its workforce. Xerox began trimming its cost base in the 1970s; the company was still at it as the 1990s moved into full swing. When *Business Week* interviewed Unisys chief executive James Unruh in June 1996, he was in the process of announcing his company's fifth restructuring in seven years. The beat goes on and on.

A list of headlined job cuts, alarming as it might be, does not even begin to portray the extent of the human carnage. The May 9, 1994, edition of *Business Week* highlighted the twenty-five largest cutbacks between 1991 and early 1994. The numbers are astounding, as shown in Table 3.1. As is clear, a lot of U.S. businesses were busy shedding their human capital.

Even this daunting table tells only part of the story. The April 25, 1994, edition of *Forbes* added its own analysis of data from the Bureau of Labor Statistics. It suggested that total employment in Forbes 500 companies (the largest companies in the economy) had declined 10% between 1980 and 1993—a body count in excess of 2 million people. Looking over a shorter time frame (1987 through 1993), *Forbes* noted employment declines of 117,553 at IBM (30% of Big Blue's workforce); 110,700 at Sears Roebuck (22%); 104,000 at GE (31%); and 102,200 at GM (14%). By January 1998, Challenger, Gray & Christmas, the Chicago-based firm that tracks layoffs in corporate America, reported in the *Financial Times* that the total downsizings of large companies had topped 4 million.

Taking a broader point of view, the Bureau of Labor Statistics reported in October 1996 that 9.4 million U.S. workers were displaced from their jobs between the beginning of 1993 and the end of 1995—4.2 million of whom had held their jobs for more than three years before getting the ax. This 4.2 million included 1.2 million managers and professionals and 1.3 million technical, sales, and administrative personnel. Restructuring in the 1990s clearly touches workers at all levels of an enterprise.

TABLE 3.1    Job Death: Twenty-Five Large Downsizings, 1991–1994

| Company | Staff Cutbacks |
| --- | --- |
| IBM | 85,000 |
| AT&T | 83,500 |
| GM | 74,000 |
| US Postal Service | 55,000 |
| Sears | 50,000 |
| Boeing | 30,000 |
| Nynex | 22,000 |
| Hughes Aircraft | 21,000 |
| GTE | 17,000 |
| Martin-Marietta | 15,000 |
| DuPont | 14,800 |
| Eastman Kodak | 14,000 |
| Philip Morris | 14,000 |
| Procter & Gamble | 13,000 |
| Phar Mor | 13,000 |
| Bank of America | 12,000 |
| GE Aircraft Engines | 10,250 |
| McDonnell Douglas | 10,200 |
| BellSouth | 10,200 |
| Ford Motor | 10,000 |
| Xerox | 10,000 |
| Pacific Telesis | 10,000 |
| Honeywell | 9,000 |
| US West | 9,000 |

SOURCE: *Business Week* May 9, 1994.

Although most of the statistics cited above are based on U.S. companies, American trends are mirrored in other parts of the world, particularly Europe. As with most management movements, there is a lag before what sweeps the United States reaches the other side of the Atlantic. In addition, local labor laws in Europe make downsizing difficult and expensive to carry out. But this did not deter firms like ABB, Volkswagen, GM-Europe, British Telecom (BT), Lloyds-TSB Bank, and many others from shedding tens of thousands of workers. By 1996 even well-known Swiss companies such as Credit Suisse and Novartis (Switzerland's largest pharmaceutical firm) were announcing job cutbacks in the thousands. Downsizing, reengineering, and restructuring have become phenomena of massive proportions.

In Europe most workers historically have been protected by contracts and laws that virtually guarantee lifetime employment. By 1996 even this had begun to change. Deutsche Telekom, eager to prepare itself for privatization, stopped offering lifetime contracts to new employees. In effect, this converted newcomers into contract workers. In doing so, it followed the lead of British Telecom, itself privatized in the early 1980s. BT replaced so many permanent employees with contract workers that the Communications Workers Union charged the company with producing a "massive sense of distrust." It was a charge duly denied by the company (*Business Week*, July 8, 1996). Laws passed in Germany, Italy, and even France allowed privatizing companies to lay off "civil service" employees. Companies like Deutsche Telekom, Alitalia, and France Telecom rushed to take advantage of these new freedoms. Elsewhere in Europe, bureaucrats are looking the other way as firms such as Air France rush to restructure their operations, despite the socialist leanings of most European governments.

Is the end of job cutting anywhere in sight? Not likely. In late 1997, Jack Welch of GE announced another $2-billion restructuring plan for his bellwether company (likely to translate into upward of 25,000 additional job losses). Where GE treads, others tend to follow. Eastman Kodak, still suffering from competition with Fuji Film, announced another 16,600 layoffs—on top of the 14,000 previous pink slips. Fruit of the Loom decided to cut 2,900 jobs—17% of its U.S. workforce—as it moves production into Mexico. Boeing, despite its record backlog and recent hiring binge to overcome production bottlenecks, revealed its plan to eliminate 12,000 workers. GM announced, as part of taking an additional $2-billion restructuring charge, its intention to shed a further 40,000 workers. AT&T said it was targeting an additional 5,000 positions in its headquarters and core long distance business (shortly followed with a plan to eliminate a further 18,000 positions). First Union Bancorp, which recently acquired CoreStates Bank, expects to eliminate the jobs of 5,500 of its 18,000 employees.

The American Management Association (AMA) has conducted a survey of its members' downsizing intentions and activities since 1988. Just over 50% of AMA's members who have responded to the survey since 1991 are engaged in "job elimination" year after year. Moreover, in a separate survey conducted by the AMA in 1995, over 95% of the members indicated they were reengineering—presumably with more job cuts yet to come. As an indication that these intentions were real, in August 1998, Challenger, Gray & Christmas reported that 321,217 jobs had been eliminated in the United States in the first half of 1998—a figure almost equal to the record-setting pace established in 1993. Cost cutting has truly come of age. For better or for worse, corporate cultures of the future will have to take this into account.

## Downsizing's Allure

Cutting costs is only one tool available to managers to improve a company's performance. A myriad of other possibilities exist, including inventing new products, entering new markets, and developing new distribution channels. Although there is plenty of evidence that companies have explored and even used such revenue-enhancing tools aggressively, there can be little doubt that the 1990s will be known as the decade of downsizing. This proved to be by far the most popular management initiative.

Why? There are two primary reasons. First, it is easier and more predictable in the short term to cut costs as a way to improve the bottom line. Inventing new products and penetrating new markets are both difficult and risky. Moreover, the financial costs of reducing staff levels are usually covered by restructuring charges, often viewed as good news rather than the write-offs of corporate assets they really are. Certainly, no one would argue that a good business should carry excess costs. If it can continue to operate successfully with fewer staff—as many large companies appear to be doing—then the cuts must be justified. So the conventional wisdom seems to go. If human costs are by-products of cost cutting, so be it. (We later discuss why this conventional wisdom may be shortsighted.)

Without a doubt, some companies needed to downsize. These include previously regulated monopoly suppliers of basic services such as telecommunications. Without competition to spur them on, it is little wonder that they developed bloated cost bases. These needed to be reduced—whatever the human cost—in order to prepare the companies for a more competitive marketplace. Not coincidentally, it often enabled companies to offer better service and value to their customers.

Companies facing competition for the first time in their core markets were also well justified in downsizing. Xerox is perhaps the best example. Xerox was not to blame that patents protected them from competition for decades. But once the patents expired and competition emerged, it would have been irresponsible for Xerox not to take action. The response inevitably implied serious downsizing, however wrenching it might have to be.

If there is fault to be found in all this, it can be laid at the doorsteps of companies that chose the "easy" way out—downsizing to inflate their short-term profits. Could they have done otherwise? Perhaps. But once the fad took hold, they had little choice but to join in.

The second major reason cost cutting became such a rampant force in the 1990s is that managers and their shareholders were rewarded for doing it. Seventeen of the companies that showed up as the biggest of the cost cutters (see Table 3.1) were listed on major stock exchanges then and now. Between 1991 and 1994, while they undertook these massive cuts, their stock value increased by an average of 57%. No wonder they thought they were on to a good thing. The good thing became even better for CEOs of the companies who cashed in their stock options. Since 1994, stocks of these cost-cutting leaders have advanced a further 127% (for a total advance of 257% since the cost cutting began). With rewards like that, who wouldn't be motivated to cut costs?

In 1995, a year in which large companies laid off 440,000 employees, the average salary of their CEOs increased by 18%, to just over $1.6 million. Including long-term incentives such as stock options, average CEO total pay increased 30%, to $3.7 million. These averages are deceptive because they hide some of the real highlights in CEO compensation that occurred during the 1990s.

Robert Daniel, the chairman of United Technologies, presided over a downsizing of 30,000 employees in the 1990s. He received compensation of $11.2 million in 1995 alone. The CEO of the company, George David, received stock options worth $6.7 million in the same year. Is it any wonder that a $64,000 middle manager at United Technologies was quoted in *Business Week* (April 22, 1996) as saying, "I used to go to work enthusiastically, now I just go in to do what I have to do. I feel overloaded to the point of burnout. Most of my colleagues are actively looking for other jobs or are just resigned to do the minimum. At the same time, the CEO is paid millions, and his salary is going up much higher than anyone else's. It makes me angry and resentful."

Of course, Daniel and David were not alone in reaping these executive rewards. The chairman of AT&T, Robert Allen, had total compensation of $15.9 million in 1995, despite taking a "pay cut" because of the company's difficulties. His contribution to the rolls of those let go: 85,000 employees. In 1993 Frank Shrontz, CEO of Boeing, announced 25,000 layoffs; his reward: a pay package worth $5.9 million. John Stafford, chairman of American Home Products, received a whopping $9.7 million and had to downsize only 4,000 employees to get it. Not to be outdone, Jack Welch of GE, architect of eliminating in excess of 100,000 employees during his tenure as CEO, was paid $22 million in 1997 alone. Downsizing is devastating for both those who are let go and those who survive. But for the CEOs of most large companies, it was just what the doctor ordered.

Were human and long-term corporate performance costs of this frenzied cost cutting taken into account? Probably. Managers are human and often humane. But with everyone doing it and being rewarded for their actions, it would be hard to resist. Can you really blame them?

### Reengineering: Farce or Salvation?

Few management trends have swept the world of corporations as completely as the reengineering revolution of the 1990s. In his book *Reengineering Management,* a 1995 follow-up to the book that launched reengineering, James Champy reported that 69% of U.S. companies and 75% of European companies, responding to a comprehensive survey conducted by the firm CSC Index, said they were engaged in one or more reengineering efforts. These projects enriched consulting firms around the world, produced massive job cuts, and one way or another touched the lives of millions of workers. Were these reengineering efforts the salvation that enabled firms to compete in the increasingly global marketplace, as their proponents argued? Alternatively, were they enormously intrusive charades designed to inflate short-term profits on the backs of ordinary workers, as their detractors argued? Or were they a combination of both, packaged for management as a panacea to overcome decades of mismanagement? The answers are, of course, respectively, yes, yes, and yes, as detailed below.

### Why Reengineer?

Companies undertake reengineering projects for a variety of reasons. One is certainly to shore up their operating statements to help them fend off unwanted advances from corporate raiders. The most important reason, however, is to enable them to become more competitive in markets they serve. Competitiveness had been eroded for many companies by the accretion of level upon level of management and white-collar staff. These functions are designed to oversee workers actually engaged in producing products for sale—a diminishing number in recent years. With historical roots in Taylorism, companies added these levels of oversight almost in direct reaction to the prevailing management philosophy. It asked workers to check their brains at the door before taking their places as cogs in the wheels of production. By the time companies had grown large, these levels of oversight had taken on a life of their own. When new competitors entered their markets, often from other parts of the world, they were not encumbered by the costs associated with these legacies. As a result, they could produce products of higher quality and lower cost than those of their more established competitors. In response to this threat, companies reengineered their operations to empower workers more directly, to use information technology to make timely decisions and eliminate the unneeded ranks of excessive supervision. That was the theory, anyway. What were the results?

### Anatomy of a Reengineering Project

Reengineering projects are big deals, both in financial terms and in terms of the number of people involved. They almost always involve large teams of outside consultants, hired for their experience as well as their objectivity (real or supposed). Many of the consultants hired for reengineering projects by large consulting firms finished reading Hammer and Champy only days before their clients did. Reengineering also involves large teams of internal staff assigned to the project for their inside knowledge and the credibility their presence might bring to whatever results. Because of the size and visibility of these projects, they almost always have top management endorsement. Most top managers are eager to support such projects because they know of no other way to reduce costs by the promised 20–40%.

Projects typically begin with a lot of fanfare. "Road shows" are launched to inform employees about how critical the project is to the future of the company. Employees are exhorted to abandon any preconceptions they have and to throw themselves wholeheartedly into a project designed to shape the corporate future.

Teams are almost always structured along process lines, since the rhetoric and religion of reengineering touts a process review as the key to identifying revolutionary new ways to do things. With project teams cutting across existing and conventional organization lines, they are likely to find new and different ways of doing business, so the theory goes. Last-minute horse trading to finalize project team arrangements often makes apparent a gap between theory and practice. Political alliances and agenda can dominate rational and functional criteria for how the teams will actually operate.

The early days of reengineering projects are exciting. The workload is enormous; enthusiasm is usually at its peak. Continuing top management exhortation buoys up even the most skeptical team members. What kind of work are they doing? Process mapping. Per reengineering gurus, a project's first step is to document, in copious detail, everyday activity. Data are collected and analyzed. Presentations to senior management are drafted and delivered. Fully aware of the impending dangers if the project fails at this early stage, top management invariably gives its strong support. After process mapping is completed, brainstorming sessions are used to invent ways for carrying out core processes. Teams are created to evaluate how each of these proposals for redesigning work processes will fly. Another round of intense data collection and analysis kicks off.

After about six months have elapsed, the consultants begin to press for a quantification of the potential downsizing likely to arise from the process redesign. The timing is predictable: After six months of high fees, even the most trusting of clients are usually demanding results.

Career-ambitious team members, usually the first to jump on the reengineering bandwagon, begin to realize the project's changes will produce winners and losers among the staff. It doesn't take long for these champions of change to decide that they want to be among the winners. Because they can claim to be key players in process re-design, they put their names forward for plum jobs needed to put the new processes in place. Those less ambitious (some might say ei-ther clueless or well entrenched in the status quo) organize to mini-mize damage to the existing organization and culture. The eventual outcome is inevitable. Politicians among team members get the best jobs in the new organization; those less skilled in trench warfare find themselves on outplacement lists. If top management is aware of the jostling for survival, they overlook or ignore it because by this stage top managers are determined to see results. They need a big win from the costly project that they can trumpet to shareholders or the press.

### Reengineering: Success or Failure?

In his 1995 book, James Champy writes that the reengineering pro-jects studied by his firm, CSC Index, "failed to attain these bench-marks [set as targets at the outset of the project] by as much as 30 percent." He goes on to add, "This partial revolution is not the one I intended." Many other students of the reengineering phenomenon have been even less sanguine in their assessment of the results. Esti-mates from various studies suggest that as many as 50 to 75% of reengineering projects fail to achieve their goals or even positive im-provements in performance.

Downsizings can be effective if they are broad in scope and un-dertaken after firms have experienced a decline in their operating performance. By contrast, downsizing efforts focused narrowly on reducing head count in particular areas often fail to meet their goals. There is also evidence that repeated efforts to downsize are self-de-structive: Failure builds on failure as a downtrodden workforce struggles to cope with repeated threats to its job security.

The report card on downsizing and reengineering projects is there-fore mixed: Some projects succeed admirably; others, perhaps even the majority, fail to realize the benefits they set out to achieve. Some firms are revitalized as a result of their ventures into reengineering. Some would even argue that the improved global competitiveness of U.S. and European companies is a direct result of their efforts to redefine the ways they went about their business and eliminate costs they could no longer carry. No one would argue that the human costs have not been enormous.

## Human Costs of Downsizing

In purely statistical terms, downsizing has hurt a lot of people. In Europe this is manifest in record high unemployment rates in most European Union (EU) countries. In the United States, which enjoyed unprecedented economic expansion throughout the 1990s, enough new jobs have been created to absorb displaced workers and still achieve historically low unemployment rates. There the good news ends.

As a result of the dislocations in the economy fueled in part by corporate restructuring and downsizing, median U.S. family income declined by $1,400 (3.4%) between 1989 and 1995. This occurred despite the fact that the average American worker is working longer hours (3% more for men and 35% more for women in 1979–1994) and the proportion of families earning two incomes is increasing dramatically (from 31% of families in 1967 to 47% in 1995).

Individuals who lose their jobs to corporate restructuring pay a huge price. On average, according to the Economic Policy Institute's report *The State of Working America, 1996–97*, workers who had lost their jobs were making 15% less (if indeed they were employed) than they had earned at their previous places of work. About 25% of these workers lost their health coverage as a result of job dislocation. Not surprisingly, job insecurity is on the rise among those still employed. Employee loyalty to employers has fallen to record lows.

The shock of permanent adjustments in workforce levels was further aggravated by the way most companies went about achieving the reductions. More often than not, reductions were orchestrated by teams of outside consultants hired by management under some popular rubric of the day, "reengineering" being a classic. Slogans about building a more productive future, eliminating waste, and "rightsizing" the organization rubbed salt into employee wounds. In effect, it blamed them for the company's underperformance. Ignoring the fact that most employees were working very hard indeed *doing their assigned jobs,* consultants, most of them young, had a field day. Without blanching at the levels of pay they themselves were earning, they produced charts and graphs and presentations that showed how most of the work being done was not only futile but was actually destructive to the company's competitiveness. Top management ate this up because it offered a quick and relatively easy way to solve problems they faced. Ordinary employees felt victimized because they had never been asked their opinions about what should be done, the rhetoric that accompanied the formal announcement of the consulting project notwithstanding.

Then the outplacement lists were drawn up, department by department. Despite claims that everything was going to be done analytically and based on reason, somehow the names on the lists did not seem to make sense. Too many of those tapped for outplacement were older. Too many of the bosses' favorites found jobs in the redesigned organization. This fueled the perception that finger-pointing was the primary basis for making decisions. Before long, the realization set in: The downsizing was arbitrary. It was mainly the luck of the draw as to whether you were picked to stay or put on a list to go.

The end result: Trust was the first victim of the downsizing. As successive waves of downsizing swept over companies (and it did over most), this lack of trust turned into cynicism about the process as well as the integrity of senior management. When record pay packages were announced for the senior executives who were the architects of these upheavals, cynicism turned into outright hostility. Everything that management espoused was tainted. Such negative outlooks were, of course, carefully disguised so people could retain whatever jobs were still available (any job is better than no job when you have a family to support). But cynicism and hostility became the core mindset of many companies. Absent any trust in future actions of management, it soon turned to fear.

The truth about many if not most downsizings is that they have fractured the institutional lives of workers. Even a casual look at local newspapers and recent books reveals thousands of stories documenting the pain. Many of us read these human interest stories but pass rapidly on to accounts of the raging bull market on Wall Street or the triumphs of local sports favorites. Here's what we overlook.

In autumn 1993, the Sunday *Boston Globe* ran a series of stories on the effects of corporate restructurings on the lives of Boston-area families. One of these stories highlighted the Costa family, who were, relatively speaking, winners in the downsizing wars. Dennis Costa worked for many years at a large and award-winning manufacturing plant of AT&T in Andover, Massachusetts. Seven months after winning national recognition as one of the most productive and progressive plants in the United States, it announced it was laying off 1,000 workers. Dennis survived the layoff—but at a price. He was offered two options for continuing his employment. The first would have involved his taking a 50% pay cut as a repair technician; the second allowed him to take only a 10% pay cut but required him to commute 500 miles each week to continue his career.

Dennis Costa chose this latter option because it was the only one he and his family could afford (he tried to find another job locally, but after accumulating some 200 rejections to job applications, he took the AT&T offer to commute). He is quoted in the article as saying, "This is survival. I'm 46 and there aren't a lot of other options out there for me."

Another survivor of the AT&T Andover cutbacks, reported in the same article, was Brenda Booze. She survived by taking a pay cut from $11.53 an hour (for work as a cable inspector in the Andover plant) to $9.50 an hour (to work at a low-grade clerical job in an AT&T facility in Florida). As Brenda was quoted in the *Globe* article: "It's like going backward. I kept my job, but we just keep going backward." And remember, Both Dennis Costa and Brenda Booze were survivors.

Less fortunate than these two was Frank Giaramita, who joined Digital Equipment straight out of college. After surviving several successive job cuts, he found himself on the street in 1993 at the age of forty-four. The *Boston Globe* quotes Giaramita, a longtime company loyalist, as saying, "I will never, never give that kind of blind dedication and loyalty to a company again." Nor will he expect it from a company again.

Are these merely isolated examples drawn from one regional newspaper? Of course not. In 1992 *Business Week* reported the story of Allen Stenhouse, a forty-eight-year-old business manager who earned $50,000 a year in Cigna Insurance's health care department. After helping a team of consultants from McKinsey & Company reduce the costs of his department by 20%, he was told, two days before Christmas, that he was one of the 2,000 staff members being let go. By the time of the *Business Week* story, Stenhouse was still out of work, had divorced, had lost his house and all of his savings, had been forced to sell possessions like a fax machine and a photocopier, owed back taxes to the IRS, and was living on a government disability pension. In Stenhouse's own words, "I have lost the fight to stay ahead in today's economy. I was determined to find work, but as the months and years wore on, depression set in. You can only be rejected so many times, then you start questioning your own self-worth."

As the decade of the 1990s careened forward, stories like this echoed across the United States and around the globe. Indeed, few of us do not know someone who has been subjected to long periods of stressful unemployment as a result of corporate downsizing. Particularly hard hit were the middle-aged—many of whom had spent decades with their previous employers—and middle managers— many of whom had never imagined that this could happen to them. The AMA survey referred to earlier indicated that between 40 and 60% of staff terminated by its member companies between 1990 and 1996 came from white-collar and managerial job categories.

When the time came to cut costs, it didn't take long for corporate executives to realize that cuts could be made more efficiently by "encouraging" older and higher-level workers to leave. Those whose salaries had become inflated by regular merit raises were often the first to go. Sometimes incentives to go took the form of early retirement packages, which allowed employees in their fifties to "retire" with reduced retirement payments. Others simply involved severance payments—typically, a few weeks to a month for each year of company service. Corporate costs of such programs were covered by the restructuring charges taken as part of the downsizing effort. Human costs, in contrast, were absorbed by individuals—either those forced out of the job market before they were ready to leave or survivors worrying whether they would be next.

In 1987, years before the wave of downsizing hit its crest, Juliet Brudney, a longtime *Boston Globe* columnist, collaborated with the author Hilda Scott on the book *Forced Out*, which profiles the experiences of some middle-aged victims of restructuring. It contains many telling examples of what happens to people when they are let go. One quote sums up these experiences: "The difference between no job and any job is the difference between being a nobody and a somebody." Or as someone who went eighteen months before successfully returning to the job market put it, "Life stops for you. At first everyone pats you on the back. Then they start avoiding you; they don't want to hear hard luck stories."

There is still more. Vincent Smith, an AT&T downsizing victim profiled in Barbara Rudolph's book *Disconnected,* graphically expresses an attitude that is becoming more dominant in corporate America: "At this point, I don't expect to find personal validation in my work. Have I always been a fish out of water in the corporate world? Perhaps. I will do my job responsibly, but I will not look to any organization to assure me of my self-worth, to tell me who I am." Maggie Stanley, another victim, echoes a similar sentiment: "I understand that if tomorrow AT&T changes its business plans, I'm a flea they'll shake off. Everyone is expendable and every lay-off starts with the peons." So much for the future prospects of loyal, dedicated, and committed employees who pour their hearts and souls into what they do.

Those thrown out of jobs are not the only ones to suffer. Survivors live a life at work different from what they knew before. Whether they admit it to themselves or not, most feel guilty that they survived while their friends and colleagues did not. Virtually all experience an increase in fear and insecurity: Will they be the next to go in an upcoming round of cutbacks? Most view their relationships with their employers in terms of increased distrust, sometimes even disrespect.

The ongoing AMA survey confirms this change in attitude among workers. In its 1995-1996 survey, 72% of AMA member companies reported a short-term decrease in employee morale following a company downsizing. Over time only 36% of the workforce still indicated that they were demoralized. This is hardly grounds for throwing a celebration. Moreover, in its 1993 survey the AMA found that morale declined even more severely (87%) in companies that had been subjected to three or more downsizings.

Sinking morale and mounting distrust of management are not the only consequences of cutting costs by terminating people. The AMA reported substantially increased disability claims among downsizing companies and a dramatic rise in the number of lawsuits filed for wrongful dismissal. More than half resulted in judgments against the companies. Absenteeism is up in most downsized companies, in part because employees are taking time out to interview for other jobs for fear that their current jobs will be eliminated.

In 1996 Nitin Nohria and Geoffrey Love of the Harvard Business School authored a working paper titled "Adaptive or Disruptive: When Does Downsizing Pay in Large Industrial Corporations?" This paper cites studies that chronicled reduced loyalty and commitment following downsizing projects. The researchers noted such specific effects as lower morale; lower levels of job satisfaction; increased stress; feelings of betrayal, anger, fright, and confusion; a breakdown of trust between managers and employees; and a disruption in the organization's functions. Nohria and Love cite other studies that document how downsizing leads to lower quality and productivity; encourages more tardiness, absenteeism, and turnover; and reduces cooperation between managers and employees. They show that downsizing can damage the legitimacy of both the organization and management, which in the extreme may trigger a downward performance spiral. Nohria and Love concluded that the majority of downsizings simply did not work, a finding consistent with other researchers on the subject.

Not only individuals were devastated by the downsizings of the 1990s, but whole communities were sent into a tailspin. The town of Poughkeepsie in New York's Hudson Valley had for years been the next best thing to a company town for the computer giant IBM. In March 1993, IBM announced a major cutback eliminating 2,700 jobs from a nearby manufacturing facility. As a result, the town's economy suffered a serious setback. Within six months, unemployment in this once prosperous town had soared to 11%, and business foreclosures had risen dramatically. The housing market virtually collapsed: Houses lost up to 40% of their value almost overnight. The situation in Poughkeepsie was mirrored in hundreds of towns and cities across America. This is also beginning to affect communities in Europe. Of course, towns, just like people, recover—even from such a rude shock. But they will never be the same again.

## Cultural Effects of Downsizing

As described earlier, the culture of an organization is the interwoven, organic system of beliefs, values, rituals, personalities, characters, and mythology that creates meaning for people at work. When it hangs together, culture produces extraordinary loyalty among the members and often extraordinary efforts in pursuit of shared goals. This in turn produces superior performance over the long term. It is vital to financial success.

Downsizing, particularly on a large scale and repeated again and again, ruins the culture of an organization by threatening or destroying core cultural elements. It attacks the core belief structure, which for most employees has traditionally meant, "Buy into the ethos of this company, work hard, remain loyal, and you will have a job for life." Downsizing signals that there is no such thing as a lifetime job—and damned little guarantee even that someone will have a job tomorrow. Under these circumstances, getting employees to buy in is widely seen as a joke. A basic belief that once held a culture together is torn apart. It cannot be stitched back together without ample time and an extended period of greater workplace stability.

The destruction of the basic commitment between employee and employer is only part of how downsizing rends the fabric of a business. Beyond this basic belief, employees have historically bought into other aspects of the company's value system, such as the famous "IBM Means Service" slogan. Lifers at IBM believed that providing excellent customer service no matter what it cost in personal terms would lead to success—both for them and the institution. When IBM laid off significant numbers, most of whom bought into this ethic, how could anyone retain his or her belief in the company's core value? Not easily, and most don't. When the company's CEO is then rewarded for cuts by unprecedentedly high compensation—certainly much more than founder Tom Watson or any of his siblings ever received—the link between the supposed values of the company and the employee are shredded.

The destruction of the bond between company and employee, though serious, is not the most serious cultural effect of downsizing. An even more crucial threat to the underpinnings of culture comes from the people who are inevitably but inadvertently let go. We talked earlier about the role played by heroic figures, priests and priestesses, and storytellers in the preservation of a company's culture. These are the informal players who make the culture real and give it a human face. Their names do not appear on organization charts, their roles are not codified in any policy manuals, but they are the people whose presence and efforts glue a company together.

When the time comes to downsize, very little attention is typically paid to these informal roles. In fact, any attention paid is often negative: "What use is that character who spends all his time talking to the young people? How can we possibly justify keeping someone whose main role in life seems to be telling stories at the watercooler or entertaining employees at company functions?" In the search for people to lay off, older individuals are often nominated first, without any consideration for their wider cultural influence.

What happens when key informal players are eliminated? The history of the organization and what makes it great goes with them. And since many are emotionally attached to these individuals—for good reason, since they were often crucial to the survival of entrants—survivors feel embittered and resolve not to fall into the same trap themselves.

James Challenger, the president of Challenger, Gray & Christmas, which has been tracking corporate layoffs for years, commented in *Bank Personnel News* (April 1996) about the attendant loss of "corporate memory." He described corporate memory as the "collective business experiences, dramas, visions, successes and failures of real people who work for the company." He went on to say,

> It is the knowledge, nuances and intuition we bring to day-to-day decision making. A little bit of this invaluable corporate memory disappears each time an individual is laid off. In the final analysis, cutting out the memory of an organization may do more harm than good to the company's bottom line. If, after layoffs are made, the company can no longer perform at the level it once did, customers will take their business elsewhere and the business will be left in worse condition than before the layoffs.

Challenger is, of course, right—but in his attempt to communicate with his constituency of senior managers, he has sanitized his message too much. Business-specific knowledge is always lost in any large scale downsizing—and most managers must realize this. More serious is the reality that the corporate soul is often wrenched out. With it goes the historical sense of how the company can succeed and prosper. In its place is a cultural vacuum—one filled by distrust and resentment.

Karen Stephenson, an assistant professor of human resources at the Anderson School of Business at the University of California, Los Angeles, describes tacit knowledge as

> the ineffable and unarticulated forms of knowledge which come from experience. As we experience life, we store our learning as tacit knowledge in memories and intuition. What we don't experience or learn, we can glean from others. Thus, people become knowledge storehouses from whom we can learn "indirectly," making them our surrogates for direct experience.
>
> . . . This form of knowledge becomes a critical (organizational) resource for innovation. A catalyst for the creation of tacit knowledge is trust. Unarticulated, tacit knowledge can find expression in collegial discussions with others, in which experiences are shared. This knowledge transfer is subtle and mediated by the trust among colleagues. Thus, trust is the medium and knowledge the message. In this way, experience is transferred from those who have it to those who don't.

When downsizings wrench people from the workplace, relationships and trust alike are betrayed. With this betrayal goes the institutional knowledge that the people in the organization had created through their shared experiences. Organizations so gutted are poorly equipped to compete in today's world. As a result, it should not be surprising that many downsizings fail to achieve the benefits they ostensibly reach for.

## Future Effects of Downsizing

For some firms, downsizing may have been the salvation they needed to compete in global markets. For most firms, however, downsizing has proven to be a cultural disaster. If maintaining a strong corporate culture is a key to producing superior long-term performance, what does the future hold? Will companies who resisted the move to downsize emerge triumphant? Or will a new culture arise in downsized companies, a culture that repackages the pieces and moves on to a brave new future? Or will downsizing just continue to decimate the social lives of people and destroy meaning, faith, and hope in the workforce?

From where we sit, we think it is unlikely that downsizing will disappear as a favored tool of senior managers, unless a clear and avoidable disaster occurs. Downsizing is just too easy to do. There are too many consultants who offer services to even skeptical managers for an exorbitant price. Their fees pale in comparison to the savings they promise. The stock market's positive reaction to announced downsizings is just too tempting for most managers to ignore. And personal rewards for managers who "bravely" undertake such cost-cutting programs are so great that only a fool would not be tempted. In a nutshell, downsizing is here to stay, and business cultures will have to adapt.

What form will this adaptation take? One aspect is fairly clear: Traditional loyalty to a company is a thing of the past. In its place, self-interest will dominate. If an employer cannot be trusted to look out for an employee's welfare (and few employers can promise that today), then any self-respecting individual is going to look out for number one. If this means pursuing other job and career opportunities, so be it. Better to jump first than to be victimized by an unexpected layoff.

Because people are social animals, self-interest alone will not be enough to sustain someone at work. People naturally need to identify with a group. And if the group is not fellow employees, people will find something more controllable to belong to—their own work unit, their professional society, or even their community. But they will always yearn to belong. This tendency to make affiliations outside conventional employment circles will lead to a gradual balkanization of the culture of most companies.

What are the likely consequences of this cultural balkanization? Having made their beds, managers must now learn to lie in them. The traditional tie between employees and their employers, a bond central to the evolution of strong cultures, was severed in the 1990s. If managers want to rekindle their employees' fire, so effectively dampened, they need to work within the constraints they themselves imposed. They must encourage the development of strong subcultures within the organization and permit employees and units to find their own ways to achieve meaningful life at work. And within what their employees will permit them, they must try to harness collective energy in pursuit of larger corporate values and goals. But managers should never forget that until this generation of workers has passed on, they will probably never be trusted again.

Downsizing and reengineering were the landmark features of corporate life in the 1990s. Their legacy is corporate cultures that have been pulled apart and reformulated along lines that employees can still trust. It will take years of concerted effort and workplace stability to rebuild the trust that has been lost. And it may take decades before strong and cohesive cultures can once again become the driving force behind long-term business success. Some legacy.

## CHAPTER 4

# Outsourcing

## Corporate Amputation

**M**odern economic systems favor specialized suppliers of products or services. Because they are specialized, these suppliers can do a more efficient job than others. In the second half of the twentieth century, specialized suppliers have thrived as corporations around the world have farmed out, or "outsourced," activities previously done in-house. The rush to outsource has spawned a massive new worldwide industry populated by contract and temporary workers. Many of these people used to enjoy full-time employment with the companies they now serve on a contract basis. In their new employment status as contractors, this new class of workers typically receives reduced wages and few if any benefits. Not surprisingly, they typically are dissatisfied and alienated from the companies that once had them on the payroll and still use them though they are employed elsewhere.

### Why Do Companies Outsource?

In the late eighteenth century, Adam Smith's *Wealth of Nations* pointed to the possibility of increasing productivity in the manufacture of pins by assigning workers more specialized tasks. Since then, managers have sought ways to specialize in order to become more efficient. Much of modern industrial development has resulted from the application of this basic principle. Outsourcing is just one recent and popular way to pursue this objective. As *New York Times* columnist and humorist Russell Baker opined, "If you sat for 40 days and 40 nights in a lonely room trying to guess what outsourcing might be, what are the chances you would see a great tycoon firing the local workforce to take advantage of cheap labor in other towns and countries?" Baker may be pulling our legs to make his point, but he cannot be far off the mark. The question is, why outsource to achieve these gains?

In some instances, the rationale is quite simple: Specialized companies can achieve a critical mass that individual firms on their own cannot. The best example of this is payroll services, one of the earliest and now most widespread specialized services performed by outside contractors. On the surface, it would seem easy to prepare a check or a pay packet for one's own employees. Given the proliferation of ever changing tax and benefit regulations, it is not. Responding to this challenge, a firm known as ADP in the 1940s began offering small and medium-sized firms in the metropolitan New York area assistance in handling payrolls. Although tax and benefit regulations were complex and always changing, they applied to all companies regardless of their business. Therefore, ADP, by developing a core of expertise in these regulations and processes, could leverage this competency across many companies at a cost lower than companies would incur in-house. Demand for ADP's payroll services were so great that it soon became a major company, perhaps the first to owe its success to the rise of outsourcing.

ADP's approach was mirrored in a legion of other companies, many in less glamorous businesses. Trucking is a case in point. Any company can buy trucks and hire drivers to get its goods to market. But between scheduled shipments, corporate trucks and drivers often stand idle. An independent trucker serving several companies can more easily keep trucks full and drivers busy. With higher productivity, independent truckers can deliver goods at a lower cost. It is no wonder that independent trucking and transport companies became a major industry in their own right.

What was true for trucking applies equally to the manufacture of specialized parts and equipment. No automobile manufacturer ever felt compelled to be in the steel business even though steel is used to make cars and trucks. Instead, car companies rely on specialized manufacturers to supply steel and concentrate on the design, assembly, and marketing of vehicles. The automotive sector's use of specialized suppliers soon extended to components and subassemblies such as seats, brake assemblies, mufflers, and so forth. Chrysler Corporation today enjoys a unit-profit advantage over its two bigger U.S. rivals in large measure because it procures almost 70% of its parts and other supplies from subcontractors. A whole industry of subcontractors was founded and thrives on this economically sound basis.

In other industries—personal computers being a notable example—brand-name companies do not even try to compete on the basis of in-house manufacturing. They farm out virtually all their specialized needs to contract manufacturers. In this niche, as early as 1994, suppliers had combined sales revenue in excess of $5 billion. A total of 70% of the guts of Apple Computer products is supplied by outside contractors. At Nike, the leading global supplier of athletic shoes, the ratio is even more skewed: Fully 100% of its shoes are produced by contract manufacturers.

The rationale and the economics for outsourcing are murkier in some other instances, if still sound enough to justify the practice. The food services industry provides a notable example. Cooking and serving food is a labor- and material-intensive service. Because edibles need to be prepared close to consumers, the food business is far from mobile. True, specialists in providing institutional services can gain some economies from bulk purchasing of foodstuffs. Moreover, because they are specialists, they should have an intimate knowledge of food provision processes (e.g., knowing the most effective equipment to purchase). Such knowledge can improve the overall productivity of their staffs, at least at the margin. Finally, as experts in the food service business, they are likely to be more experienced in planning menus. As a result, the quality of their food may well be perceived as superior to that prepared by in-house staff. Although these factors may seem somewhat marginal compared to the economies achievable by independent truckers, they should still be significant.

All said, it is hard to see how these marginal economic edges would be sufficient to account for the current popularity of outsourcing food services. For example, 92% of U.S. hospitals contract out food services. Another factor must be at work, and indeed it is.

Many companies farm out functions like food services because they are simply not interested in being in the business. Even the marginal attraction of slightly improved efficiencies is sufficient to convince them to look elsewhere for goods and services. Some of the growth in outsourcing can therefore rightly be attributed to corporate ennui, buttressed by marginally better economics.

Until the beginning of the 1990s, the rationale for contracting functions outside centered on improving economics and eliminating annoying peripheral tasks. In the spring of 1990, this changed with the publication of two influential articles in the *Harvard Business Review*. The first was "Beyond Products: Services-Based Strategy," by James Brian Quinn, Thomas L. Doorley, and Penny C. Paquette. The second sentence of the article's abstract stated: "Sustainable advantage is more likely to come from developing superior capabilities in a few core service skills and outsourcing as much of the rest as possible." A broader rationale for outsourcing was on the horizon.

This newly emerging rationale was underscored in a landmark article by C. Prahalad and Gary K. Hamel, "The Core Competence of the Corporation." Drawing on detailed case studies comparing the evolution of NEC (the Japanese powerhouse) and GTE (the U.S. company), the authors argued that companies that understood and concentrated their energies on improving core competencies would succeed and prosper over the long haul. The article warned of dangers, such as outsourcing for temporary economic advantage at the expense of losing expertise needed to augment a core competency. But the article's greatest impact was in producing a strong new rationale for farming out anything peripheral to core functions.

The fire sale was on. Companies around the world hired consultants and set up teams to define core competencies. This might have been too expensive were it not for the exercises' cost-effective by-products: a raft of strategic disposals and the wholesale outsourcing of noncore functions. As the reengineering juggernaut was running out of steam, along came the core competencies rationalization to spur on the downsizing movement. Banks could now justify shedding large information technology (IT) staffs. Banking, of course, was their core competence, not running operations. "Outsource the buggers and let's get on with the business of banking" became the de facto rallying cry. Similarly, marketing-oriented companies could finally justify jettisoning manufacturing people. Although much of the impetus might well have come from armies of newly trained MBAs not eager to spend their time on plant floors, the public justification became: "Let's concentrate on marketing, our core competence." Even important functions such as product design could be jettisoned if a company convinced itself that its core expertise was selling a product already conceived.

Examples of this new centrifugal philosophy were legion. In September 1997, the *Economist* reported that Sara Lee, the Chicago-based multinational company, planned to sell its textile and yarn manufacturing businesses. Heretofore these operations had supplied its Champion-brand sportswear and Hanes apparel. The company was not getting rid of either Champion or Hanes. It was refocusing on what it did best: managing and marketing the brands. To free itself (and also to free up a sizable amount of cash), it decided to outsource the manufacture of the key raw material used in creating its brand-name products.

The same article also noted that Heinz, the ketchup company, was closing its tomato paste plant in California. It preferred to buy paste on the open market. At the same time, Campbell's, the soup company, was selling its chicken farms, and Pillsbury, the processed food provider, was moving out of vegetable canning operations. All three of these major corporations are planning to continue their respective businesses of selling ketchup, soup, and canned vegetables. Getting out of processing operations would ostensibly allow them to concentrate on brand management—what they do best.

Manufacturing has no monopoly on outsourcing, however. Other businesses and services are also joining the crowd. A *Business Week* article reported how a small consulting firm serving pharmaceutical clients prospered by farming out its basic accounting operations. In a July 1995 issue, the same magazine reported how American Airlines (among others) had contracted outside for ticket agents at several airports. The reason: lower costs. American pays its own agents $19 an hour plus benefits. The contractor paid its staff between $7 and $9 an hour, with few or no benefits.

With such obvious savings, it is not surprising that companies look for an ever increasing number of functions to farm out. By September 1995, *Business Week* highlighted the growing trend among manufacturing companies, such as IBM, Rubbermaid, AT&T, and Steelcase, to outsource product design functions. The payoffs included lower costs, faster new product design, and reduced investment in high-cost computer-aided design (CAD) systems and technology. Earlier that year, the *Financial Times* commented on the growing tendency of companies like British Petroleum and Courtaulds to contract out their basic R&D activities. The *Financial Times* added that the idea had really caught the fancy of consultants, who were increasingly arguing for companies to move to "virtual R&D" operations, a new buzzword to capitalize on the burgeoning trend.

If product design or R&D would appear to be peripheral to a company's core competencies, consider ill-fated ValuJet's decision to farm out airplane maintenance. *Business Week* reported speculation in June 1996 that the cost-cutting strategy might have contributed to the crash of Flight 592 bound for Atlanta. ValuJet is not alone: Many major airlines outsource maintenance. They just don't bother to tell their customers that someone else is looking after their planes. Bob Ayling, CEO of British Airways, goes as far as talking about turning the "world's favorite airline" into a "virtual airline" by the year 2000. This would help to achieve economies the company believes it needs to remain the world's most profitable carrier.

From its early role of achieving economies and eliminating distracting peripheral tasks, outsourcing appears to be moving into a dominant position in business life. Many firms contract out even their customer care functions, ranging from telemarketing to providing direct customer service. Users of such contracted services include major companies in telecommunications, banking, insurance, consumer products, and even retail. The voice you hear on the phone is no longer likely to be working for the company you think you're calling. A *Harvard Business Review* article in November 1997 noted that because of downsizing and the perceived ineffectiveness of internal planning staffs, companies are contracting more and more strategic planning activities to consulting firms. One wonders what's left of a firm if even thinking is contracted outside. Is nothing sacred?

## The Scope of Outsourcing Today

Although outsourcing is apparent across the board, determining with precision the scope of its impact is difficult. A 1994 *Conference*

*Board* survey reported that 45% of executives polled (a good representation of American industry) outsourced payroll management, 38% contracted tax administration, and 35% farmed out benefits management. The *Journal of Commerce* (July 1996) reported that contract trucking was a $25-billion-a-year business. The Outsourcing Institute, which periodically reports on trends in the industry, claims that 85% of banks with IT budgets larger than $5 million a year are either outsourcing their IT or planning to do so. Although there are no precise statistics, a huge percentage of firms contract out security services to specialized firms.

The Outsourcing Institute also estimates that by mid-1996 the industry was at least $100 billion in size and growing at a rate of between 20 and 30% a year. A poll conducted by consultants A. T. Kearney (cited in *Business Week* in 1996) claimed that 84% of U.S. companies contract out at least some services (up from an estimated 52% in 1992). Our guess is that both of these estimates are on the low side.

Reading press reports, one is staggered by both the scope and size of activities being farmed out in recent years. *Business Week* reported in a March 1997 article that the $3-billion, ten-year contract DuPont gave to Computer Sciences Corporation to run its computer operations was one of thirty-five "megacontracts" of this sort. Other large companies getting out of the IT business included J. P. Morgan, Mutual of New York, and Lucent Technology. As also reported in the article, IBM, although a late entrant to the industry, had built a $16-billion unit by early 1997 to provide services to other companies.

As the outsourcing industry gained momentum in the mid- to late-1990s, a few critics emerged to warn that companies were in danger of eviscerating skills needed to build a successful future. Moving headlong toward "virtual company" status has potential costs. An April 1996 *Business Week* feature article carried the title "Has Outsourcing Gone Too Far?" If future restraint was a measure, it appeared that most readers ignored the article as some kind of April fool's joke. Companies continued the rush to hand off anything they could to external contractors.

A sense of the industry's growing size can be gleaned from labor statistics, especially those focusing on outsourcing arrangements. In the October 1996 *Monthly Labor Review,* the U.S. Department of

Labor published a specialized survey: "Workers in Alternative Employment Arrangements." At the time of the report, approximately 12 million American workers, nearly 10% of the U.S. workforce, were contract employees. Not all were contractors as a result of outsourcing, but a considerable number were.

Independent contractors—in effect, self-employed people—totaled 8.3 million of the 12 million workers. Although some may have been outsourced from permanent jobs (quite common in the area of computer programming and systems analysis, for example), most are independent contractors by choice. They value the freedom nontraditional work arrangements afford. This is not true for the 2.2 million people who work for temporary help agencies or the 650,000 contract employees. The vast majority of these workers (in excess of 70%, according to the survey data) would prefer to have the security of conventional, full-time jobs. They work for one client company, provide services on site, and are supervised by client company managers. Yet they are not on the company's payroll, nor do they participate in the company's benefit programs.

In addition, 2 million others were classified as "on-call" workers. Some, substitute teachers, for example, do so out of choice. Others, such as construction workers, are forced into this work arrangement because of the seasonal and project nature of the industry. Still others, such as food service workers (waitpeople and cooks, primarily), work on call because this is the only work available. A goodly number of these have been outsourced. Although external contracting is not responsible for all workers in alternative (and often less-than-satisfactory) work situations, a number have had their jobs farmed out to contract companies.

Fueling all this growth is the economics of cost reduction. Joseph G. Sponholz, chief administrative officer at Chemical Bank, said, "Once we are convinced we have driven down the cost of purchased goods and services as far as we can, we will go back and think about whether there are things that can be outsourced." No outsourcing contract was ever let with promises of increased costs. So Sponholz is right: If you can't cut costs any further, outsource.

KPMG Peat Marwick, the accounting and consulting firm, forecast that the outsourcing business, worth $100 billion in 1996, would grow to a $282-billion industry by 2000. Since the source of their forecast was a survey of CEOs' intentions, there can be little doubt that outsourcing is here to stay.

## Who Wins and Who Loses at the Outsourcing Game?

Companies believe they win at outsourcing because of the substantial cost savings involved. Although individual contracts vary, typical deals promise annual savings of 15–30%. Promised gains are difficult to challenge. Many deals are large and/or long term, making it extremely unlikely that there will be anyone around to assess the bottom-line impact once they finally expire. In the meantime, companies bank the short-term savings that flow from the initial contract and go on to look for costs they can cut elsewhere.

Managers, too, are rewarded for implementing bold outsourcing programs. As the *Economist* pointed out in September 1997, "Wall Street loves the talk of 'adding value' and the 'focus' that accompanies . . . restructuring. Sara Lee's share price rose 14 percent . . . on the day of the announcement" that the company was getting out of manufacturing yarn and textiles for its apparel and hosiery divisions. With that kind of feedback, tied directly to executive pocketbooks because of stock options, an immediate movement away from outsourcing is unlikely.

Some employees also benefit, or think they do, from being outsourced. This is especially true of employees who possess a set of professional skills or credentials they can bring with them to a new specialized supplier. For example, a payroll specialist working alone in a company will likely have fewer career advancement opportunities than such an individual would have if employed by a company like ADP. Such an employee would leap at the chance to be "outsourced" to ADP, all other things being equal. Information technology specialists tend to have a similar view. Career paths open to an IT specialist employed by IBM or Computer Sciences Corporation are likely to be far more fulfilling than the opportunities available to the same person working in a small to medium-sized bank. All such technically qualified individuals likely command premium salaries from their new employers because of the value of their technical knowledge. What have they got to lose from being outsourced? Relatively little.

Surprisingly, some employees seem to prefer contract status because of the independence it provides. We have friends who built a nice business by capitalizing on this factor. The business began when a major company downsized its IT function under orders from corporate headquarters. Believing that it might be risky not to have continued access to experienced employees it was dumping, the company turned to our friends: "Why don't you hire our former employees and sell them back to us on a contract basis?" It didn't take long for our friends to respond. They hired the former employees, offering them salaries and benefits comparable to those at their previous employer, and then sold them back to the company for a 35% markup. It was a win-win deal. Our friends were happy because of the gold mine they discovered. The company was happy because it got its valued employees back, sort of. And the employees were ecstatic: They worked for a computer company now and could tell their previous employer to go to hell if they felt like it (although most didn't since they actually liked working for the company). If you are shaking your head at this arrangement, think again. There are a lot more outsourcing deals out there with similar characteristics. All involve employees with a scarce set of skills who can in effect write their own tickets regarding how and for whom they work.

Workers without such in-demand skills are not so lucky. They tend to be the big losers in the outsourcing game. These include food service workers, security guards, clerical workers, cleaners, maintenance workers, telephone operators, receptionists, and so forth—the bottom of the working world's food chain. These workers see their salaries cut by 20–40%, depending on the job markets in their areas. Under the new terms, they typically lose all or most of their non-wage benefits. Often they are asked to go from full-time to part-time status, always to accommodate work requirements of their new employers. These people go from real jobs to "McJobs"—the term economists use to characterize the new service economy.

Between 1982 and 1995, temporary workers in the U.S. economy increased from just over 400,000 to around 2.2 million, almost 2% of the U.S. workforce. These temps were split almost equally between white-collar and blue-collar workers. Many were placed on the temporary rolls as their new employers insisted on more flexible working hours to deliver savings promised in the outsourcing deal.

Most temporary workers are ineligible for routine benefits. One estimate is that fewer than 10% of temporary workers receive health benefits. They earn wages on average 29% lower than full-time employees in similar job categories. For example, temporary precision production craftspeople earned $8.33 an hour compared to $13.21 for their full-time equivalents. Temporary clerical workers earned on average $7.83 an hour compared to the $10.25 earned by full-timers. The plight of an outsourced, temporary worker is not always easy.

Not all companies gain from outsourcing arrangements either. Some, like the company described above, enter into unfavorable arrangements in response to political pressure to reduce permanent costs. If they end up paying higher costs to hire the same workers back on a temporary basis, so be it.

Other companies incur higher costs from contracting arrangements through ignorance and the loss of valuable in-house skills. A large paper mill in Canada decided a number of years ago to outsource many of the technical operations associated with the mill, including the preparation of operations manuals and the engineering of equipment additions to the plant. Although the initial decision to outsource may have saved money in the company's operating budget, no budget we know can account for the potential losses that might have accrued were it not for the watchfulness of a long-term plant operator.

At the time, the mill was engaged in a major upgrade of its equipment. Engineering work for the project was outsourced to an engineering contractor with no previous on-site experience. One day the team of engineers arrived to supervise the installation of four huge heat exchangers. The exchangers' function was to take waste heat and convert it into clean process steam for use in paper making. A low-level steam operator from the old plant asked them what they were doing. After listening patiently to a long explanation of how the heat exchangers would work, he asked the engineers, "Why don't you just use that?" He was indicating an 8-inch pipe that ran from the old plant all the way down the middle of the factory to where they were standing. The engineers peered at the pipe and asked, "What's that?" When told it was an unused steam line to carry excess steam from the old plant to an outside exhaust vent, they were amazed. The heat exchangers were put into storage and the new machines were connected to the existing pipe.

To add insult to injury, shortly after this money-saving decision was made, the team of technical writers hired on an outsourcing basis to write operations manuals for the new plant delivered their first product. The manuals explained in copious detail how to operate the now redundant heat exchangers. These expensive white elephants now also occupy space in storage, adjacent to the unneeded heat exchangers. Mistakes made in the construction and operation of a huge facility like a paper plant are highly visible. We wonder how many other contractors have incurred similar costs through a comparable lack of relevant knowledge.

Companies outsource to save money for functions they need but can get more cheaply elsewhere. Sometimes savings achieved are real, often because of depressed wages and benefits paid to contract workers. Other times savings are illusory—hidden by management or gobbled up by inefficiencies that arise out of the outsourcing arrangement. The human costs for those outsourced are almost always real. They are the real losers at the outsourcing game.

## A Case Study: The UK Civil Service

All examples so far have been drawn from the corporate sector. But outsourcing continues as a major preoccupation of public-sector managers as well. As far as we know, the largest single public-sector program was carried out by the United Kingdom's civil service during the last years of Conservative Party rule, between the mid-1990s through 1997. Typical of the public sector, a different terminology was used: Rather than labeling its program "outsourcing," the UK called it "competing for quality," or CfQ. CfQ became the buzzword that preoccupied Britain's civil servants during the 1990s.

CfQ was officially announced in November 1991. Chancellor of the Exchequer Norman Lamont presented a white paper to Parliament that introduced the policy of extending competition throughout the public sector. It identified a series of specific actions and initiatives to achieve its goals. In the years prior to 1991, the British government had been experimenting with outsourcing through an initiative called "market testing." This initiative had yielded promising small-scale results, as shown in Table 4.1.

TABLE 4.1    History of Market Testing in the UK

| | Value of Activity Tested (millions of £) | Level of Savings Generated (millions of £) | Savings as a Percentage of Value of Activity Tested (percent) |
|---|---|---|---|
| 1986/87 | 39.6 | 9.4 | 23.7 |
| 1987/88 | 32.3 | 8.1 | 25.1 |
| 1988/89 | 47.0 | 13.0 | 27.6 |
| 1989/90 | 29.0 | 7.4 | 25.5 |
| 1990/91 | 43.4 | 12.5 | 28.8 |

SOURCE: *Competing for Quality Policy Review* (HMSO, 1996).

Not surprisingly, with savings running over 25%, the chancellor was highly motivated to expand the program.

The new CfQ program had as its objective a "significant extension in the volume and range of services exposed to competition in order to improve value for money" (for UK taxpayers, of course). The high-level aims of the CfQ initiative were (1) to improve value for money in the delivery of public services through competition and (2) to bring about a step change in the level of competition for the delivery of public services. To achieve these broad objectives, a number of different approaches were proposed. These included the abolition of the service in question, privatization, and internal restructuring. Its most important suggestions involved bidding processes: "market testing," which allowed civil servants already performing the service to make an in-house bid for their jobs and "strategic contracting out," which involved simply auctioning off the service to outside contractors. Elaborate procedures were established to ensure the process was fair and aboveboard. These included providing consulting services to in-house teams in preparing their competitive bids.

As noted in the Cabinet Office Policy Unit review (which we used extensively in drawing up this case), the CfQ initiative was launched in an era when an extremely activist Tory government was pursuing a number of initiatives to improve civil service effectiveness. For example, its financial management initiative sought to heighten awareness of how much program and management decisions cost by delegating budgetary responsibility and accountability to lower ranks of the civil service. The "next steps" initiative tried to determine whether existing civil service activity was needed by instituting a so-called "prior options" review. Another initiative encouraged private firms to assume the risk of providing capital for public-sector projects. Finally, the concept of "efficiency plans," an umbrella program, encouraged increased efficiency in the provision of public services. Of all these competing and often overlapping programs, CfQ was to have by far the greatest impact.

The array of functions exposed to CfQ inquiry was broad. They included

- 299 reviews of a variety of office services to the British government
- 94 reviews of property management (for example, for the various facilities used by the armed services both in Britain and overseas)
- 43 reviews of functions that dealt with money (tax receipts and so forth)
- 100 reviews of engineering and maintenance activities (including such esoterica as maintenance of electronic equipment in military aircraft)
- 103 reviews of accounting and legal operations
- 70 reviews of IT operations
- 60 reviews of scientific and R&D operations
- 62 reviews of training and personnel operations
- 48 reviews of general information service activities
- 56 reviews of printing and reprographics activities

To the best of our knowledge, no review was conducted of the efficiency of the legislative process itself, but virtually everything else seemed fair game for the CfQ process.

Just how great was the impact of CfQ? From the time the program was launched in November 1991 until the Policy Unit of the Cabinet Office reviewed its efficacy in 1997, close to £2 billion of annual spending on civil service activities was subjected to some form of market test. This resulted in gross annual savings in excess of £330 million—estimated at 18% of the annual costs of the functions reviewed and net savings in the range of £240–280 million after program costs and consulting fees were taken into account. From April 1992 through

March 1995 (the last date precise statistics were available), 20,186 staff had exited the civil service as a result of the CfQ initiative.

What of the people who worked in units subject to the CfQ process? A total of 69,283 were subject to reviews, and 95% of them said their morale was negatively affected by the process. By mid-1997, 34,518 remained in the jobs they had before the process began; 14,579 were working elsewhere in the civil service; 11,924 were employees of the company that had won the contract, providing roughly the same services they had previously provided (usually working in the same location but no longer "protected" as civil servants); 2,572 took early retirement; 2,917 were made redundant involuntarily; and 2,773 simply left (the phrase "natural wastage," used in the government report, hardly seems to do justice to these people). To repeat, all these people were civil servants who had once held the world's most secure jobs.

What exactly became of civil service status as the CfQ process rolled forward? The answer is quite complicated. Civil servants in the UK are protected by what are called "Transfer of Undertakings (Protection of Employment) Regulations," widely known by the acronym "TUPE." This is a complex law. It essentially seeks to protect workers' rights during times of change. Under its provisions, a protected worker can "voluntarily" agree to a change in the terms and conditions of employment or request a transfer to another civil service job. Roughly 10% of employees who transferred to private companies agreed to have their pay reduced. Quite a few more accepted different working hours and shifts from their new employers. Often these agreements came about because the worker had few other options for work in the region (many military facilities in particular are located in remote parts of the country). The vast majority of the 14,579 who transferred to other parts of the civil service likely did so by exercising their TUPE rights.

One provision of the TUPE legislation says that a worker needs to be offered redeployment only on a best-efforts basis. If redeployment is not possible and the worker still does not want to go to work for the new contract company, he or she is deemed to have resigned and forfeits protection under the law. The contracting company is under no obligation to offer employment to every worker in a function subject to CfQ's market test (how else could the savings of roughly 20% of annual operating costs be achieved?). On balance, the worker has few options—despite the protection afforded by TUPE. That having been said, workers in the UK were treated quite fairly in the CfQ process. Many expressed increased satisfaction and career choice in their new private-sector jobs.

Clearly, what's good for the (corporate) goose is good for the (public-sector) gander. The CfQ program in Britain, one of the largest organized efforts to outsource services ever, has widely been judged a roaring success.

## Effects of Outsourcing: Cultural Alienation

Many would argue that downsizing—forcibly removing people from their jobs and livelihood—is the single most *culturally* destructive management trend since the late 1970s. We beg to differ: Outsourcing is. Downsizing severs an individual's ties with the culture he or she previously identified with. It permanently scars the perceptions of those left behind, looking nervously over their shoulder to see whether they, too, are likely to fall victim to a downsizing initiative. What could be worse?

Try the following scenario. You've avoided being downsized. Now you've been outsourced. You still have a job but are working for a new company. You still have an office, the same one you have had for years. You still have the same colleagues. Now, however, some of these officemates still work for the company that farmed you out. They now have perks you no longer have: benefit plans and tenure (whatever that is worth these days). You have neither since you are now a new kid on the block, starting over. Your former colleagues have the usual pressures to perform found in most work situations. You experience the same pressures, aggravated by the fact that your salary in the new company may be substantially lower. Your paycheck has been reduced and your workload increased. You understand why: Your new employer promised savings of 20% from what it used to cost for the work you once did. You aren't happy, but at least you have a job. You're grateful for that but resentful that your old company's savings are coming out of your pocket.

A fanciful scenario? Not really. A lot of outsourced workers are facing a similar situation. Some of the specifics may be different, but the general scenario is typical. What effect does this have on people's participation, loyalty, and commitment? On a superficial level, probably not much at all, at least early on. Since you show up at the same office and interact with the same people, it is unlikely that your day-to-day behavior will change for a while. What you think and feel will be very different, however. Try as you might, you cannot avoid feeling betrayed by your former employer. And that sense of betrayal will increase every time you compare yourself with your former colleagues. Without meaning to, they will probably rub you the wrong way every time they comment about something in your old company.

The sense of betrayal will be accentuated if your former employer is profiting financially. When your former colleagues remark on how well their company's stock is performing, and many are doing quite well, you would not be human if it didn't cross your mind: "Why did they have to farm me out if they are doing so well and they still need me to do the work I have always done?" It's a fair question.

What if the terms of your new working arrangement require you to transfer from the full-time payroll to some form of temporary or contract work? In order to manage costs of taking on contracted functions, many firms resort to similar kinds of arrangements for workers they have taken on. As the executive of one temporary agency explained to the *Wall Street Journal* in a January 1997 article, "The business that's really growing is downsized workers who are hired back through us."

In May 1995, Jackie Krasas Rogers published an article in *Human Resource Management Journal*. It was based on in-depth interviews with a cross-section of temporary workers. The point of her research was to establish a sense of the nature of temporary work and how the conditions affected the individuals involved. She uncovered a highly alienated group of people, disengaged from the work itself and detached from fellow workers. She also found self-alienation caused by the loss of self-esteem associated with becoming a temporary worker. The words of her interviewees tell a dramatic story:

- "It's because you are a temp. They . . . look at you as a sort of disposable factor."
- "That's what can be really hard. Because most people don't really wanna get to know the temps . . . because they figure you're not worth the investment. . . . That was probably one of the biggest frustrations."

- "I think since they don't see you as being permanent they sort of dismiss you as being expendable, like you're not worth it."
- "Well, it's like a small community, everybody has their friends. . . . When you're just about ready to break in, they actually invite you out on a Friday night for drinks with everyone else . . . you leave."
- "There was no Christmas present for you under the tree like the rest of the company would get."
- "You just felt like a moron."

As Rogers comments, "Alienation is a complex concept. [It] signals a lack of control, a certain powerlessness felt by the individual and derived from the structure of social relations. . . . [In a temporary work situation, temporary workers tend to be isolated from their co-workers because] their co-workers did not think they were worth getting to know."

In the case of outsourced workers who return to a workplace on shortened hours, co-workers no longer want to hang out with them. They are afraid they may contract the "disease" themselves and be shoehorned out of their jobs. Outsourcing alienates both those who are outsourced and those who remain. This has a destructive effect on corporate culture.

Think about the cultural implications. Your former co-workers bend over backward making you feel still part of the gang. But gradually they will come to see you as an outsider and will begin to distance themselves. They'll stop including you in news about the company because they are worried about possible leaks of information. They'll even exclude you from the grapevine. You'll lose out on who's doing what to whom because you just aren't one of them anymore. Some may even grow resentful—especially if your new employer is one of the firms benefiting from the outsourcing boom and adding volume at an incredible pace. They'll start thinking, "Why couldn't I have been so lucky?" conveniently forgetting the pay and benefit cut you took in moving to your new employer.

What about transferring your loyalty to your new employer? The company that now signs your paycheck may even encourage you to belong, doing things like inviting you to corporate outings. But it is devilishly hard, surrounded as you are by your old environment. It is even more difficult when your only real contact with your new employer is the person who dispatches you to work on a day-to-day basis or forwards your diminished paycheck. Rogers tells of a sixty-year-old white woman who decided to attend the Christmas party for her new firm. The only person she knew at the event was the woman who sent her out on her temporary assignments; all of the others were strangers.

In effect, outsourced workers are put into a position of attending an extended wake. They mourn the old culture they worked for, and their grieving will likely not end until they move on to new jobs somewhere else. Downsizing may be brutal, but it is quick, final, and clean. People can and do adapt to such change over time. It pales in comparison to the near torture people are put through when they are outsourced and forced to work in the same cultural environment.

## CHAPTER 5

# Merger Mania

# Shotgun Marriage

Corporate mergers are not new. They have been a prominent feature of the business world for many years. Companies that today are household names, such as General Motors, were cobbled together from a series of acquisitions years ago. However, since ideas of shareholder value surfaced in the late 1970s, mergers have grown enormously both in number and scale. They have also taken on a more frightening face within the corporate world. From a cultural point of view, mergers often try to blend companies with strong, conflicting corporate identities—a task no one has found easy. Partly as a result, many mergers do not realize the synergies intended when they were first announced. Despite this evidence, the urge to merge goes on, as industries around the world rush to achieve the scale they believe they need to remain competitive. The effects on culture are often devastating.

## The Growth of Mergers

The advent of the shareholder value craze sparked an explosion in corporate mergers that continues unabated to this day. Figure 5.1 (see page 110) shows the increase in number of deals for both Europe and the United States year by year since 1981.

109

FIGURE 5.1    Growth in Numbers of Merger Deals

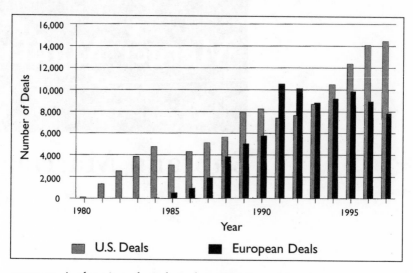

SOURCE: Authors' analysis based on IFR Securities data.

NOTE: These figures detail only the number of deals announced in any one year, but the correlation between deals announced and actually completed is quite close. In any case, the announcement alone is often enough to throw most companies into turmoil, even if the deal is later abandoned.

These staggering growth figures, however, pale to insignificance compared to the magnitude of the deals. As early as 1981, the value of deals surpassed $100 billion. By 1995 it hit an astronomical sum of more than $1 trillion; by 1997 it almost doubled to $2 trillion, as shown in Figure 5.2. The falloff in the size and number of deals in the late 1980s and early 1990s was likely both a reaction to the minicrash of the stock market in October 1987 and a response to the excesses of the LBO era, most aptly illustrated by the ill-fated KKR takeover of RJR Nabisco. But by the early 1990s, whatever restraint existed earlier evaporated. The value of deals began to soar into the stratosphere.

Along with the growing aggregate value of deals, the size of individual deals was increasing. Table 5.1 (see page 112) highlights the growth in deal size since 1980, skipping over the temporary anomaly created by the RJR Nabisco deal in 1988. In the early 1980s, the bulk of the very large deals were resource related. They involved the acquisition of mineral resources like oil reserves or mineral deposits. By the late 1980s, takeover artists arrived on the scene, and the mag-

FIGURE 5.2    Growth in Value of Deals

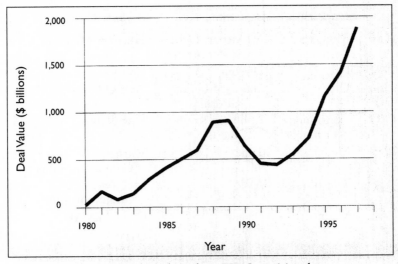

SOURCE: Authors' anaylysis based on IFR Securities data.

nitude of deals began to grow. The focus also expanded away from natural resources to encompass other industries.

The 1990s, when raider activity declined in the face of a rapidly rising stock market, was the era of the corporate merger. Across the board—in pharmaceuticals, telecommunications, media, banking, and other industries—scores of senior managers jumped on acquisitions as a primary means of building shareholder value. Given the size and strength of corporate balance sheets (and the important fact that many of the deals were "friendly"), the value of transactions skyrocketed. Many executives got very rich as a result. Trailblazers like Craig McCaw, the founder of McCaw Communications, cashed in on their entrepreneurial efforts. Hundreds of others cashed in as well simply by jumping on the bandwagon. As the turn of the century neared, the merger craze showed no sign of abating.

## Why So Many Deals?

All deals are different, or so deal makers proclaim. If we look at the top twenty-five corporate mergers, shown in Table 5.2 (see page 113), we see that their claim certainly appears to have some validity.

Please note that each of the twenty-five deals in this table involves more than $10 billion. Only three of the deals, the RJR Nabisco

TABLE 5.1   Increase in Deal Size

| | Industry | Acquirer | Acquired | Value of Deal ($ billions) |
|---|---|---|---|---|
| 1980 | Minerals | McMoran Exploration | Freeport Minerals | 2.5 |
| 1981 | Oil | DuPont | Conoco | 9.5 |
| 1984 | Oil | Standard Oil of California | Gulf Oil | 13.4 |
| 1988 | Consumer Products | Kohlberg Kravis Roberts | RJR Nabisco | 30.6 |
| 1989 | Media | Time | Warner Communications | 15.1 |
| 1993 | Telecom | AT&T | McCaw Communications | 16.7 |
| 1995 | Media | Disney | Cap Cities/ABC | 18.8 |
| 1996 | Telecom | Bell Atlantic | Nynex | 30.8 |
| 1997 | Telecom | WorldCom | MCI Communications | 35.3 |
| 1998 | Banking | Travelers | Citicorp | 70.0 |

SOURCE: Authors' analysis, based on IFR Securities data.

takeover, the Time Warner merger, and the takeover of Kraft by Philip Morris, occurred in the 1980s; the rest were products of the merger boom of the late 1990s. Several names in the list recur. WorldCom, for example, is an upstart company largely assembled through acquisition. Its deals simply keep getting bigger and bigger. NationsBank, similarly, started life as a small regional bank in the southeastern United States. Convinced that banking consolidation was inevitable and would change the face of banking forever, it, too, has been steadily acquiring bigger and bigger targets. Many of the others on the list, such as Travelers and Grand Met, are regular acquirers (some might say predators) as well, but their earlier mergers did not break the $10-billion barrier.

Six different rationales were advanced for the deals:

1. LBO. The RJR Nabisco deal is the only LBO among the top twenty-five. Its primary purpose, like any LBO, was to make money for the deal makers. It is doubtful that it ever did (except for the insiders at KKR), because in this instance at least the deal makers overstepped themselves. But their

TABLE 5.2 Top Twenty-Five Deals of All Time, Through Midyear 1998

| | | Value ($ billions) | Acquirer | Acquired | Rationale |
|---|---|---|---|---|---|
| 1 | 1998 | 70 | Travelers | Citicorp | One-Stop Shopping |
| 2 | 1998 | 62 | NationsBank | Bank America | Scale |
| 3 | 1998 | 39 | BancOne | First Chicago | Scale |
| 4 | 1997 | 35 | WorldCom | MCI | Scale |
| 5 | 1988 | 31 | KKR | RJR Nabisco | LBO |
| 6 | 1996 | 30 | Sandoz | Ciba-Geigy | Scale |
| 7 | 1996 | 21 | Bell Atlantic | Nynex | Scale |
| 8 | 1995 | 19 | Disney | Cap Cities/ABC | Distribution |
| 9 | 1996 | 16 | SBC | Pacific Telesis | Scale |
| 10 | 1997 | 16 | Grand Metropolitan | Guinness | Diversification; scale |
| 11 | 1993 | 16 | AT&T | McCaw Com. | Diversification |
| 12 | 1995 | 15 | Lloyds Bank | TSB | Scale |
| 13 | 1997 | 15 | NationsBank | Barnett Bank | Scale |
| 14 | 1995 | 14 | Glaxo | Wellcome | Scale |
| 15 | 1989 | 14 | Time | Warner Com. | Diversification; scale |
| 16 | 1996 | 14 | WorldCom | MFS Com. | Diversification; scale |
| 17 | 1997 | 14 | Starwood Lodging | ITT | Financial |
| 18 | 1988 | 13 | Philip Morris | Kraft | Diversification |
| 19 | 1996 | 13 | Boeing | McDonnell Douglas | Diversification; scale |
| 20 | 1997 | 12 | CUC International | HFS | Distribution |
| 21 | 1997 | 12 | Morgan Stanley | Dean Witter Discover | Distribution |
| 22 | 1996 | 11 | US West | Continental Cablevision | Diversification |
| 23 | 1995 | 11 | Wells Fargo | First Interstate | Scale |
| 24 | 1996 | 11 | Axa | UAP | Scale; diversification |
| 25 | 1995 | 10 | Chemical Bank | Chase Manhattan | Scale |

SOURCE: Authors' analysis, based on IFR Securities data.

stated purpose was clear: make money. (Reading between the lines, it might be argued that the real purpose of this particular deal was to massage the egos of the protagonists, but since ego plays such a large role in most major deals, that may be a moot point.)

2. "One-stop shopping." Equally unique is the rationale for the Travelers-Citicorp merger: Put the companies together to build a supermarket of financial services for clients. The two CEOs justified the economics of the transaction by calling attention to the potential synergies achievable by cross-selling. That such synergies have failed to materialize in previous deals did not seem to daunt them.

3. Financial engineering. Starwood Lodging's "white knight" takeover of ITT (a major hotel operator through its Sheraton chain) was motivated by pure financial engineering. As a real estate investment trust (REIT)—a specialized company for managing real estate holdings—Starwood could take advantage of U.S. tax provisions none of the other ITT suitors could match. Game, set, and match to Starwood, at least in this particular instance.

4. Distribution. Several companies justified mergers as providing expanded outlets for one another's products. Here the Disney–Cap Cities merger is probably the best example. How much this will improve their respective economics is still to be seen. But this did not prevent Wall Street from giving the deal its blessing.

5. Diversification. A related rationale to distribution is diversification. Grand Met adds value by pushing Guinness through its distribution channels, and beer (or more precisely, stout) provides them a new product. Similarly, Boeing adds McDonnell Douglas's military planes to a portfolio of mainly commercial aircraft and achieves economies where processes overlap. Almost all deals that involve diversification also point to overlapping functions of the companies.

6. Scale. Most mergers of the late 1990s were justified on the need to build scale in consolidating industries. Here banks and telecommunications firms were most prominent. Whether or not consolidation occurs to the extent companies are betting on, the economics can usually be justified by

potential staff reductions once the union takes place. For example, NationsBank and BankAmerica expect to shed 8,000 staff members once their transaction goes through. The $2 billion a year in operating savings this will generate more than justifies the merger to Wall Street observers.

How valid are these (and other) rationales put forward to justify mergers? Does the economy at large or the economics of the merger partners ever provide a strong enough case for the transaction to offset the accompanying turmoil? The answer is mixed at best. Michael Porter, the famed Harvard business strategist, studied acquisitions of major companies over a period of thirty-six years. He found that more than half the "unrelated" acquisitions were subsequently divested—a clear signal of defeat. *Barron's* pointed out in April 1998 that Travelers was getting only a 5% return on the capital it was investing in its joining with Citicorp. Similarly, WorldCom is expected to earn only 2.1% on the capital involved in its recent takeover of MCI. These are hardly robust returns. *Barron's* also cited a study by McKinsey & Company showing that 61% of 116 acquisition programs failed to earn returns greater than the annual cost of capital required to do the deal. Successful acquisitions, it seems, are hard to come by.

Despite these difficulties, some acquisitions are necessary to enable companies to remain competitive in their industries. With business going global at a seemingly ferocious pace (see details in Chapter 7), some companies are compelled to join up just to keep up. Major corporations abhor dealing with hundreds of little telecommunications suppliers as they spread their tentacles worldwide. Mergers between phone companies to build capability on a global scale probably make sense. None, however, has occurred (although the joint venture between British Telecom and AT&T announced in 1998 was focused foursquare on this emerging market). Most of the recent telecommunications mergers have attempted to build capacity crossing the boundaries separating local and long-distance service as well as voice and data service offerings. In the case of the local and long-distance wars, we recognize that the grass always appears greener on the other side of the fence. Whether this phenomenon can be translated into service advantages for consumers remains to be seen.

The shift of communications away from voice to data, in contrast, is very real. As people rely more and more on the Internet for information and communications, providers of Internet access (and this means phone companies) have simply had to adjust. New switches have to be installed to handle the longer "packet lengths" of data traffic. More carrier capacity is needed than the historical twisted pairs of copper wire can provide to give demanding customers faster access. Some companies have explained their recent acquisitions as methods of buying required increases in capacity. If they can manage the acquisitions as successfully as they have managed capital investment programs, their vision may be confirmed.

In the case of banking, the bulk of recent transactions have focused on extending the market reach of the acquiring banks. In some banking business segments, this search for greater scale is well justified. Credit card processing is so scale intensive that long before the recent spate of bank mergers, a few megaplayers (Citibank and GE Capital, for example) had emerged to dominate the market. Similarly, in securities services such as Global Custody, requirements of scale have already forced a tremendous industry-wide consolidation. Consolidations have been justified economically by the need to amortize the required heavy investment in computer systems and operations management across as broad a base as possible. Bankers are betting in recent mergers that other product categories will follow suit. Mortgages offer one such prime candidate. Whether individual customers will flock to this new class of "low-cost providers" remains to be seen—especially for services usually purchased locally. The big players in the merger game are betting that they will.

On balance, therefore, the case for mergers is unclear. Most fail, according to recent studies. Using only highly personal and selective data (firsthand observation), we would speculate that a lot of failures happen when firms merge across the cultural typological framework summarized in the Introduction to this book. For example, many years ago we witnessed two mergers: the first was between Wheelabrator-Frye, a macho conglomerate assembled in the early 1980s by Mike Dingman and several colleagues, and Pullman, a classic bet-your-company capital goods firm in the Midwest. Watching executives from the two companies try to communicate was like attending a session at the United Nations General Assembly: They simply did not speak the same language. Needless to say, the integration of the two companies did not run smoothly, and neither company is now part of the contemporary corporate landscape (although that is another story altogether).

The second was a merger between Millipore Corporation and Waters Associates. Although both were high-tech companies operating in related markets, the merger never realized the benefits anticipated when the deal was first put forward. Millipore, which had grown up with a strong sales culture and epitomized the work hard/play hard environment, never succeeded in instilling its sales values and practices in the slower-moving world of Waters. The reason was as much cultural as any other: Waters had been built through invention (the high-pressure liquid chromatograph and its related peripheral devices being the company's primary product). Given its origins, Waters operated like a bet-your-company capital goods company, far from the go-go style of its more sales-oriented acquirer. Quick decisions made by Millipore executives and inserted into Waters were often off the mark. More thoughtful decisions by Waters executives were usually off pace, causing them to miss out on opportunities—this, of course, to the chagrin of their new owners. In due course, Millipore spun off its newly acquired possession, unable to make the cultures mesh. How much the problem was recognized as cultural is still open to conjecture.

Still, some other acquisitions succeed. Moreover, some of the more recent mergers have a strong rationale behind them, but it will take time to find out whether the assumptions are valid. With such mixed explanations for the merger craze, there must be something else going on to fuel the movement.

## Wall Street Loves a Merger

In the week Travelers and Citicorp announced their record-setting merger, the two companies' market capitalization increased by $30 billion (a $20 billion increase for Travelers, $10 billion for Citicorp). The same week, the value of stock and options held by Sandy Weill, Travelers CEO, was reported by CNBC to have risen by $124 million. John Reed, CEO of Citicorp, saw the value of his holdings rise by a much more modest $24 million. Not a bad week in the office for either gentleman. No wonder CEOs love mergers. But since the merger was announced and subsequently executed, the stock of the combined groups has sold off considerably as Wall Street skepticism grows over the ability of the combined management team to deliver on the promised synergies. (Although this sell-off has undoubtedly hit the pocketbooks of Weill and Reed hard, we have no doubt that new incentives will be found to keep them motivated at the task of delivering on the results they promised.)

Taking a somewhat longer-term view, we analyzed stock price movements of the ten largest mergers in 1995 and 1996. We wanted some distance from the euphoria that often follows the announcement of a megadeal (as was immediately the case for Travelers-Citicorp). Therefore, we tracked the movement of the stock through the year of the announcement and then to the subsequent year's end. Two of our sample stocks showed little movement over the period. One was Boeing, which encountered difficulties in its commercial airliner business. The other was AT&T, whose merger with McCaw, though large, was not of sufficient size to change things materially for AT&T. The results for the other eight companies are shown in Figure 5.3.

Stock value growth for the eight remaining companies the year of the announcement was 14%. The average gain by the end of the second year was an even more impressive 46%. Companies would have to sell a lot of product or make a slew of good loans to achieve anywhere near these gains.

Our sense is this: The merger game is not driven by an increase in "real value" but by short-term-oriented institutional money managers who are intensely focused on finding any news that justifies buying or selling a company's stock. Megamergers are front-page news. They grab everyone's immediate attention. Whether a deal will prove to be good or not requires time to determine. So why not look favorably on it at the outset, then move on to something else? Short-term-oriented money managers generally buy stock immediately when a merger is announced and then wait to see what happens. Hence the positive treatment of mergers on Wall Street.

This doesn't escape the notice of corporate managers, who use mergers as a way to garner favorable attention from Wall Street and thereby puff up their stock price. And if the deal is slow to mature, as was the case with NationsBank's 1997 acquisition of Barnett Bank, there is always a bigger deal to trumpet to cover up the shortfall (such as the merger NationsBank proposed with BankAmerica in early 1998). And so the deals go on and on.

FIGURE 5.3    Postmerger Stock Gains

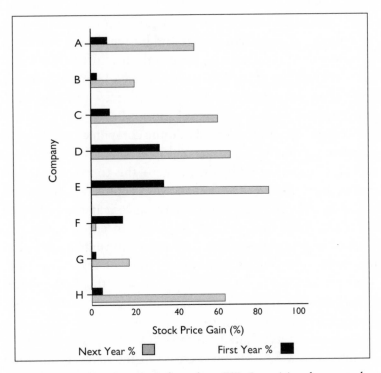

SOURCE: Authors' analysis based on IFR Securities data; stock prices from Dow Jones.

Wall Street analysts are not totally clueless about the potential value to be derived from mergers. They often look carefully at the proposed transaction and over time adjust their calculations about what the deal will produce.

For example, on April 6, 1998, Citicorp and Travelers issued a joint press release titled "Citicorp and Travelers Group to Merge, Creating Citigroup: The Global Leader in Financial Services . . . Transaction Has a Value of over $140 Billion." That this modest headline was proclaiming the world's largest ever business combination seemed lost in the announcement's subdued rhetoric. In the body of the press release, John Reed, the CEO of Citicorp, said, "With this merger, we instantaneously broaden our services to our customers around the world. . . . Now we have the capability to serve customers . . . with convenient, efficient access to all the expertise and the full range of value-added products and services they need—a capability unmatched by anyone, anywhere." Not to be outdone, Sandy Weill, Traveler's CEO and the deal's initiator, added, "Because the world economy changes at an unprecedented pace today, and regions, markets, continents and businesses are more and more interdependent, consumers, corporations, institutions and governments around the globe increasingly need a financially strong and reliable source for financial advisory services and products. . . . Together, we will be that company."

Jointly, Reed and Weill proclaimed that the companies expected to generate substantial incremental earnings from the significant cross-selling opportunities afforded by the merger—this together with potential cost savings. They noted that the transaction was subject to regulatory approval. They glossed over the fact that the proposed transaction was, at the time the deal was announced, in direct violation of the Glass-Steagall Act. This legislation prevents commercial U.S. banks from operating as investment banks or insurance companies. They projected that the deal would close in the third quarter of 1998 (and, presumably, that the legislative barriers to its consummation would have been removed).

Despite the various associated caveats, Wall Street rewarded the announcement with a $30-billion increase in the market valuation of the two companies. Given that both companies were trading at above twenty times earnings at the time, their combined earnings would have to increase by about $1.5 billion after tax (just over $2 billion before tax) to justify the combination. Before long, some of the deal's premium was removed from the two prospective partners' stock prices since the initial expectations from projected cross-selling and cost savings seemed overinflated.

The Citicorp-Travelers merger stands out because it was the biggest transaction proposed up to that time. It is also interesting because much of the synergy demanded as justification for the deal was predicated on potential cross-selling. Earlier in his career, Weill had lost his job as president of American Express when similar promised product cross-selling synergies failed to materialize. Even though the virtues of cross-selling are widely trumpeted, financial service customers historically shop around for products rather than put their eggs in one basket. Only time will tell whether Reed and Weill are visionaries championing a concept whose time has come—or just pigheaded executives in pursuit of personal gain and glory.

Recognizing the potential pitfalls in the Citigroup merger, NationsBank and BankAmerica (the second largest deal in history) made no mistake in detailing how their combined synergies were to be achieved. At the press conference announcing the merger, Hugh McColl, the CEO of NationsBank slated to become the new company's chairman and CEO, said: "While this merger is *not* all about cost-cutting, we will gain efficiencies in three key areas: limited franchise overlaps; consolidation of common national business lines; and corporate overhead." The CFO of NationsBank, James Hance, quantified these expectations by forecasting $2 billion in before-tax cost reductions within two years. Cost recoveries would materialize by reducing manpower in the combined companies by 8,000 people, roughly 10% of their staff. Predicated on head-count reductions completely under the control of management, these were numbers you could virtually put in the bank. Wall Street agreed, bidding up the combined values of the two banks by roughly $10 billion in the week following the announcement—more modest than the initial markup for Citicorp and Travelers but still substantial.

These two examples, albeit both from banking, lay bare the anatomy of the merger. Mergers produce stock market gains if Wall Street can see enhanced earnings as a result. The surest route to enhanced earnings is to reduce head count and costs. Virtually every deal thus takes this expected path. With only a few notable exceptions, Wall Street is quite skeptical about other, less bankable synergies, and most managers know it. Nevertheless, it is managerial focus on Wall Street's reaction, not real business gains, that have fueled much of the merger boom of the 1990s.

## Mergers and Culture

Although substantial cost reductions may be a primary justification for mergers, they are not among the most important effects. Mergers affect cultural patterns. They do so in three critical ways, separated in time from the date the deal is announced. First, there is the look-over-your-shoulder effect. Personnel try to figure out where cuts will be made. Second, there is the winners-and-losers effect. One party to the deal almost always wins, and the other, usually the acquired, almost always loses as jobs in the new entity are allocated. Third and most important, there is the cultural isolation effect. It occurs when survivors discover that the company they now work for is significantly different from the one they worked for before. Let us examine these three effects in more detail.

### *Looking over Your Shoulder*

As soon as a merger is announced (and to achieve maximum stock market advantage they have to be announced with great fanfare), staff in both the acquired and the acquiring company begin nervously wondering where the ax will fall first. In a brilliant series of articles in the *New York Times* later combined into the book *The Downsizing of America*, Louis Uchitelle and N. R. Kleinfield chronicled the experiences of a middle manager in a large pharmaceutical company being absorbed by another. Because the middle manager was fearful of losing her job, she consented only to letting the reporters review her diary entries in the weeks following the merger announcement. These entries offer a poignant insight into the expected staff anxieties that follow merger announcements:

- A huge cloud of uncertainty hangs over each employee. Officially, we still haven't been told a thing about the acquisition and must learn about it from the newspapers. The sleepless nights begin.
- Every day I have lunch with my friend G, a great guy with a good sense of humor and rock solid values hard to find in industry. He will probably have to relocate out of state. This is ironic because the company just moved him here twenty months ago from halfway across the country. We will probably not see each other again.
- The company has been sold. It would be sick to suggest that this merger—which will result in the loss of thousands of jobs—is in the best interests of employees.
- My friend M was told that there were two lists: those who would be offered jobs and those who wouldn't. Her name was on the second list. Are they crazy?
- My boss left last month. There's no one left to report to.
- I ran into B today. He wasn't offered a job and is devastated. He is scared he may not be able to pay his kids' college tuition and may have to ask them to transfer to local schools. Any sense of joy I had at being on the 'Schindler's list' of em-

ployees who've got jobs with our new parent corporation has been wiped out by experiences like this.

- I have been here four months and am convinced that I will never fit into this cold foreign corporate culture. I'm reminded of the old adage "Be careful what you wish for," since just a few months ago, I was praying they'd offer me a job here.

Looking over one's shoulder and gossiping about who might go or stay are part of the experience of a merger. The experience is even more demoralizing than when employees fall victim to a conventional downsizing (certainly demoralizing enough). In mergers everyone knows the exercise is a numbers game to find enough bodies to justify the deal. Most think that little or no thought is given to the merits or skills of individuals who will lose their jobs as a result. Welcome to life during merger mania.

### Winners and Losers

We participated in the merger integration planning and implementation for a combination of two magazine publishing groups some time ago. If ever a merger was designed in heaven, this was it. Both companies were based in New York and shared a "streetsmart New Yorker" perspective on the world. Both had strong titles that complemented each other in the marketplace. Both companies had good people up and down the ranks, and the talents of these people were their keys to business success. Although the price paid by the acquiring company was thought to be on the high side, with the amalgamated talent in the new company, everyone expected nothing but positive results.

The cultural integration was planned very carefully—from the location of individual offices (so that no one group would feel slighted) to the allocation of expanded responsibilities in the newly enlarged company (so that managerial opportunities were given to the best people from each company). What could go wrong? A lot, it turns out. Within less than a year, virtually all of the senior managers in the acquired company had left. What happened?

What ensued was a cultural clash between the people in the two tribes. The cultural cleavage was exacerbated by the fact that the acquiring company was staffed predominantly by ethnic Catholics and the acquired by a mixture of mostly gay, predominantly Jewish people. Although all were native New Yorkers, they could not have come from more different worlds. Within weeks, the two camps were at loggerheads. The macho ethnics of the acquiring company went out of their way to avoid meeting with their new and different colleagues. The people acquired felt doubly discriminated against and withdrew into their own protective enclaves. Soon decisions were being made unilaterally by members of the acquirer's management team; soon thereafter the newly acquired managers started their exodus. It was a screwup in integration planning, you could well argue. But there was more to it than that.

Every merger involves winners and losers. Typically, the winners are drawn from the ranks of the acquiring company and the losers from the ranks of the acquiree. Letting tribal nature take its course, the winners congregate as they always have. They make decisions without consultation as they always have. They impose their wills on those around them as they always have. As a result the losers withdraw, barred from the corridors of power, banding together against the inevitable injustice they see on the horizon. Before long, the excluded losers start taking their talents elsewhere; the winners discount this exodus, in effect saying, "Who needed them in the first place?" N. R. Kleinfield, the reporter for the *Times* series that featured the Chase–Chemical Bank merger among others, uncovered a joke going around the old Chase: Downsized former Chase employees were known as "Chemical waste."

Are these merger experiences unique or typical? Clearly the latter. Bell Atlantic takes over NYNEX, and it is NYNEX that must change its ways to become part of the brasher and more marketing-oriented Bell Atlantic. Glaxo takes over research-oriented Wellcome and the intellectual researchers soon adapt their style to that of the more aggressive Londoners. The first year or so after a merger is consummated is when the losers learn what losing is all about: Staff cuts fall disproportionately on the acquired company. Key management jobs go to the acquirer. Systems in the acquired firm are replaced with systems from the acquiring firm. In most cases, the rhetoric of those involved in the merger doesn't match the reality: If you are acquired, you lose. This transition period establishes winners as winners. Losers come to realize that they really are losers. It is a prelude to a darker reality that lies ahead: the submersion of the acquired culture under that of the acquirer. Because culture changes very slowly, this often takes several years, but it does happen and is any merger's most lasting cultural impact.

## *Submersion of the Acquired Culture*

"SBC Communications' Takeover of Pacific Telesis Transformed Company's Culture," screamed the April 7, 1998, headline in the *San Francisco Business Times*. How did this self-professed "merger of equals" result in such a newsworthy transformation of one company's culture? It is easily understood in light of what was revealed in the three-article series written by the *Business Times* staff writers Steve Ginsberg and Lorna Fernandes. They noted the typical winners-and-losers effect of the merger: Of the thirty-five top officers in the company before the merger, only thirteen survived after a year; all seven members of the executive committee of Pacific Telesis (PacTel) were disposed of, as were 250 of the top 1,000 management jobs in the company. In their place, SBC inserted, with dazzling speed, SBC veterans who knew and were comfortable with the culture of the acquiring company.

Just what was the SBC culture, and why was it so different from that of PacTel? Basically, it was a Texas business culture, conservative about such things as dress code but highly aggressive in terms of business practices and decisionmaking. This was all quite alien to the easygoing Californians who composed the rank and file of PacTel. Longtime PacTel employees, accustomed to dressing informally (one executive was quoted as saying he would normally wear a tie only once every two weeks), soon itched in the buttoned-down starchiness of their new Texan owners. Women executives were informally coached to wear skirts rather than pants when attending company meetings in San Antonio. An executive reported that around the old PacTel office they joked that to fit in, women "better get big hair and red nails."

Dress codes (and there is no actual formal dress code at SBC) are of course only cosmetic. What other, deeper cultural changes ensued? One of the largest involved transfer policies: As a way of melding its culture together, SBC had a history of frequently transferring staff to different areas of the country. Typical career paths for senior managers involved up to five such moves. By contrast, PacTel had a history of accommodating employees' desires to stay in one place. SBC took over and began offering PacTel employees transfers to other parts of the country, often to much-diminished jobs. This was their way of testing an employee's loyalty to the new company. It is hardly surprising that many chose to leave instead. This suited SBC, since it opened up a whole raft of transfer opportunities for its own loyal employees. It also sent shock waves through the traditional culture of PacTel.

More important, SBC's top-down decisionmaking style rattled consensus-oriented PacTel employees and managers. "PacTel had a culture that was gentle, considerate, caring, conciliatory, consensus-driven and communication-rich," a surviving executive of the company was quoted as saying. In the words of a former PacTel executive, SBC's "new regime brought a sense of urgency—a drive to get things done. While there is time for hearty debate, it is limited. And executives who miss it are out of luck." Another former executive added, "If I had concerns about decisions in the organization structure . . . there was no one who I trusted that I could turn to." Clearly, times and culture had changed at Pacific Telesis, and those who remained would have to learn to adapt—or leave.

This example of cultural takeover is typical. The scenario occurs in most mergers. When WorldCom took over MCI, the brash newcomer from Mississippi was taking over an establishment-oriented long-distance carrier. Once an upstart itself, MCI had transformed itself over the years into a company that emphasized technology and service. In the course of doing so, it had embraced the telecommunications establishment. Will WorldCom's relentless drive for profits and reduced costs to support its high-flying stock price change MCI? We would not bet against it. NYNEX's emphasis on price and quality has certainly been subsumed by Bell Atlantic's brazen and combative approach to both regulators and customers.

Cultural collisions, almost without exception, result in cultural isolation for the surviving employees from the acquired firm. In a *Washington Post* article in February 1997, the amalgamation of Morgan Stanley Group with Dean Witter, Discover, and Company was described as the "white shoes and white socks" merger because of the massive disparity in the cultures of the two companies. Allan Sloan, *Newsweek*'s Wall Street editor, predicted "trouble ahead because of 'clashing corporate cultures,' which is a polite way of saying that Morgan Stanley's highly paid investment banker types aren't likely to become bosom buddies with Dean Witter's lower paid employees." Only time will tell whether he was right in his prediction, but as the *Times* articles on downsizing so powerfully reveal, there is every reason to believe that "survivor syndrome" and "cultural isolation" will prove crippling forces in almost all blended companies.

Not every takeover involves the total submersion of the acquired company's culture. But the handful of exceptions go further toward proving the rule than setting a different example. For example, when AT&T bought McCaw Communications in 1994, it purposefully set out to preserve the entrepreneurial, philanthropic, and casual culture of McCaw. McCaw insiders were left in charge of the newly acquired company. James Barksdale, president of AT&T's wireless operations, was quoted in the *Valley Daily News* on September 20, 1994, as saying, "AT&T has shown absolutely no interest in telling us (McCaw) how to run our business. If anything, it's our desire to change a few things AT&T does." We should not read too much into this, however, since wireless was a new business for AT&T and a hands-off attitude made sense. It certainly did not keep its hands off NCR when it acquired and subsequently disposed of that ill-fated company.

Similarly, though likely tempted to be more meddlesome, IBM did not interfere with the culture of Lotus Development Corporation, which it acquired in 1995. This did not prevent a number of talented Lotus employees, including CEO Jim Manzi, from leaving the company after the merger. But the flavor and culture of Lotus has remained largely unchanged. This is not the outcome Lotus employees anticipated when they were first acquired. A story in the March 26, 1998, edition of *USA Today* described an early meeting at Lotus between IBM senior vice president John Thompson and a group of Lotus senior managers. In preparing for the meeting, the Lotus crew had donned conservative suits and ties they thought were expected in the traditionally buttoned-down IBM. They were shocked when Thompson, trying to play to the culture dictates of Lotus, showed up for the meeting in a T-shirt and jeans. At a much more fundamental level, several weeks later they were even more surprised when in response to their request to lower the price of Lotus Notes in a major attempt to gain market share for the trendsetting product, the CEO of IBM, Lou Gerstner, told them, "You're running the place. Do what you want."

Three years after the merger was completed, the two companies were still wrestling with the little "details" required to allow them to work well enough together to gain the advantages from being unified. These "details" included things like showing up for meetings on time (which is sacrosanct at IBM but not at Lotus) and remembering to return phone calls (a requirement at IBM, more often than not ignored at Lotus). In due course, these cultural wrinkles will undoubtedly get ironed out. In the meantime, one is left to wonder what opportunities may have been lost in the interests of preserving the cultural integrity of the smaller firm.

In any case, the McCaw and Lotus examples (and there are others) are atypical of the cultural scenarios of large mergers. In both these cases, the acquisition was that of a new business or a new technology—assets that could be protected only by preserving existing cultural identities.

## What Lies Ahead

Mergers are big business for the investment bankers and investment managers of Wall Street. In today's business climate so intently focused on share-price appreciation, they are also high on the agenda for managers. Nothing on the horizon suggests this will change soon. Many industries are still highly fragmented, both nationally and internationally. Even industries that are part of the biggest recent deals, like banking and telecommunications, remain ridiculously fragmented. Megadeals will no doubt continue in these industries for decades. Other fragmented industries, like insurance and construction, have yet to begin consolidating and are likely to join merger mania before too long. In only a handful of industries—defense, aerospace, and consumer products—have the pairings reached saturation. Companies in the (until recently) rapidly growing Far East have been relatively protected from the deal making. This is so for a variety of cultural and regional reasons. But as we discuss in Chapter 7, the increasing pressure to globalize markets will draw foreign countries into the deal-making process. Mergers are a fact of modern business life, and they are most likely here to stay for the foreseeable future.

Does this mean that the world of corporations will contract until there are just one or two large corporations in the world? Will cultural diversity disappear as more and more companies merge and subsume the cultures of others? We think this is highly improbable. On the contrary, if anything is likely to put a brake on runaway merger activity, it will be the pressure to retain cultural diversity in merged firms. Culture changes only reluctantly. Even in firms that are acquired and whose cultures are aggressively subsumed by their acquirers, the culture of the old firm lives on in the hearts and minds of the employees who survived the merger. It will rear its head from time to time for decades to come—perhaps even until a whole new generation of workers arrives on the scene, a generation unfamiliar with the original culture and its origins.

Moreover, vestiges of an entrenched culture fight back: They will do so in divisions where critical masses of old employees still survive; they will do so in times of stress, when going back to long-proven methods of work will appeal most to embattled employees; and they will do so in sheer rebellion, rebellion kept silent while the greatest risks to livelihood were still extant.

The implication of these coming battles for cultural survival or even renewal is that productivity in companies pieced together by mergers will suffer. Productivity and performance will remain weak until management realizes the need to come to grips with the problem of merging, not subsuming, cultures. Managers will need to devote serious time and energy to identifying the best practices of merging partners and forging a new, robust, and shared culture.

There is potentially an upside to all this as well. Companies worth acquiring in the first place typically have cultures that have stood the test of time in their own marketplaces. If acquiring companies recognize this and try to build a new blended culture that combines the best features of each of the companies being joined, there could emerge a series of companies whose cultures are stronger because of the diversity they embrace. Managers contemplating mergers often trumpet the synergies to be achieved and the new skills and expertise being acquired. Some of these potential synergies and skills are cultural, a factor not always given much thought. Unfortunately, Wall-Street-driven pressure for immediate results combined with the human hankering for meaning at work make such goals elusive. Yet for anyone bold enough to reach out for it, the prize is there for the taking.

## CHAPTER 6

# Computers

## Cultural Isolation

Computers have been an important factor in corporate life since the 1950s. The first primitive machines had little effect on the great mass of workers, so they had virtually no impact on company cultures. In certain industries, such as insurance, masses of records had to be maintained. As a result, in the late 1950s workers became accustomed to wrestling with massive printouts as a normal part of their workday. But the machines themselves were largely hidden from view, maintained by small teams of computer-literate pioneers.

In the early 1960s, all this changed. IBM introduced its revolutionary 360 series of computers. Because their price performance capabilities were many times those of predecessors, workplace after workplace acquired the new machines. Frequent interface between people and computers became a regular feature of working life. This was particularly true after 1965, when IBM introduced its 360 Model 65 computer. It was the first computer of any significance to introduce the quaint notion of time-sharing: Workers in remote locations could now interact directly with the central computer through the keyboards attached to their "dumb" computer terminals.

Through time-sharing, the computer factory came into being for clerks responsible for processing insurance claims or updating bank account records. Hundreds of other similar applications spread across almost all industries. By the early 1970s, these computer factories had become an important part of corporate life practically everywhere. Coincidentally, this was about the same time the number of white-collar workers first exceeded the number of blue-collar employees in the workplace. Who would have predicted then that the revolution in work practices was just beginning?

In 1971 a struggling young semiconductor firm introduced the Intel 4004, the first of a family of microprocessors. Originally, only electronic hobbyists took note. When Intel followed in 1974 with its Intel 8080, a handful of these hobbyists, working out of a converted shop in an Albuquerque mall, put together the first real microcomputer, the MITS Altair 8800. This new device inspired another pair of hobbyists, Steve Wozniak and Steve Jobs, to chuck what they were doing and begin work on their own microcomputer. After a few detours, by 1977 they succeeded in introducing the Apple II—the first microcomputer aimed at regular users, not just hobbyists and geeky tinkerers.

On the software side, inspired by the Altair, two young programmers, Paul Allen and Bill Gates, developed a version of the Basic programming language to run on the Altair. The company they founded to sell this program was and still is called the Microsoft Corporation, and ownership of its stock has made Gates the richest man in the world.

These exciting developments in a fledgling industry would likely have been insignificant had not IBM, then undisputed leader of the computer industry, decided to enter the fray. In 1981 the company launched the IBM PC with an operating system supplied by Microsoft. The microcomputer revolution was off and running.

## Who Does and Doesn't Use Computers Today?

In October 1993 the Census Bureau's "Current Population Survey" sampled thousands of U.S. households to determine just who relied on computers in the workplace. It found that fully 45.8% of all American workers used a computer at work. If you consider that almost 45 million people (35% of the total workforce) are involved in jobs like food preparation and handling (6 million), cleaning services (over 3 million), personal services such as barbering and hairdressing (almost 3 million), construction (over 5 million), farming, fishing, and mining (almost 4 million), trucking and taxi service

FIGURE 6.1    Relative Computer Use by Age

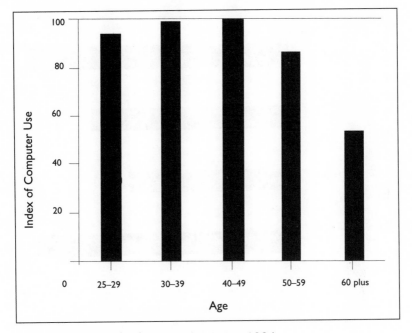

SOURCE: *Digest of Education Statistics*, 1994.

(over 5 million), laboring outside the construction sector (over 5 million), and machine operation of various kinds (almost 8 million), the conclusion is inescapable. Even as early as 1993, virtually everyone who could worked with computers.

As we might expect, it is modern society's dispossessed who are excluded from active computer use. The microcomputer revolution imposed a new set of work requirements: Familiarity and facility with modern computer technology. The poor, uneducated, or unlucky simply cannot obtain what they need in order to compete. Consider, for example, the penetration of computer use at work by age, as shown in Figure 6.1.

Not surprisingly, the use of computers at work is most prominent among those between the ages of thirty and forty-nine. These people grew up with the technology. Only half of those over sixty still working at the time of the survey make use of computers on the job. With the ranks of unemployed full of older workers, is their lack of jobs due to an inability to master the new computer skills? If we slice

FIGURE 6.2    Relative Computer Use by Race

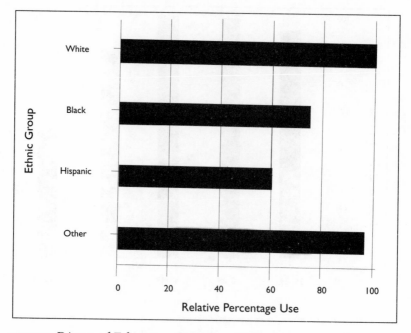

SOURCE: *Digest of Education Statistics*, 1994.

computer users along racial lines, as shown in Figure 6.2, we find that whites and Asians (who make up the bulk of the "Other" category) are the winners at the computer era's job game. Blacks and Hispanics are underrepresented. Looking at education levels, we see that more education makes people stronger participants in today's computerized society, as shown in Figure 6.3.

Are these patterns likely to persist into the future? If home ownership of computers is any indication, as shown in Figure 6.4 (see page 136), the answer is a resounding yes. Computers are still an expensive investment for most families; the more affluent are the most likely to own computers. Home use of computers will undoubtedly lead to a higher level of computer literacy for all members of wealthier families. The advent of lower-priced computers, just becoming a reality in the late 1990s, may help close the gap in computer access. Until then, the computer will create another barrier to economic mobility.

Eliminating unwanted and unintended social barriers imposed by the computer age is one of the major challenges policymakers will face in the years ahead. Unless they are successful, computers will

FIGURE 6.3    Relative Computer Use by Education Level

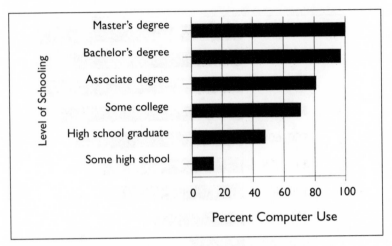

SOURCE: *Digest of Education Statistics*, 1994.

further disrupt the socioeconomic-ethnic composition of society. How will computers affect people at work?

## Effect of Computers on Blue-Collar Work

The nonfarm, blue-collar worker emerged in medieval times as craft guilds undertook the task of providing for the material needs individuals could not easily supply for themselves. These craftsmen included blacksmiths, weavers, shoemakers, and carpenters. Apprenticeships, typically taking from five to ten years to complete, provided entry to a craft. Young workers learned craft secrets from masters to whom they were apprenticed. It was a tough system; young apprentices in many cases were treated little better than slaves while they learned their crafts. Once they became master craftsmen in their own right, their futures were as secure as those difficult times would allow. The guild system set requirements for self-regulation and quality control of the craft professions.

In the 1770s and 1780s, this all began to change. James Watt, drawing on the work of others, perfected the steam engine, which more than any other invention launched the industrial revolution. The steam engine allowed fledgling industrialists to cluster workers in one location, forming the era's nascent factories. Machinery was run by pulleys and belts driven by the power of the Watt engine.

FIGURE 6.4    Home Ownership of PCs by Income Level

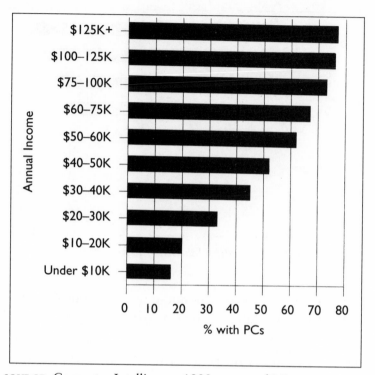

SOURCE: Computer Intelligence 1998 survey of PCs.

This machinery changed the jobs of workers dramatically: For the first time, they became subsidiary to machines. Unlike the earlier craft shops, factory workers did not need to know every aspect of a craft in order to be productive. A long apprenticeship was no longer necessary. In a few weeks, days, or even hours of training, workers were taught specific and specialized tasks to keep the machinery running. Anyone could rapidly became a productive member of the workforce. Because of the tremendous gains in productivity, output skyrocketed and industrialist-entrepreneurs made serious fortunes. Growing capital fueled further expansion of the industrial revolution.

Industrialization of the world economy increased the number of available jobs and spurred huge growth in the blue-collar workforce. This expansion was both caused by and the product of the growing specialization of blue-collar workers. New disciplines were introduced into the workplace by the creation of new and ever larger factories.

These early industrial enterprises did not really function the way modern industrial organizations do. They retained in their operations vestiges of the old craft systems. For example, until late in the nineteenth century, it was common practice, even in heavy industries like coal mining and steelmaking, for the owner-entrepreneur to engage the services of a master-foreman who would then recruit his own workers (often children paid pittance wages) to carry out tasks contracted to the foreman by the owner. This foreman retained some measure of control and status within his area of responsibility similar to that of a master craftsman.

But with the principles of "scientific management" espoused most aggressively by Frederick Taylor, this all began to change in the nineteenth century. As noted, years earlier the redoubtable Adam Smith had analyzed the potential for improved productivity in the manufacture of pins through work specialization. But Smith's observations had been those of an economist and thinker, not the practitioner and zealot Taylor was in his search for ways to simplify work.

The son of a lawyer, Taylor was sent by his wealthy Philadelphia family to Exeter, where he was supposed to prepare himself to follow in his father's footsteps to Harvard. Instead, he dropped out and found employment as a craft apprentice in a small firm. After completing his apprenticeship, he took a job as a common laborer at the Midvale Steel Works. There his career as the leading exponent of scientific management took form.

As detailed in Harry Braverman's classic work, *Labor and Monopoly Capital,* Taylor, soon after arriving at Midvale, began a series of experiments. These eventually totaled between 30,000 and 50,000 over the next twenty-six years. From his experiments, he constructed the optimum combination of steps to be taken in a given machining process. Years later he codified these rules in a book he called *Principles of Scientific Management.* As reported in Braverman, the two main principles were:

1. "The managers assume . . . the burden of gathering together all of the traditional knowledge which in the past has been possessed by the workmen and then classifying, tabulating, and reducing this knowledge to rules, laws, and formulae."
2. "All possible brain work should be removed from the shop and centered in the planning or lay-out department."

Around the dawn of the twentieth century, entrepreneurs had few reservations about adopting Taylor's principles. The die was thus cast for the future evolution of blue-collar labor. When Henry Ford invented the moving assembly line for manufacturing automobiles, he pushed these principles to their logical extreme. Blue-collar workers became little better than cogs or tools performing simple functions in the manufacturing process.

A similar scenario played out for blue-collar workers in the computer era. When computer technology arrived in modern factories in the late 1950s and early 1960s, they came in under the guise of numerically controlled machines. These were programmed to perform a sequence of tasks previously determined by the machine operator. Before their advent, machinists worked from shop drawings, making a series of decisions about how a particular process was to be carried out. To learn this process, machinists trained for months (far shorter than the training required to become a master craftsman but still substantial). With the introduction of numerically controlled tools, decisions about production and machining processes were made in the engineering department. The role of the machine operator was reduced to starting and stopping the machine or moving material into place. Training for this new type of blue-collar work was reduced considerably.

The impact of computers on blue-collar work has thus been to continue the deskilling of jobs that Taylor and his disciples began. The more recent, widespread adoption of computer-aided design (CAD) and computer-aided manufacturing (CAM) systems is extending deskilling to higher levels of the workforce, into the ranks of engineers who had earlier taken over such a large part of blue-collar workers' jobs. Engineers in environments that rely heavily on CAD and CAM are little better than terminal operators. Many of the tough engineering decisions are taken over by the systems themselves. More and more people are thus becoming blue-collar workers. But what about white-collar work?

## Effect of Computers on White-Collar Work

White-collar work is an invention of the twentieth century. As documented in Braverman's book, clerks existed in the nineteenth century, but they were few and most were male. They functioned mainly as assistant managers for entrepreneurs who employed them. For example, the U.S. census of 1870 listed only 82,000 persons claiming the occupation of clerk (0.6% of the workforce). Similarly, the 1851 census in Great Britain counted only 70,000 to 80,000 clerks (0.8% of Britain's workforce at the time). Censuses conducted in both countries in 1900 showed that the clerical proportion of the workforce had risen to 4% in Britain and 3% in the United States. Today clerical workers account for 15% of the workforce, a proportion that has grown steadily over the years. White-collar employment (including managers, professionals, etc.) accounts for over 50% of all jobs in our modern economy.

Although the total number of people involved in white-collar work has expanded enormously, its gender composition has changed just as dramatically. Focusing once again on purely clerical workers, the 1851 census in Great Britain identified only nineteen clerical workers who were female. In the 1900 U.S. census, three-quarters of clerical workers were still male. In contrast, the Bureau of Labor Statistics estimated in 1996 that 76% of clerical workers in the United States were female.

The nature of white-collar work has also changed in the intervening years. So has the compensation. Braverman notes that wages of a clerical worker in 1900 were $1,011 per year, more than twice that earned by the average manufacturing employee. By 1971 the Bureau of Labor Statistics reported the average weekly wage of a clerical worker in the United States as $115—two-thirds of that earned by a blue-collar worker and the lowest of any group in the labor market, excepting service workers. With lower pay, different gender composition, and lower status, clerical work experienced the same intense pressure for productivity gains that Taylorism had advocated for blue-collar occupations. In short, white-collar workers were prime candidates for computerization.

So computerized they were. Taking the banking industry as an example, Richard Franke, a professor of management, used American Productivity Center data to track the nearly fourteenfold rise in capital investment in banking between 1948 and 1983. Most of this capital was invested in computer equipment to automate white-collar clerical functions. Despite this massive investment in computer technology, little was gained in terms of productivity of the banking industry—at least as measured in classical economic terms (see Figure 6.5). This was of course a big disappointment to management.

FIGURE 6.5   Trend in Banking Investment and Productivity

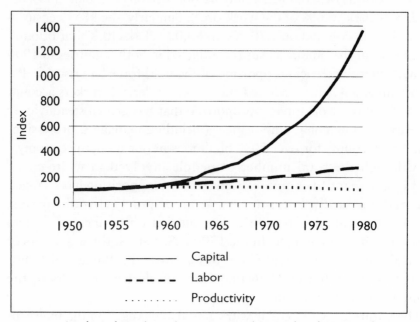

SOURCE: Analysis based on data contained in Richard H. Franke, "Technological Revolution and Productivity Decline" (*Technolgical Forecasting and Social Change* 31 [1987]).

But with the advent of microcomputer technology, this jolt to expectations was also about to change.

Dazzling advances in computer technology since the 1980s have allowed most work environments to be wired and networked. People who work are linked with each other through intranets, joined to the outside world through the Internet, and coached in just about everything they do by software-driven wizards and help screens. Management no longer has the primary say in how workers spend their time. This task has been conceded to Microsoft's software engineers and a legion of others in the information technology industry. But designing work is far too important to delegate to techies at a time when technology is increasingly beyond the capacity of many managers to understand.

As a result of these advances, the use of computers is pervasive in today's banking industry, as in most other white-collar industries. Computer technology is most visible to customers in the guise of au-

FIGURE 6.6   Trend in ATM Use and Employment of Tellers

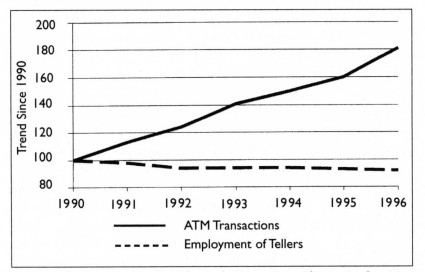

SOURCE: Sheila McConnell, "The Role Computers Play in Reshaping the Workforce" (*Monthly Labor Review*, August 1996).

tomated teller machines (ATMs). These have proliferated since the early to mid-1980s, leading to real productivity gains and a significant reduction of teller employment, as shown on Figure 6.6. Employment in banking fell by almost 70,000 during the 1990s, almost all the decline felt by clerical workers, especially tellers.

But changes in the level of employment in white-collar professions is only part of the story. Adoption of computer technology has caused significant alterations in the nature of work, the environment in which this work is performed, and the relationships among workers. Instead of liberating humanity from mind-destroying boredom, computers are in danger of enslaving workers in a new kind of high-tech prison. Failure to grasp this nettle will make all other efforts to improve working life pointless.

## Changes in the Nature of White-Collar Work

In 1984 Harvard Business School professor Shoshana Zuboff published a remarkable new book, *In the Age of the Smart Machine: The Future of Work and Power*. She attempted to chronicle in meticulous detail how automation has changed both blue- and white-collar jobs.

She based her analysis on three detailed case studies: a pulp mill, the back office of an insurance company, and a bank. Although her work has drawn some controversy, it is a definitive worm's eye view of what the advent of automation has brought with it.

Early in the book, Zuboff describes the nature of white-collar work:

> The knowledge traditionally associated with clerical work is not limited to the substantive knowledge of the methods by which a task should be executed. Such substantive understanding has been embedded in a much wider, richer, more detailed, and largely unspecified interpersonal reality. It is through "informal" contact with peers and supervisors that appropriate courses of action generally are determined. Office work is chatty, but that chattiness is more than a social perquisite of the job. It is the ether that transmits collaborative impulses, as people help each other form judgments and make choices about the work at hand.

What happens to this informal system when technology is introduced?

Computer systems are designed and installed in a way that isolates workers from their peers. It ties them instead to computer screens. Computers redefine the nature of work performed by white-collar workers. Because computers are usually quite inflexible, the context surrounding work is changed as well. Workers are expected to stay in front of their machines, tied to their workstations. This eliminates social interaction, once so much part of the job. Returning to Zuboff's observations:

> Oral culture and the associated action-centered skills were eroded as the organization's work—objects, events, and processes—was translated into explicit data and displayed in the medium of an electronic text. This is not the first time that technology has displaced oral culture and the know-how associated with action-centered skill. The mechanization of work drained the craft worker of his or her skills and altered the traditions of group life in which craft knowledge had once thrived. Work was made more explicit but not in a way that enriched the worker. In the office, mechanization provided the occasion for the creation of a new stratum of routine clerical tasks. Office work, at least

at its lowest level, finally could be subjected to the explicating rigors of scientific management. Again, the clerk's work became available for rational control and analysis but not in a way that enriched the clerk.

The white-collar world of the late twentieth century has come full circle. We are now in danger of re-creating the Tayloristic world of the late 1900s. Workers have finally been transformed into cogs in computer-driven machines. They are reengineered and reorganized at the whim of their bosses' newest priority. In the short term, the dilemma of low payback investments in white-collar functions is being solved.

Although Zuboff's is a major voice in cautioning people about the potential downside of modern computer technology, she is not alone. In a book titled *Whose Brave New World?*, Heather Menzies, a respected Canadian writer, raises similar concerns. She cites a number of Canadian studies that look at the effects of computerization:

As systems software automatically issued the claim notices, maintained the claim portfolios, and dispatched claim settlement statements, the proportion of clerical workers fell from 43 percent to 26 percent of the total in the four companies studied. A 1987 update revealed a continuing shrinkage in clerical ranks as well as a "hollowing out" of middle management as integration made self-management by professionals and semi-professionals part of the new "entrepreneurial" or postbureaucratic corporate culture.

Workers complained about the inappropriateness of [computer-based] monitoring as a measure of performance. "The place runs on statistics," one interviewee said. "The keyboard becomes the actual site of work measurement." It creates an airtight job ghetto.

One claims clerk was reported to have said, "Everything is programmed. You have to do what the machine wants." Another worker in the same study said, "I used to go really fast because I thought they'd notice me and maybe I'd get promoted. Then one day it hit me—why should they move me? I'm a top performer. It's sort of a Catch 22."

In June 1985, management set a minimum performance level of 11,400 key strokes per hour, warning that anyone falling short would receive counseling and training, and anyone still falling short after three months would be demoted and possibly "released" from employment. Not so surprisingly, the women who received the memo said they were, "insulted, humiliated and degraded."

Critics of Zuboff's work and those like Menzies who follow it do not take great exception to Zuboff's basic argument. Instead, they argue that the changes may not be all that bad. In a 1990 article, Rob Kling, Suzanne Iacono, and Joey George presented early results from a three-year longitudinal inquiry into desktop computing. They measured a variety of factors, including patterns of computer use, access to equipment, and quality of worklife. Their research encompassed both clerical and professional users.

They found that both professionals and clerks used their computers about the same amount each week—17.1 hours. Clerks had to share access with on average one other person; professionals, in contrast, tended to have their own computers. Surprisingly, clericals and professionals reported increases in both job enrichment *and* pressure for job performance. These findings were sharply at odds with what they called the "degraded work" theme advanced by Braverman and Zuboff. Kling, Iacono, and George argued that computerization is shaped by the character of the host social system rather than acting as an autonomous force. This may be a compelling argument, but since the pattern of computer use is already well established and jobs have been restructured and social mores changed as a result, it may well be a case of locking the barn door after the horses have fled.

Others point out that modern computer networks have added capabilities that never before existed in the workplace. These in turn enhance the quality of worklife for everyone. The favorite candidate for praise is electronic mail, the sine qua non of communication in the late twentieth century. Just how has e-mail enhanced the workplace?

Ronald E. Rice and Douglas E. Shook suggest in the March 1990 *Journal of Management Studies* that e-mail had already had a significant impact. They were surprised that the impact was greater at an organization's executive level than its clerical level (see Figure 6.7).

There is no question that widespread availability of e-mail has changed fundamentally the nature of work and communications in highly computerized organizations. However, much of this "job enhancement" appears more concentrated in senior ranks than among an organization's lower-ranked employees. Enhancements such as e-mail are unlikely to be effective as a substitute for face-to-face communication junior members are deprived of while tied to their computer screens.

FIGURE 6.7    Use of E-Mail

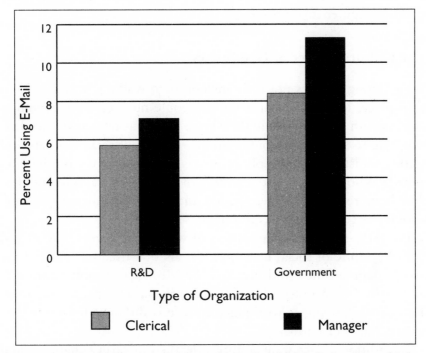

Type of Organization

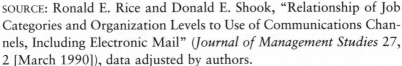

SOURCE: Ronald E. Rice and Donald E. Shook, "Relationship of Job Categories and Organization Levels to Use of Communications Channels, Including Electronic Mail" (*Journal of Management Studies* 27, 2 [March 1990]), data adjusted by authors.

There is a more widely perceived and highly negative aspect of computerization: the ability of management closely to monitor employees. Even Kling, himself a defender of modern computers, admits that close monitoring of keystrokes performed by data entry clerks has tended to increase error rates rather than productivity. Fear of surveillance is felt, especially by lower-level employees.

We suspect it may be decades before an accurate balance sheet can be drawn up on the efficacy of computer technology. But something much more immediate strikes us. Modern computers change behavior in the workplace and drastically alter traditional patterns of communications. Since behavior and communications are central to the maintenance of corporate cultures, computers have changed cultural patterns far more than the raft of managerial actions profiled in the previous chapters. Just how have cultures changed in the wake of the computer revolution?

## The Cultural Effect of Computers

Who among us does not have memories of walking into a modern workplace, looking out at a sea of people huddled over computer screens with glazed looks in their eyes? Who has not experienced attempting to strike up a conversation with one of these workers and getting a distracted nonreply or a suggestion that we send them an e-mail? Who has not stood next to workers for several minutes after they have returned to their screen and continued their rapid keystrokes, virtually oblivious to our presence?

The large-scale computerization of white-collar work has altered the very fabric of social behavior. Rituals that used to be social are now machine-timed and dictated. Face-to-face communication is more often than not replaced by impersonal electronic exchange. This new white-collar workplace culture is different from any that history has ever known.

In traditional corporate cultures, detailed in earlier chapters (and in our earlier book), cultures were human creations designed to bring meaning to time spent at work. Cultures consisted of thousands of rituals of workday activity, reinforced by people's telling stories about what so-and-so had done and what it meant in the grand scheme of things. Routine was punctuated periodically by social gatherings—celebrations of cultural values. These reassured people that adhering to cultural practices would serve them in good stead over the long haul.

All this has now changed or is highly threatened. Actions by managers since the early 1980s, as we have noted, have undercut the prevailing belief systems of corporate life. The operative assumption for decades had been, "Work hard and stick within the norms of this organization and you will have a job for life or for as long as you want one." The new corporate dictate is clearly, "Look out for yourself and don't trust the organization to provide you with anything but a temporary job, as long as it serves its purpose to do so." That's the legacy fifteen years of inspired management has given the world of tomorrow.

Around all this, the very fabric of organizational life was changing, especially for white-collar workers—more than half of today's workforce. Many of these changes were stimulated by new technology, particularly the computer. Previously, life at work was a social experience: The old hands in the organization took newcomers under their wings. Disputes were mediated by unanointed but well-known priests and priestesses, who interpreted the history, told parables, and offered guidelines about how to behave. Much of an organization's cultural life was conducted in informal gatherings— around the coffeepot or in the local pub. For most people, it worked and gave meaning to the majority of their waking hours, which they spent in the workplace. For companies that cared about the social context of the work environment, all this kept the company together and led to superior performance over the long haul.

Contrast this to the computer-mediated life in the modern corporation: An employee comes to work in the morning and probably avoids greeting colleagues for fear of interrupting them as they work at their terminals. After hanging up his or her coat and pushing around a few papers, the employee performs the first official task of the day: firing up the computer. The employee checks and returns electronic messages, some with fellow workers and many with acquaintances in other parts of the company or the outside world. For the many employees who do routine work, their daily agenda is dictated by the computer. The employee logs into the appropriate system or file and begins to move forward the transactions of the day.

Even with top-end computer technology, a user gets tired. Inevitably, after a couple of hours, it's time for a break. The employee logs off, stretches to ease the strain in back and shoulder muscles caused by working at a console, and ambles off to the kitchen or coffee station. There is no set time for this break. Employees know how much work is expected and pace themselves to meet the required standard. As likely as not, there is no one else in the kitchen. Cup of coffee in hand, the employee returns to his or her workstation, alone. The chance for a routine conversation is not a regular part of the break. Sipping coffee, the employee checks the company jokeline to find out the laugh of the day. If the content is particularly amusing, he or she passes the jokes along via e-mail to those who have a similar sense of humor. Then it is time to log back on and get back to work.

We are not trying to paint a universal picture of a draconian workplace with little charm and few social opportunities. Rather, we are trying to portray a generic image of what life in a computer-mediated environment is like. Since most modern organizations are saturated with computer technology, our portrait translates into a picture of life at work today for many people. It has its perks. The use of e-mail to arrange life's events (meetings or social engagements) and stay in contact with people outside one's immediate work group is certainly something few would choose to live without. But these pluses are offset by diminished social interaction with one's peers and a sterile interface with a computer rather than a supervisor. Of course vestiges of old ways persist. Supervisors still hold meetings with underlings. Colleagues still mingle to iron out difficult problems. But overall the social fabric of the workplace has undergone significant change.

In this new environment, there is little time for telling stories. References to the way things used to be are for the obsolete, not the in-crowd. The pecking order is different: The whiz kids who can fix software glitches or the computer system itself are the stars of the culture. They are carefully cultivated to ensure systems are up and running to meet company output targets.

Modern communications capabilities are superb. But how often are they used to reinforce core cultural messages rather than just to communicate the latest corporate downsizing? Skills associated with working in a modern computerized environment are valuable and transferable. But how often are staff trained to do anything more than simply learn the minimal set of skills? How often are staff encouraged to go beyond the confines of current jobs to look for new ways to add value to the collective good? Not too often.

Computer technology is a double-edged sword. Computers can be used to enhance the skills of workers and broaden their impact on a wider field of corporate endeavor. But they can also be used to trap workers in dead-end jobs. Although the jury on computer usage is still out, it seems unlikely that from a cultural view the verdict will be favorable.

## CHAPTER 7

# Globalization

## The Cultural
## Tower of Babel

It is impossible to pick up a newspaper or read a business magazine without seeing references to the globalized economy. Headlines feature the financial crisis in Asia and its likely effect on the U.S. or European economy. This phenomenon cannot help but catch the attention of readers in all walks of life. Go into any supermarket and you are offered products from around the world. Go into an American electronics store and notice that most of the products are manufactured by Asian companies. Observe automobile traffic and see a United Nations parade of automobiles go by. Global products and global markets are reshaping the world. These market and economic trends are greatly changing the culture of companies now competing internationally.

### A Brief History of Globalization

Reflect on these two quotes:

International finance has become so interdependent and so interwoven with trade and industry that . . . political and military power can in reality do nothing. . . . These little recognized facts, mainly the outcome of purely modern conditions (rapidity of communication creating a greater complexity and delicacy of the credit system), have rendered the problems of modern international politics profoundly and essentially different from the ancient.

New world of globalization—a world in which the integration of financial networks, information and trade is binding the globe together and shifting power from governments to markets. . . . A country, by integrating with the global economy, opening itself up to foreign investment and empowering its consumers, permanently restricts its capacity for trouble making and promotes gradual democratization and widening peace.

What is remarkable about these quotes in not that they harp on the same theme but they were published eighty-seven years apart. The first is from *The Great Illusion* by Norman Angell. Published in 1910, the book argued that growing world trade was a guarantor of future world peace. It sold a million copies worldwide, and its author won the Nobel Peace Prize, largely because of the book's influence. The second quote is from a 1996 series by Thomas Friedman published in the *New York Times*. Both quotes appeared in a *New Republic* article by Peter Beinart in October 1997.

Why this seeming convergence across the gulf of the twentieth century? Because despite one hundred years of tumultuous events, by the century's end international economic developments were only just surpassing the achievements of a much earlier era, as shown in Figure 7.1. As the figure makes clear, it was not until after 1970 that the modern world economy equaled levels of world trade like those prior to World War I. (The internationalists of the modern era might take heed in their predictions of a glorious global future for the world. Norman Angell shared their worldview in 1910, just years before the onset of thirty years of almost unparalleled conflict among nations.)

There were of course differences between these two high-trade eras. Most economic historians would argue that expansion of global trade in the early part of the century had two causes. One was a result of improved communications and transportation (the telegraph, railroads, and the steamship). The other was the declining British empire's attempt to expand its hegemony worldwide. Modern economists

FIGURE 7.1    Trade as a Percentage of GDP

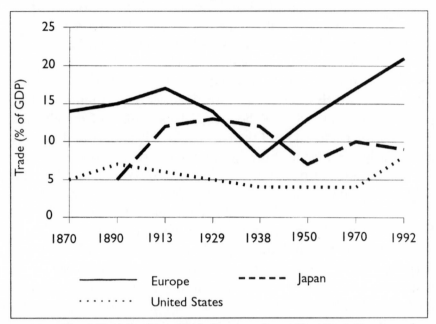

SOURCE: Dani Rodrik, *Has Globalization Gone Too Far?* (Institute for International Economics, 1997).

would also cite improved communications and transportation (tele-communications and air travel) as the keys to the modern explosion of trade. But they would see another influence: the United States' attempt to extend its declining global economic hegemony. Not much new under the sun, although the major players have changed.

But is increased world trade synonymous with globalization? What about the effects of foreign investment on the world economy? Surprise again. Net capital outflows from Britain, Germany, France, and the Netherlands in the fifty years leading up to World War I were massive, peaking at about 9% of gross domestic product (GDP). By contrast, although the sums were much larger, capital outflow from the United States in the late 1980s peaked at between 4 and 5% of GDP. Foreign investment and trade are the most direct means of globalization. What was true at the turn of the nineteenth century rings true again at the turn of the twentieth.

There is one major difference between the level of contemporary globalization and that of an earlier era: the number of people directly affected by these trends. This results from the speed associated with modern communications and transportation technology. At the dawn of the twentieth century, there were global entrepreneurs. But they were a very special breed. A trip to the New World from Europe took months; a trip around the globe could be measured in years. As a result, these highly individualistic and self-determined entrepreneurs thrived on the lucrative market opportunities and experiences available all over the world. This pattern of the globalist entrepreneur persisted until the late 1960s. Then advanced aircraft, particularly the advent of the 747 jumbo jet, revolutionized travel.

To get an idea of the early entrepreneurs who specialized in "the world," consider the head of export sales for the General Electric Company, one of the earliest global companies. His exotic claim to fame was being the salesman who sold the turbines for the Cahora Bassa Dam on Mozambique's Zambezi River. He was once asked what it was like when he was trapped in Lagos during one of the many revolutions that swept postcolonial Nigeria. He responded, "It was hell." After a short pause he went on to add, "We ran out of scotch on the second day." With the dawning of the jumbo jets, such colorful people were no longer the only ones capable of tapping world markets. Anyone who can buy an airline ticket or pick up the telephone can qualify.

Trends in international telephone calls and overseas trips (shown in Figures 7.2, and 7.3) graphically depict the rapid diffusion of international business in the post–World War II era. As Figure 7.2 indicates, overseas long-distance calls skyrocketed after 1975, reaching the staggering total of 2.8 trillion calls by 1995. To put this in context, there were fewer than 1 million such calls in 1950. Overseas travel (Figure 7.3) experienced similar but not quite as explosive growth. The trend rises significantly after the dawning of the jet age in the early 1960s. Before this, roughly 1 million Americans ventured overseas in any given year. By 1990, 16 million Americans took trips abroad. At the same time, a comparable number of overseas travelers were coming into the United States. Given the increased volume, travel and telecommunications costs plummeted. For example, between 1960 and 1988, the real cost of international travel fell by 60%. This helped spawn a 3,000% increase in overseas travel.

What are the consequences of such a massive rise in the flow of calls and travel overseas in such a short period? People all over the

FIGURE 7.2    Trend in Overseas Phone Calls

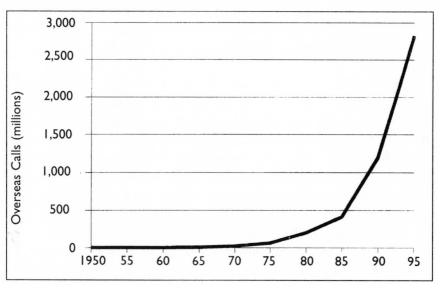

SOURCE: *Statistical Abstract of the United States*, various years.

FIGURE 7.3    Trend in U.S. Overseas Travel

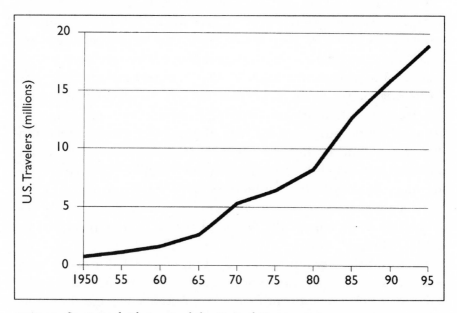

SOURCE: *Statistical Abstract of the United States*, various years.

world are getting to know each other better. They are doing more and more business across national boundaries. This globalization of the late twentieth century contrasts to the colonially based globalization of the century's beginning.

## The Effect of Globalization on Labor Markets

In its earliest days, globalization followed a fairly predictable pattern. A manufacturer in one country, most often one of the world's more-developed economies, found itself with excess manufacturing capacity. As a result, the company would send salespeople into the field to drum up business. Salespeople who worked in foreign countries would send home orders that became exports—important to the trade balance of the manufacturer's home country. As the overseas demand grew, the manufacturer often found it necessary to invest in overseas plants located in key markets. These plants were an essential element of the strategy to protect the manufacturer's overseas market share. Although opening these foreign plants affected production volumes in the home market, the effect was marginal. Within this classical model of globalization, foreign investment naturally followed as the market grew more global in character.

Countries highly dependent on foreign trade to sustain their domestic economies are therefore subject to the risk of shipping domestic jobs overseas. As a result, they tend to compensate home markets by providing a higher social safety net for their own citizens than countries where trade is less significant. In high-trade countries like Luxembourg, Belgium, Ireland, Norway, Sweden, Great Britain, France, and Spain, government expenditures as a percentage of gross domestic product (GDP) are almost twice those in relatively low-trade countries like the United States and Canada. There are limits to how much such social safety nets can be expected to protect domestic employment from the suddenly globalizing world. But the very fact that they exist shows that policymakers around the world are conscious of the potential threat to jobs from foreign trade and investment.

Foreign investment to protect position in growing overseas markets was only one part of the picture in the late Victorian era. Other kinds of foreign investment focused on resource exploitation benefiting the world's more-developed economies. The very word "colonialism" conjures up pictures of vast tea and rubber plantations. The word also conjures up images of mostly white, foreign overseers living in the lap of colonial luxury while their Third World laborers sweat away their lives in the fields. Although much has changed, many of these images are still valid today.

The new commodity exported from Third World countries is not so much the products of tropical climates but cheap labor. For example, in 1960 100% of Motorola's workers were in the United States. Today only 44% work here; the rest are spread around the Third World. Motorola is one of the largest (and most highly respected) employers in Malaysia. General Electric is the largest employer in Singapore.

Countless other U.S. and European firms have been following suit, exporting significant amounts of manufacturing capacity to Third World countries, where wages are low and the supply of workers willing to work for less is almost limitless. Close to the U.S. border, the low-cost maquiladoras in northern Mexico are a good case in point. In 1990 the manufacturing arm of AT&T closed its Radford, Virginia, factory for making transformers and other devices, eliminating 2,100 jobs. Jobs were moved to factories in Mexico, where workers received approximately $2.35 an hour in wages and benefits in contrast to the $13 the company had to pay in Virginia. Even adjusting for possible differences in the productivity rates of workers in the two countries (and this is changing fast as foreign workers develop better skills and education levels), AT&T undoubtedly came out ahead.

Lower-tech industries like textiles and footwear offer more extreme examples of the benefits gained by employing workers in overseas plants. Nike, world leader in athletic footwear, contracts all its manufacturing operations to Third World countries. In a 1991 survey of Nike plants, *Indonesia Today* estimated that the average *daily* wage rate for an experienced female Nike employee in Indonesia was $0.82. This wage compensates for an eleven-hour workday, six days a week. Toy manufacturers are shifting production from Thailand to China, taking advantage of emerging wage differentials: For $20 a month in China, employees work twelve-hour shifts, seven days a week. Few workers in developed economies would compete to retain such jobs. As a consequence, the movement to source labor from Third World countries grows exponentially.

Economists for a long time have argued the relative merits and de-
merits of expanded trade and foreign investment. Classical economists claim that exporting jobs overseas to capture lower labor costs
is good for everyone involved. It represents the next step in specialization among nations so they can take advantage of their own competitive advantages. According to these arguments, everyone comes
out ahead because countries are concentrating on doing what they do
best. The large-scale exploitation of low-cost overseas labor in recent
years, however, has not been quite so benign. As the economist Dani
Rodrik argues in his recent book *Has Globalization Gone Too Far?*
the world's labor markets are connected. More trade and the shifting
of labor costs to overseas markets increases the elasticity of labor
costs on a worldwide basis. Thus, it is not terribly surprising that the
real wages of high school dropouts in the United States declined by
about 20% since 1979—the period when the most aggressive investments were being made in overseas, low-cost-labor plants.

Moreover, the line between trade in the classical sense and foreign
investment has become heavily blurred as a result of the massive
overseas investments of companies from member countries of the
Organization for Economic Cooperation and Development
(OECD). One-third of the U.S. trade gap with Taiwan in the early
1990s was the result of reimporting products made by U.S. companies operating sourcing plants in Taiwan. At around the same time,
international sales of all U.S. multinationals exceeded $1.2 trillion—
29% of their total sales worldwide. By 1997, estimates pinpointed
25% of recorded foreign trade as the movement of goods and ma-
terials inside multinational companies. Overall, companies, especially U.S. companies that lead with investment overseas, have not
lost their competitiveness; they have just shifted their base of operations (overseas)—to paraphrase a comment by Robert Reich in a
1990 article in the *Harvard Business Review*.

While American companies in particular have been pushing their
manufacturing overseas to benefit from lower labor costs, Japanese
and European companies have been investing heavily to establish
their positions in the lucrative U.S. market. Because of the relatively
low value of the dollar compared to other currencies, in recent years
foreign investment in the United States has almost matched investment outflow from the United States to other parts of the world
(shown in Figure 7.4). Although fully 90% of the investment into

FIGURE 7.4    Trend in Investment Flows

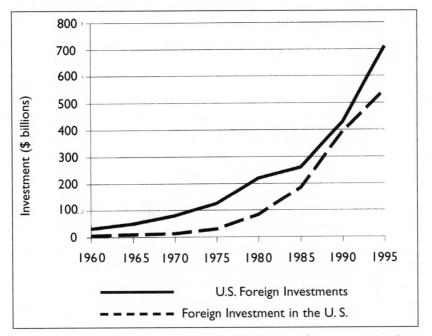

SOURCE: U.S. Department of Commerce, Bureau of Economic Analysis.

the United States was coming from the developed economies of Europe, Canada, and Japan, almost 40% of U.S. investment overseas was going into the developing world. Other OECD countries were buying up corporate America at a time when corporate America was busy shipping its manufacturing jobs overseas.

There are other differences in the foreign investment patterns of countries around the world. Overseas plants of U.S. foreign investors, particularly those in Third World countries, export a substantial share of goods and services back to the United States. By contrast, Europeans and Japanese make investments to gain preferred access to the U.S. market. U.S. investors consistently import much more to the United States than they export from their U.S. base of operations. Because of this, U.S. affiliates of foreign companies contributed almost $120 billion to the chronic U.S. trade deficit in 1995 alone. Good corporate citizens they may well be in some respects, but this does not prevent them from exploiting their U.S. market position for gain in their home countries' economies.

Nevertheless, the impact of foreign investors on the U.S. economy has been substantial. Foreign-owned firms by 1991 controlled half of the U.S. consumer electronics industry, one-third of the chemical industry, 20% of the automobile industry, 70% of the tire industry, and almost 50% of the film and recording industry. Since 1991 these percentages have undoubtedly risen. Foreign takeover interest in U.S. companies has continued to grow.

All these shifts in capital and ownership are shaking up world markets. With tongue slightly in cheek, Norman Glickman and Douglas Woodward in *The New Competitors: How Foreign Investors Are Changing the U.S. Economy* noted that:

> An American can buy Chicken-of-the-Sea tuna (owned by an Indonesian company) from A&P (Britain) or dresses from Bonwit Teller (Canada) with a credit card from Marine Midland Bank (Hong Kong). She may drive a Plymouth Laser (Japan), fill up at a Texaco station (Saudi Arabia), read a Doubleday book (West Germany), swig a Lone Star beer (Australia), and listen to Willie Nelson on CBS Records (Japan).

The effect of such large-scale foreign investment in U.S. companies has generally been quite positive. Reich's article in the *Harvard Business Review* noted that overseas owners of U.S. plants were paying wages almost 20% higher than were U.S. domestic manufacturers. This conclusion is disputed by authors like Glickman and Woodward, who after careful analysis of the numbers suggest that these foreign investors are no better or worse than U.S. companies in terms of how they pay their workers. (We are inclined to agree with Glickman and Woodward.) Others have argued that most of the full-time job growth in the United States in the early 1990s was the result of jobs created by foreign investors. Once again Glickman and Woodward believe this is a massive overstatement: Although foreign investors have added jobs to the U.S. economy, they have also eliminated others as they sought to rationalize their new U.S. operations. Their net effect is, therefore, only mildly positive.

Overall the net effect of foreign investment on jobs, both inward and outward, is a picture of winners and losers in the job game. This comes as a result of the rush to globalization. Low-skilled workers in the United States and Europe have seen their jobs disappear overseas to low-labor-cost countries as wage rates decline and unemployment grows. Developing countries have until very recently experienced above-average growth in their economies. This yields standard-of-living improvements despite the low wages paid by their overseas employers. Some workers in developed economies, particularly skilled workers in the United States, have benefited from jobs created by foreign investors. Truly a mixed bag of results—depending on just where you sit in the global economy.

What is not in doubt, however, is that virtually everyone has been affected by the rapid globalization of the world economy. It is estimated that 73 million people in today's global workforce work for foreign owners. Twenty-five million of these work for U.S. companies overseas. Only about 12 million of the 73 million, however, are in the developing world. Upward of 5 million U.S. employees work for a company owned and managed by foreigners. Each day at work, they are confronted with the need to adapt to the foreign culture of their overseas owners. Other Americans are part of the phalanx of workers spreading the gospel of American values all over the world. And millions of workers in foreign countries mirror the experience of their American counterparts as they go to work for foreign-owned companies. The number of workers involved directly in cross-border work is of course much more difficult to estimate, though it is clearly growing year in and year out.

## Cultural Differences at Work

In a 1991 article in the *Harvard Business Review,* highly respected academic Rosabeth Moss Kanter reported the results of a massive survey of managers in countries around the world. The conclusion: Managers from different countries in the world are different. For example,

- Managers from Germany, Austria, France, Belgium, the Netherlands, and the Scandinavian countries are more cosmopolitan (meaning, among other things, they tend to speak more than one language).
- Managers from Japan have the greatest work ethic (and the greatest concern about the work ethic of their compatriots at work).

- Managers from Australia, Canada, Great Britain, New Zealand, the United States, and Singapore—the Anglo-Saxon axis—tend to think alike. Among the things they agree on, for example, is that family is more important than work.

Of course people from different countries are different. People have different values inculcated by growing up in different cultures. They are educated in different educational systems. Their native tongues vary, the structure of their languages strongly influencing how they think. They behave according to what their own societies dictate. People see the world through different lenses, depending on their history and traditions. In today's global world, these unique species are thrown together willy-nilly in the workplace and expected to make things work.

How must an American manager of Motorola's semiconductor plant in Malaysia feel when he looks around the lunch table? His team of managers is composed of a Scottish engineer, a white-skinned Indian from Johore whose father had worked on colonial estates, and a mix of Chinese, Malay, and Indian Malaysians. What possible common grounds can they find for dealing with each other and solving day-to-day problems? They are asked to run a high-tech business employing 5,000 people in a tropical climate while communicating with a parent company located in America's Midwest. It is a tribute to human adaptability that they succeed and even excel. Not all are so lucky.

In Forrest City, Arkansas, a Sanyo TV and microwave oven plant was the scene of a bitter strike in 1985 (as reported by Glickman and Woodward in *The New Competitors*). One of the big points of contention was attitudes toward work. One of Sanyo's Japanese managers was quoted as saying, "They come here for eight hours' work and eight hours' pay. As long as they get that, they don't care what happens to our production." As Kanter's survey demonstrated, Japanese managers' preoccupation with the work habits of their workers was predictable, as was the workers' interest in life outside work. Lacking this insight into cultural differences, the company shifted most of the production in the plant to Mexico.

Elsewhere in the United States, a division of Sumitomo, the giant Japanese trading company, ran into trouble with its workforce. The company tried to apply conventional Japanese wisdom to female workers in its U.S. subsidiary. In Japan working women are a significant part of the labor force but are almost always assigned to low-level clerical positions and rarely considered for promotion. Japanese culture assumes that (young) women who work are simply marking time until they get married, when they will have children and leave the workforce to care for their families. Sumitomo made this same assumption with its U.S. workforce and was hit with a major lawsuit charging the firm with sexual discrimination. It was finally settled favorably for the plaintiffs in 1987.

This is not at all to pick on the Japanese as paragons of overseas mismanagement. On the contrary, countless examples around the world show the merits of imported Japanese management techniques, such as quality circles and employee participation. Nevertheless, substantial language as well as cultural differences make the task of Japanese managers unusually difficult. It also creates daunting challenges for workers who report to them. Peter Gruber, for a time the head of Sony's Columbia Pictures operation in the United States is said to have remarked about one of his American colleagues (Michael Schulhof), "I give him three things. Balance—he doesn't get ruffled easily. Intelligence—he has a high quotient of intelligence. And No. 3, he speaks Japanese. I don't mean he literally speaks Japanese, but after 18 years in the company, he understands the significance of what's not said."

Yet the Germans, who (as Kanter noted) tend to speak several languages as a matter of course, have had a great deal of difficulty adapting to cultures other than their own. In Germany managers operate in offices behind closed doors guarded by a phalanx of secretaries. The number of secretaries in this "palace guard" is directly related to the perceived seniority of an individual manager. For the truly senior manager, the secretarial force will invariably include a male executive assistant, the mark of real importance. Moreover, Germans are very formal, even with longtime colleagues; they address each other by formal titles even when they have worked side by side for many years. Paul Overby, an American manager working for a subsidiary of the German giant AEG, reflected that the formality is in part linguistically imposed. The German language demands precision that has spilled over into the culture.

Beyond the language, of course, there are other assumptions about how things are supposed to work. Another American manager, Herbert Goller, worked for a German company. After completing a year in which he increased the sales of his unit by 45%, he met with his German bosses and asked them how he was doing. The response he got, "We haven't had any complaints," at first shocked him. Later he reflected on the fact that he had learned that "an American boss criticizes by not praising and a German boss praises by not criticizing." Although seemingly trivial, these small differences in the assumptions about what constitutes correct workplace behavior are the elements that so often lead to distrust and resentment.

The German penchant for detail and precision has caused some problems in its overseas operations. Bertelsmann, the 150-year-old German company that is now the largest book publisher both in the world and the United States, entered the U.S. book market in 1977, when it bought Bantam Publishing. Nine years later, it expanded its U.S. operations by acquiring the venerable Doubleday from the heirs of its founders in order to gain access to the Literary Guild, at the time the largest book club in America.

As described in Richard Barnet and John Cavanagh's *Global Dreams*, Bertelsmann rose out of the ashes of World War II by launching the first major German book club. The club sold used books door to door to impoverished Germans eager to get their hands on anything to read. The book club was so successful that by 1954, less than ten years after the end of the war, it had in excess of 1 million members in Germany. By buying Doubleday and its book club subsidiary, Bertelsmann executives were convinced they could export their book club expertise to the world's largest book market.

Initially, management of the U.S. operations was left in the hands of an American, Alberto Vitale, who had been acquired by Bertelsmann as part of the Bantam deal in 1977. An experienced book manager, he had within three years made substantial improvements in the operations of Doubleday. His German bosses were not happy, however, because of his lack of focus on the opportunity they saw in the book club area. In frustration, Vitale quit and took a similar job with a competing publisher. There followed a succession of managers in the top job at Doubleday. In addition, Bernard von Minckwitz, the head of Bertelsmann's worldwide book-publishing activities, began spending a week a month on-site overseeing the U.S. operation. The president of Doubleday, Stephen Rubin, reported saying to Minckwitz that his hands were tied (with the intrusion of so many German "experts" into the day-to-day affairs of the company), only to have the German executive look at Rubin's hands to try to see what the problem was. It would never have occurred to Minckwitz that so much German expertise was not the solution. The Bertelsmann story, of course, had a happy ending. After many years of trying, the Germans finally got the formula more or less right for the American market. The company went on to expand its U.S. operations in the late 1990s with the acquisition of Random House.

The size of German, French, British, and Japanese foreign investment is small compared to the size and scope of U.S. foreign investment around the world. As a result, for the millions who do not live in the United States, it is the image and style of Americans overseas that represent the unwelcome face of foreign ownership of assets. Much has been written about this topic; two of the classics are Eugene Burdick and William Lederer's *Ugly American* (first published in 1958) and Jean Jacques Servan-Schreiber's *American Challenge* (which appeared in 1968). We will not, therefore, dwell on it here. Suffice it to say that some themes raised in these books (for example, arrogance, self-satisfaction, and implicitly, ostentatious wealth) many years ago still have validity today.

Two newer American cultural patterns continue to cause problems as Americans expand their world holdings. The first of these is informality. That this should be seen as an American fault may at first blush seem quite odd. Surely informality is a virtue when measured on the world scheme of values. It would be if the rest of the world were not more formal than is customary in the United States. Both Europeans and Japanese, for example, are very formal in addressing each other. In other parts of the world, physical contact between casual acquaintances is frowned upon, if not looked upon as downright rude. Into this existing cultural milieu, breezy, informal Americans, intent on getting their business done, move about with slaps on the back, friendly grins, and first names. For people brought up in more reserved societies, this is offensive. Granted, the American presence overseas is now so long-standing that most people have come to accept American styles for what they are. But this does not mean that they are less offended by them.

When American informality is coupled with the American emphasis on youth, the cultural effects can be even more extreme. In most of Europe (the UK being the only major exception), professionals and managers enter the workforce relatively late in life (when they are twenty-seven to thirty years old). They enter company service after years of study in pursuit of professional qualifications or advanced degrees. In most of the world, advancement beyond entry-level positions is relatively slow: People are expected to pay their dues before climbing the seniority ladder. When such people are confronted with hotshot, young (twenty-four- to twenty-seven-year-old) American MBAs, many entrusted with significant responsibilities, they are often appalled. But given the circumstances, they do not feel free to express their dismay.

There is as well a lingering sense in many parts of the world that life in the United States is easier (because of the amount of space available for housing and the proliferation of convenient retail outlets). This, coupled with informality and stress on youth, makes dealing with Americans abroad a continuing challenge. The pervasiveness of American mass-market culture through movies, TV reruns, and so on often rubs salt in these cross-cultural wounds.

Differences in cultural ways and traditions will not soon disappear. And in the workplace differences have to be accommodated. Companies that operate in this increasingly global world will have to learn to adjust to radically distinct worldviews, work styles, and behavior patterns. The world is too diverse to yield simple answers as to how people from unique cultures can learn to work together.

## Culture in the Workplace

How has globalization affected the culture of the workplace? In a number of ways, and most of them not for the better. First, there is the issue of trust. Trust is earned differently in various societies around the world. In some countries, such as the United States, trust is a function of immediate performance: "What have you done for me lately?" A foreign manager working for an American boss in a non-U.S. plant or operation is likely to be appalled by demands placed on him (or her, but more often than not him) for short-term performance. It is common to hear grumbling about the short-term orientation of American managers, which is often perceived as destroying the capability of local managers to build a long-term presence in their home markets. Most employees, however, don't confront the issue head-on. They value holding on to their jobs. They do what they are asked, no matter how wrong they feel it is. But resentment builds and creates a barrier between people who might otherwise have come to know each other on much better terms.

In other parts of the world, particularly Japan and Germany, trust is something that is earned over the long term. (It is sometimes a function of family relationships or long-term knowledge.) A short-term-oriented American manager working for a German or Japanese manager is likely to feel isolated. Instead of getting immediate kudos for a job well done, he or she experiences stone-faced silence. An American will tend to interpret this as disapproval, even though that is not what is intended. This often produces a bitter reaction. Walk around a corner in a foreign plant or office and you're likely to find American employees muttering about "those goddamned Japs (or Krauts)." Such things are seldom said face to face, but implied racial slurs are often picked up by overseers and further contribute to a sense of mutual distrust. Trust is basically about setting and meeting expectations. When trust is fractured because of cultural misunderstanding, individual and collective performance suffers.

The second major cultural barrier to cooperating across national boundaries at work is language. A commonly observed phenomenon in cross-cultural companies is the sight of two expatriates in a corridor or a conference room conversing in their native language. They do this because they are starved for the social contact this familiar interaction affords. They often fail to recognize the degree of exclusion their bonding creates for others. Left unchecked, this leads to resentment and more isolation for the expatriates.

A more serious language barrier arises when teams of people from different countries work together to solve business problems. The typical functioning of multinational teams would be comical if the consequences were not so dire. The primary problem relates to verbal language. But nonverbal signals can be even more significant. The Japanese team member smiles in a friendly but noncommittal fashion. His gesture is taken as acquiescence by the ever optimistic American. It is seen as disagreement by the ever pessimistic German. The Italian engineer agrees to a deadline as part of a multicountry conference call without ever meaning to adhere to it. His intent in agreeing is just to be agreeable. Confusion abounds, deadlines slip, fingers point, and people walk away frustrated and disrespectful of their foreign colleagues. Such scenarios occur too often. Over time, if people try hard, they will learn to work together and overcome communication problems. But stereotypes formed in the meantime have a lasting and negative effect on the ongoing culture of the enterprise.

The third major obstacle to effective cross-cultural communication is ritualistic behavior. One example is the European habit of rapping knuckles on a conference table to signal approval of a presentation. The first time this happens to American managers they are totally confused and wonder what went wrong. Obviously, it doesn't take long to learn what such rituals mean in the specific context. The immediate crisis passes. But the sense of being an outsider remains and acts as a barrier to building stronger cultural bonds.

More serious are the meaning of rituals associated with meetings. Meetings in different parts of the world are conducted differently, often with different purposes. An operations review in North America is usually meant to root out, discuss, and resolve problems. A similar meeting in continental Europe is more likely just a show-and-tell. Formal discussions and decisions are taken to a more private place. Because both the context and the required content are so different, miscommunication abounds and frustration and resentments grow. Of course most of these cross-cultural misunderstandings abate over time, though not before permanent damage is done. Too often the fabric of the corporate culture is left in shreds in the wake.

## Learning to Live in a Global World

Over 40% of the market for Coke, Gillette, Lucent Technologies (the old manufacturing arm of AT&T), Boeing, and the power systems operations of companies like GE and ABB are located in Asia. In response, these companies have been moving for years to shift the balance of their resources to the parts of the world where markets exist for their products. For example, ABB shrunk its European head count by 40,000 people in the 1990s while adding 45,000 employees in Asia. Other companies like Gillette and Coke have been at the transformation to a global enterprise for so long that sudden shifts in manpower are no longer even an issue. Those who would learn to live comfortably in a global world can learn a lot from these early pioneers. (They can also learn a bit about the downside associated with truly global operations: Gillette recently announced a significant reduction in its workforce in response to the economic problems undermining its position in Asian markets.)

Take the case of Gillette as an example. With sales of almost $10 billion a year, net income approaching $1.5 billion a year, and a market capitalization in excess of $55 billion, Gillette is one of the premier consumer products companies in the world. Since its founding over a fish market in downtown Boston in 1901, it has also become a global power. Three-quarters of its 44,000 employees work outside of its home base, the United States. Its products are sold in over 200 countries and territories around the world. It operates sixty-three manufacturing facilities in twenty-six countries across the globe. Going global is not something new to Gillette. It opened its first overseas sales office in London in 1905; in 1906 it opened a blade-manufacturing plant in Canada, a European distribution center in Germany whose sales extended as far away as Russia, and a sales operation in Mexico. Given such a start for a fledgling company, it learned early how to operate in a global environment, but it has taken the bulk of its years in existence for Gillette to codify its learning into a truly distinctive set of management practices.

As Gordon McKibben reports in the book *Cutting Edge,* Gillette has learned that it takes about twenty-five years to build an expatriate workforce capable of routinely filling the jobs that open up around the world. It launched its first formal expatriate program in 1967; by the mid-1990s fully 400 managers were involved in the program. Even before this program was launched, however, Gillette had come to appreciate the overseas work experiences of its key managers. The current president of the company, Michael Hawley, spent time in Hong Kong, Canada, the United Kingdom, Colombia, and Australia on his way to the top of the company. Moreover, the organization is full of executives with a wide range of global work experiences. For example, in the mid-1990s a British citizen replaced a Mexican as the head of the company's Turkish operation, a Swedish-born British citizen was running the operations in Russia with a staff made up of British, Argentinean, and American managers (as well as indigenous Russians). All operations in Africa, the Middle East, and Eastern Europe reported to a Spaniard who lived in London.

The evolution of Gillette's global recruitment and promotion policies did not take place overnight. McKibben highlights the career and influence of Tony Levy, one of the many managers who made Gillette so global in its thinking. Born a Jew in Egypt, Levy emigrated at an early age with his family to Brazil, where almost by chance he ended up working for Gillette. Having risen to sales manager in Gillette's Brazilian operations, Levy was subsequently promoted to higher positions in England, Canada, and the home office in Boston. In 1973 he was sent back to Brazil as head of Gillette do Brazil. Within seven years, Levy had converted the Brazilian offices into an operation managed almost exclusively by local nationals. When he took over as head of international operations in 1987, he converted his Latin American operation from an importer of talent to an exporter of management around the Gillette system. Brazilian-trained managers played significant roles in the evolution of company operations in India, Russia, Turkey, China, or wherever else the company needed them. Gillette does not require its employees to take transfers outside of their home countries: All transfers are voluntary. However, it has become part of the culture of the company to participate directly in the adventure of building its presence around the world.

Building an international culture into the very fabric of the company is the challenge facing all firms eager to succeed in the modern global economy. As C. K. Prahalad and Kenneth Lieberthal wrote,

> How many of today's multinationals are prepared to accommodate 30% to 40% of their top team of 200 coming from China, India, and Brazil? How will that cultural mix influence decision making, risk taking, and team building? Diversity will put an enormous burden on top-level managers to articulate clearly the values and behaviors expected of senior managers, and it will demand large investments in training and socialization. The need for a single company culture will also become more critical as people from different cultures begin to work together. Providing the right glue to hold companies together will be a big challenge.

This is a challenge to the basic mind-set of companies and to the foundations of their cultures. Companies like Gillette, with years of experience in the world's markets, have learned how to make international culture a part of the normal life of the company. For most others, the process is just beginning.

CHAPTER 8

# Corporate
# Cultures After
# the Deluge

Since the 1980s, the business community has experienced unusual turmoil. Core assumptions have been rewritten. Long-standing, implicit contracts between workers and employers have been abrogated. Significant gaps have opened between senior management and employees. Even friendly compacts among employee groups show signs of strain. Mergers have revamped the corporate landscape: Companies with different identities and styles have been thrown together. Technology has revolutionized the workplace. Computer and communications innovations have changed behavior patterns and altered traditional working relationships. Engaging in deals abroad has called into question our parochial ways of doing business. All of these changes have in one way or another undercut traditional views of how cultural patterns form and thrive and left in their place denial, fear, cynicism, self-interest, distrust, anomie, and growing underground subcultures.

Still, cultures endure in every workplace. They persevere because as social animals we yearn for some sort of existential anchor. We need cultures to give meaning to our lives at work. We need to define and learn acceptable rules of workplace behavior. We need them to justify, or at least rationalize, hours spent on the job. Although the cultural cores of many companies have been eroded by radical shifts in the environment or the actions of management, those that survive continue to perpetuate corporate and individual well-being. At their best, business cultures offer a positive force for the good. They need to be nurtured and shaped. Things will never, of course, be as they were in less turbulent times. But how can cultural cohesion once again be salvaged and strengthened to improve the quality of life for employees? How can we revitalize values that demand high standards for products, service, and customer satisfaction? How can we shape robust workplaces that yield superior long-term performance?

## Corporate Cultures on the Edge

Preceding chapters have highlighted several revolutionary changes in management thinking and the business environment. Each of these trends has contributed to significant rifts in the cultures of many corporations. In the place of positive, cohesive enterprises that encouraged employee loyalty and commitment, we now see negative influences that threaten the ability of businesses to thrive and compete.

### A Culture of Denial

The balanced image of a corporation as servant of many constituencies has shifted to a single focus on shareholders. The shift has undermined an implicit, long-standing belief in the mutuality of interest between employer and employee. This widely shared belief carried the promise that if employees worked to the best of their abilities, a company would provide positive working conditions, ample pay, and a stable career.

Why is this belief fundamental to preserving a positive work culture? It seems simple enough: People need to believe. Belief provides the faith and symbolic unity that allows people to get on with their work. Beliefs, many of which are unspoken, provide individuals an opportunity to anchor themselves in a meaningful workplace. Undermining a belief system triggers a crisis of confidence that makes it difficult if not impossible to sustain people's loyalty, commitment, and best efforts.

What happens when a basic belief is suddenly compromised? First comes disbelief: "They can't really mean that." Then people become angry: "How could they do this to me?" Employee anger roared in the 1990s, triggering union militancy, strikes, and sabotage. Once the anger has subsided, people get depressed. Survey after survey has recorded the high levels of depression among employees across institutions. During major downsizing, suicide levels increase. Unprecedented levels of family violence and breakup occur. Although not all of this can be blamed on the erosion of beliefs underlining the employer-employee relationship, it has had a decided impact. Following depression comes grudging acceptance of the new conditions. In many companies, the transition to a new set of beliefs goes relatively smoothly and it's business as usual. In other places, the new order is a long way off and confusion rules the day. Only when a new reality becomes widely shared can businesses reclaim the cultural unity they once enjoyed. The question is, What form will the acceptance of a new employment compact take? Will a new and improved workplace emerge? Or will a resentful and cynical acceptance of the status quo prevail because there is no hope for anything better? The future of workplace cohesion and performance may turn on this pivotal question.

## A Culture of Fear

Continuing waves of downsizing have led to widespread fear that jobs are constantly up for grabs. There is nothing so debilitating as the fear of losing one's livelihood. The loss of a job is akin to losing a way of life and its attendant meaning. Traditionally, individuals have drawn a boundary between life at work and at home. A thread that connects the two is the guarantee of a paycheck. People work for a living. When this guarantee is equivocal, people worry. When the guarantee is canceled, personal chaos results. The corporate rug has been pulled out from under people, sometimes throwing them onto the streets with no means of support.

As we have discussed, it is not just those cut loose who suffer the consequences of job loss. Employees who survive the ax live in fear that they will be next. In place of the old promise of security, fear rules the workplace. It doesn't make any difference how hard you work, how long you've been around, or how loyal you've been: You're an expendable commodity. If the company needs a bump in profits, the employees' futures are on the line. Shareholders, not employees, rule the roost.

## A Culture of Cynicism

Stock-option-based compensation ensures that senior management's interests are aligned with those of shareholders, the newly anointed dominant business constituency. Coupled with the recent explosion in stock market values, this caused executive compensation to skyrocket. It fueled an ever widening fissure between the pay of those at the top and that of rank-and-file employees, fracturing the potential for a shared agenda or common purpose between management and the workforce. Workers, especially those struggling with flat or diminished personal earnings, are not motivated to follow the leadership of greedy managers whose first priority is their own pockets.

This creates a troublesome situation. Leadership is vital to cultural stability and evolution. Tom Watson Jr., CEO of IBM during its halcyon days, voluntarily took a pay cut because he felt his earnings were too high relative to others in the company. His successor several times removed, Lou Gerstner, negotiated an even more lucrative contract extension for himself before agreeing to stay on as IBM's CEO. As an IBM employee, which one of these two leaders would earn your loyalty and commitment? Which one would induce you to put in long hours or contribute special effort? The answer, we believe, is obvious.

## A Culture of Self-Interest

Another aftermath of downsizing is the emergence of self-interested workers. If a company is not going to champion employee interests, intelligent people are going to look after their own. In self-defense, people now put their personal interests well ahead of what might be good for the company.

This emerging work ethic substitutes loyalty to oneself or one's profession for loyalty to a company. Most workers today are eager to go to job interviews. They'll do it on company time if they can. They spend discretionary time networking with personal or professional colleagues to keep career options open. This time and attention often detracts from company business. It is not seen as an overt or conscious act of disloyalty. After all, the company showed its stripes first by dropping the primacy of long-term job stability. The new reality for workers involves taking care of number one.

## A Culture of Distrust

Think about how it feels: Your company appears to abandon you. Your boss focuses on his or her personal agenda. Many of your former colleagues now work for contractors who provide outsourced services to your company. The next wave of job cuts is looming. Under such conditions, it is not surprising that people don't trust either management or one another. As a result of big changes in the business environment, distrust has replaced positive cohesion in many companies. It is no longer wise to share your deepest thoughts with colleagues. They may become rivals for your job. It is no longer a good idea to express your disagreements with management too forcefully. You might be singled out as a troublemaker and placed on the next list of planned redundancies. Contributing your ideas for how the company should move forward no longer seems politically smart. If your ideas are out of step with higher-ups, you may find yourself out of work. The end result: you keep your mouth shut, do only what you have to, and psychologically check out.

Well-run, healthy corporate cultures have historically encouraged widespread and open debate and straightforward dialogue. As a corporate member in good standing, you were encouraged to use all your faculties, including your brain, to advance the common cause. In doing so, you felt safe. Not any more. Now the premium is on keeping your mouth shut, your rear covered, and your nose clean. It took years to break down the level of trust built up in strong culture companies. It will take many more years to get back to the former level.

## Cultural Anomie

Since the late 1940s, nearly 20% of large U.S. companies have merged or been involved in some form of an affiliative transaction. Changes in management philosophy and practice resulting from these mergers have chipped away at core cultural beliefs and attitudes. Mergers toss a culture into total disarray. Winners of merger battles typically impose their practices and ways on the losers, abandoning promises made prior to the deal. The result is a loss of cultural identity for acquired companies.

What does it mean to lose your cultural identity? Imagine yourself at a fancy dress ball with people you have never met before. You're dressed in a tuxedo or a gown, clothes you haven't worn since your wedding day. You are expected to engage in sparkling conversation with strangers while juggling a champagne glass in one hand and a napkin of canapés in the other. Assuming that this is not something you do often, you will likely be very uncomfortable. You may perspire more than usual. As you engage in small talk, you may become uncharacteristically tongue-tied and unsure of yourself. You feel at sea and insecure. You want to leave but feel obligated to stay.

That's what it's like to be a member of a newly acquired company. You attend meetings that are foreign in content and process. All the cues are wrong, and you don't know when or whether to speak up. What about time and expense sheets? Are you expected to submit them exactly on time with appropriate receipts? Or is expense reporting informal, like it used to be in your old digs? You attend a casual social gathering designed to help the blended staff get to know one another better. But you don't know what behavior is now acceptable. Do people tell off-color jokes? Are the rumors about how ruthless the new owners are really true?

These are not trivial concerns. Learning to live with a new owner is like starting over, learning a whole new set of permissible behavioral norms and practices: what to say to whom and when; how to write memos or send e-mail; when to speak up and when to lie low; even what to wear. Everything you have previously taken for granted is in flux. You are exhausted from the daily grind of trying to learn what is acceptable. These are symptoms of losing your cultural identity. In the corporate world today, this jolting experience is common.

### The Rise of Underground Subcultures

If you've been acquired and confronted with new cultural patterns, you may try to adapt while still mourning the familiar ways you are leaving behind. If you didn't feel the pain, you wouldn't be human. It's human nature to cling to old symbols, rituals, and values. People do, but often not publicly. Nostalgia or deviance might send out an alarm that you are less than happy with the new situation. You take your feelings either behind the scenes or underground. When you get together with former colleagues, you talk reverently about old times and gripe fervently about the new situation. In this way, people cultivate secret subcultures that hark back to more satisfying, comfortable, and meaningful times. The net result is a hodgepodge of secret subcultures held over from the latest merger. Aggressive companies, cobbled together from a series of mergers, are often hollow at the core: Companies acquired typically lose their cultural identity; the acquiring company trying to absorb the new entities find their culture diluted or unraveled.

• • •

All this adds up to a troublesome situation: Corporate cultures as we wrote about them in the early 1980s have changed dramatically and too often not for the good. Employees are confused as to their purpose at work, distrustful of most everyone, and motivated to pursue self-interests (as do their bosses). They feel isolated, reactionary, and afraid. They are detached, disillusioned, and prone to gather in underground subcultures. This hardly looks like a recipe for future business success. But we hope there are grounds for optimism: Although corporations have led an unprecedented assault on their cultural foundations, some have survived the attack. In a few instances, some have actually thrived as the next examples illustrate.

## Enduring It All: The British Telecom Story

British Telecommunications (BT) is the major supplier of telephone and telecommunications services to people in the UK. Founded over one hundred years ago as a state-owned monopoly, BT was housed in the General Post Office Department of the British civil service. In the early 1980s, the winds of change in telecommunications were blowing as strongly in the UK as in other parts of the world. BT positioned itself for privatization. It was the first major privatization by the Tory government then in power.

BT's move toward privatization began in 1983 with the licensing of Mercury, its first UK competitor. Soon thereafter, in a complicated transaction befitting such a groundbreaking change in status, the government issued shares of BT to the public. This was done in three successive tranches: November 1984, June 1985, and April 1986. Not surprising, at the time it was floated on the stock market, BT was Britain's largest capitalization company and its largest employer. Since the initial flotation, the quality of work life has gone steadily downhill for employees.

FIGURE 8.1    Trend in BT Full-Time Employment

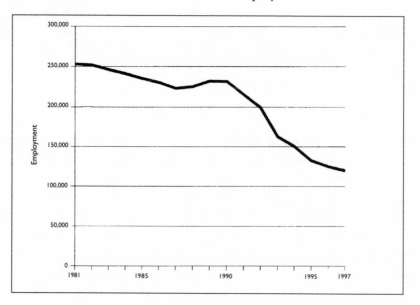

SOURCE: Communications Workers Union, "British Telecom: Staffing Problems and Processes" (August 12, 1997).

As shown in Figure 8.1, BT's employment plummeted from a 1981 high of 253,000 to a 1997 complement of just under 120,000. Although a 53% decline in employment can hardly be taken as business as usual, few inside BT—or even in the UK at large—disputed the company's need to address problems of overstaffing. In the run-up to privatization, BT functioned as a classical public services monopoly. Not only was it overstaffed, but it provided poor and unresponsive customer service. That said, BT was still considered to be an excellent employer. It offered fair (if not generous) wages, interesting jobs, employment for life (if one performed at a minimally acceptable level), and generous pensions. Many Brits admired the company. At the same time, others despaired over the transformation required to turn BT into a world-class competitor. That was management's nagging dilemma.

Iain (now Sir Iain) Vallance has been at the helm of British Telecommunications from 1986 until the present. Son of a post office worker and lifetime BT employee, Vallance was placed in charge of one of the world's greatest corporate transformations. To succeed and survive, he needed to draw on both his long experience with the company and his vision for the future.

Early on Vallance articulated a set of values as the company emerged from the public services womb:

1.  We put our customers first;
2.  We are professional;
3.  We respect each other;
4.  We work as one team;
5.  We are committed to continuous improvement.

These values were challenged as the process of transforming BT rolled along, but they have survived and passed the test of time. Vallance now describes the early articulation of these values as the single most satisfying action he took in his years as CEO.

The core values were developed as an integral part of a total quality management (TQM) program launched by the company in 1986. In those early days BT, like many Western companies, was impressed with gains made by Japanese companies worldwide. Through the TQM process, management hoped to turn the company on its ear, producing dramatic gains in productivity and quality. Headed by a senior BT manager, Colin Williams, and spurred forward by an extremely energetic younger manager, John Jarvis (who now heads BT's operations in the Far East), TQM succeeded in turning BT upside down. But it was still not enough to make the company a world-class competitor. Other actions were needed and subsequently taken.

In 1991 BT launched "Project Sovereign," a major initiative to reduce a bloated cost base. Headed by Mike Grabiner (now the CEO of Energis, a direct competitor of BT), the project was designed to turn BT from a strictly functional organization into a series of "customer-facing" divisions. In reality, the project was a cover for a significant reduction in head count. It succeeded in cutting staffing complements by upward of 40,000 persons. On July 31, 1992, 19,480 people left the company under generous outplacement terms. But management believed this was still not enough to whip the company into shape. More cuts were needed.

In early 1993, a reengineering project was launched under the name of "Project Breakout." Over the next three years, this massive and complex effort succeeded in reducing staffing levels by another approximately 70,000 persons. Included in the reductions were nearly 30,000 jobs categorized as operators (88% of all such jobs in the company) and 55,000 engineering jobs (half of such jobs in the company). Many of these changes were enabled by the adoption of new, digital technology. For example, virtually all the company's old analogue switches were upgraded to digital switches in the late 1980s and early 1990s. Field engineers were equipped with handheld computers to guide them from one service call to another, saving them from making time-consuming trips into regional parts depots. Operator services were automated to such an extent that BT was able to build a major presence in the UK telemarketing industry. It did so on the back of its automated technologies.

Managers and clerical workers fared somewhat better as downsizing cut away at staffing levels. Only 5,000 of the former and 7,000 of the latter lost their positions (this understates the number who lost their jobs, as some positions were added in marketing and sales whereas others were eliminated in operational functions). Approximately 7,000 jobs were outsourced during the downsizing effort. Temporary and contract employees, many of them fill-in operators, increased from around 10,000 in 1980 to approximately 21,500 by 1997. Outsourcing and redefinition was clearly part of BT's restructuring mix.

Most important was that all jobs were eliminated without relying on compulsory redundancies. BT placed respect for the individual high on its list of core values and beliefs. Chairman Vallance was adamant that the values be observed. Even so, given the virtual bloodbath, pressure on individuals to take voluntary redundancy was intense. This caused fear and suspicion to creep into the company. Moreover, redundancy terms strongly encouraged early retirement for those over fifty. During the process, this group of employees suffered some of the most severe cutbacks.

While all this turmoil was raging, the company took a number of steps to position itself as an international competitor. In 1993 it launched Concert, a joint venture with several other partners. This effort focused on providing communications services to large, multinational companies worldwide. In September 1994, BT announced its purchase of 20% of MCI's outstanding stock. MCI was the second largest long-distance carrier operating in the lucrative North American market. In November 1996, BT announced a plan to merge with MCI. Subsequently the plan fell apart when WorldCom entered the bidding for MCI with a substantially higher bid. In the meantime, BT initiated a series of joint ventures, primarily on the European continent. This allowed the company to participate in the liberalization of EU telecommunications markets scheduled by Brussels to begin on January 1, 1998. In midyear 1998, BT announced a plan to merge its international operations into a new joint venture with the international operations of its arch rival, AT&T. Globalization had come to BT—even though fewer than 5,000 employees worked in BT's international operations as of late 1997.

To summarize, BT, a single company operating in a single, albeit highly competitive, industry, experienced all of the major business and cultural crises characteristic of the 1980s and 1990s:

1. Reorientation of values: Because of privatization, BT was forced to add shareholders to the list of constituents it served. Better than most companies, at the same time it resisted the urge to submerge the interests of other constituents—that is, customers and employees.

2. Downsizing: In two successive waves, BT reduced its staff in excess of 50%. Few cost cutters around the world could cite similar levels of efficacy.

3. Outsourcing: Though a less dominant element of its downsizing strategy, BT outsourced a sizable number of workers. Most still perform services for the company but under the guise of a different corporate affiliation.

4. Mergers: Although it has not yet been able to pull off the one big transforming deal, BT has been a weighty player in the global merger game. Its employees have certainly been affected by the discussions and near deals.

5. Technology: Adopting modern computer technology was a key factor in enabling BT to achieve needed levels of downsizing. Few in the company have been untouched by this technological revolution.

6. Globalization: Not yet a major player on the global telecommunications stage, BT is still firmly committed to moving in this direction. Increasing numbers of BT employees have therefore accumulated exposure across national boundaries. For a former public services monopoly like BT,

> the impact on employees of a move into the global market-
> place should not be underestimated.

Yet the culture of BT has survived. It is no longer devoted primarily to service and cradle-to-grave paternalism. But the company
continues to command a high degree of loyalty from its current employees. There is even a surprising beneficence from former employees. Good feelings were secured as most former employees received
generous severance payments. Most landed very attractive jobs in
the upward of 200 competitors who entered the UK telecommunications market once it was completely deregulated in 1993. BT's
successful experience warrants closer examination for the management lessons to be learned.

Despite the turmoil since the early 1980s, BT has benefited from
having Iain Vallance's constant hand at the helm. Given the CEO's
long-standing ties to the company, employees have been willing to
give him the benefit of the doubt in evaluating the company's various change programs. Though they seldom voiced the thought, most
people assumed that Vallance would never undertake any action
contrary to the company's best interest. Even when he was seen as
the force behind major layoffs, those directly affected readily conceded that something had to be done so the company would remain
competitive in world markets. Along the way, many senior managers
as well as rank-and-file workers did disagree, sometimes vehemently,
with what he was doing. But they were willing to go along to see
how things would eventually turn out. In early 1998 Vallance announced that he was stepping down as full-time chairman and turning day-to-day operations over to Peter Bonfield. Bonfield is an
executive recruited by BT after a stint as head of the British chemical giant ICL. It remains to be seen how much slack today's employees will cut the new CEO as he takes over the reins.

The second reason many cite for the continuing coherence of the
BT culture is widespread support for the value statement written by
Vallance in the mid-1980s. It served as a guide to management actions throughout the restructuring of the company. These values emphasized putting customers first. When customer-facing divisions
were created by "Project Sovereign," the process was disruptive to
thousands of BT workers. Still, most employees understood the
steps were necessary if BT was to live up to its values. BT values also

emphasize respect for the individual. As a result, when layoffs became necessary (and most believed they were), they were carried out voluntarily with generous severance payments. BT's values also emphasize professionalism and a commitment to continuous improvement. Because of this, continual churning through the early 1990s was no great surprise. The engineering-oriented culture of BT posed it as just one more problem people had to overcome. The value statement of BT has served the company well during this period of turmoil. But only because senior management was sincerely committed to it—in both word and deed.

Is today's BT culture identical to what it was when this period of turmoil began? Of course not. BT is now much more of a results-oriented, performance culture than it was before. From an employee perspective, there is more fear than existed earlier. But the fear is not about being treated unfairly. Rather, people are afraid of not measuring up to tough new performance standards required for success. As a result of this and the lingering memories of massive redundancies, today's BT employees are much more self-reliant. They pay more attention to job advertisements; they take calls from headhunters recruiting for other companies; they avail themselves of virtually every training program available on company time to enhance their marketable skills. Despite this, they still work hard—mostly because they want to; in part because if they don't, their jobs will be at risk. They are also very loyal to the company but not so committed that they wouldn't leap at a good job opportunity elsewhere. The new BT culture is more self-centered and more suspicious, but it still has cohesion and buoyancy. People pull together when they need to. Surviving employees are proud that the company they work for is one of the finest in the UK. We wonder how many large U.S. companies still command the same loyalty from their employees.

The key lesson to be learned from BT's difficult yet successful cultural transformation is consistency. Despite a revolving door in senior ranks just below the top, BT had a single CEO for the duration of its trauma. He was also a trusted insider, not an external hired gun. In visible ways, the company adhered to a consistent set of values even when it might have been easier to ignore values in the interest of getting on with the needed changes. It retained a meaningful respect for individual employees even when it was necessary to achieve the transformation at their expense. As a result, BT came out of the restructuring process functioning well—culturally intact and commanding loyalty and respect from the bulk of its employees, both current and past. BT is living proof that shaping a viable culture in a chaotic environment requires bifocal vision: One eye on the necessary changes, the other eye on preserving tradition and creating cultural cohesion.

## Back from the Abyss: Continental Airlines

It was hard to imagine how a business could be worse off than Continental Airlines in 1994. Among the top ten U.S. airlines, it was dead last in on-time performance. It had the worst record of mishandling baggage. It received almost three times more customer complaints than the industry average and more than 30% more than the ninth worst airline. Its only performance success came with overbooking: It was among the top three. It had suffered through a seemingly never-ending wave of cost cuts. It had been in chapter 11 bankruptcy twice. Its stock value had declined to rock bottom. It had been through a series of leaders and management schemes. Morale was horrible. People were not happy to come to work. They were surly to customers and to each other. Most were ashamed of the company's performance. The rate of on-the-job injuries was astronomical, as were turnover and sick time. Employee groups haggled over scarce resources. Covering one's backside was more important than solving problems. In 1994 Continental Airlines was a company and culture on the edge.

Enter Gordon Bethune, Continental's new CEO. Starting in early 1995, the airline was in the top five on-time performers every month. Lost baggage claims became consistently among the two or three lowest. Consumer complaints fell continually below the industry average and were usually the lowest. When overbooking occurred, Continental was the best in the industry in taking care of bumped passengers. Wages had gone up an average of 25%. Sick leave was down more than 20%; turnover, down 45%. Worker's compensation claims were down 51%. The number of on-the-job injuries had been cut in half. Beginning in 1995 the company had eleven quarters of record profits. The stock price went from $3.25 a share to $60 by the end of 1998. The company has stacked up awards for customer satisfaction. *Air Transport* magazine named Continental Airlines the 1996 airline of the year.

How was this miraculous turnaround achieved? CEO Bethune credits the company's focus on people and culture: "We didn't just change the symptoms of what was wrong with Continental. We changed Continental. We changed its corporate culture from top to bottom. In fact, we changed more than any corporation this decade."

In making these fundamental changes at Continental, Bethune and his colleagues relied heavily on cultural strategies. Here are some highlights of their remarkably successful effort:

1. Those at the top have to want to change. Bethune was totally committed to making fundamental changes and insisted on being the person in charge. He made it known that he was in the captain's seat and had signed on for the duration: "I'm here, I'm not going away, and we're going to do this." As Bethune put it: "If you want change, you have to have a strong leader—an identifiable person at the top when change begins in a highly visible way. It can't be done by a committee of this or an office of that. It's got to be done by somebody."

2. Resisters have to be put on notice. Any cultural change creates resisters—people who have a vested interest in maintaining the status quo. The person in charge needs to point out the costs of standing in the way or sabotaging the progress. Bethune made it crystal clear: We will change. The reason: "Because I said so, and I'm the guy at the top, and that's the way it's going to be."

3. Dramatic events need to signal that things will be different. At Continental Bethune opened the doors of his office in the twentieth-floor executive suite. Prior to this time, the CEO's office had been an armed fortress. After the doors were propped open, employees were invited to visit at open-house events with food and drinks. Bethune took employees into his office, opened the closet doors, and said, "See, Frank Lorenzo's not here anymore" (referring to the former CEO of Continental who had initiated large-scale cost cutting and run the airline into the ground).

Soon after he opened the executive doors, he and some employees went to the company's parking lot carrying stacks of employee manuals. In the old Continental, these cumbersome collections of rules dictated in minute detail what employees were supposed to do in every situation. To the delight of everyone, the manuals were set afire. It was a dramatic gesture that showed that in the future employees would be asked to use their judgment rather than blindly follow the rules.

Bethune also ordered all planes to be repainted. Appearance is a powerful symbol. Prior to this, Continental's planes were a hodge-podge of paint schemes, many peeling versions of former colors of aircraft Continental had inherited from acquisitions of other airlines. When the operations people told Bethune it was impossible to paint all 200 of Continental's planes immediately, he was fairly clear about his expectations. He told his people it was indeed possible to accomplish the task and gave them a reason: "Because I have a Beretta at home with a 15-round magazine, and if you don't get these planes painted by July 1, I'm going to come in here and empty the clip. You're wonderful people and I love you, but you're going to get those airplanes painted or I'm going to shoot every last one of you."

4. Cultural change needs a clear blueprint. You can't just tell people to change; you've got to tell them how. And it's got to be in a form that people understand. Continental's change strategy was simple, comprehensive, and memorable. The blueprint was outlined in the "Go Forward Plan." The plan had four parts: a market plan, a financial plan, a product plan, and a people plan.

"Fly to Win," the marketing plan, outlined several simple premises: Stop doing things that lose money. Fly to places people want to go. Find out what customers want and provide it. And run a competitive operation. "Fund the Future," the financial plan, set some fiscal priorities: Stop the bleeding of cash flow. Develop systems to let us know where the money is going. Wrest some concessions from creditors. Don't make the bottom line the only line. "Make Reliability a Reality," the product plan, focused on developing a top-quality airline: Reach destinations on time—with passengers' bags. Provide clean, safe, and reliable service. Work together to make it happen. Get rewarded when it does. "Working Together," the people plan, focused on treating people with respect, getting out of their way, letting employees do their jobs, and creating a sense of teamwork—"Every piece of a watch counts," in Bethune's words.

There is an interplay among these four aspects of the new cultural blueprint. Together they added up to a plan for success and became a checklist for making key decisions. Interests of all important constituencies—customers, shareholders, and employees—were incorporated into the plan for moving forward.

5. Measure progress by rewarding people for making it happen. It's one thing to have a plan but quite another to put it into practice. To keep track of how well it's working, you've got to measure the right things and then reward employees when they do things right. And when a company is so up on teamwork, the team rather than individuals should get the rewards. Continental told its employees: "Get us there on time and it's worth $65 to each of you. Don't and you don't get the dough—none of you. That's all or nobody—we win and lose as a team." Every month the airline is in the top three for on-time performance, every employee receives a check for $65.

6. Encourage ritual and ceremony to reinforce changes. At Continental Bethune shifts his place at the conference table in the board room for each meeting he holds there. The message he wants to convey: Change is in the air. All meetings start and end on time. Message: on-time performance is one of our dominant values. At the beginning of Continental's turnaround, Bethune invited the company's best customers to his home. "We told them we were wrong and that we were going to fix things. And to prove it, we invited them over to my house one evening. We sent out invitations to 100 of our best, most frequent flyers, and we asked them to bring their spouses. When they got there, we had cocktails and tables of food. We gave them a little leather ticket case as a gift, and we flat out apologized." Message: stick with us and you'll see some changes you like.

7. Convey values through stories. Bethune seemed to understand the importance of stories and shaped his behavior to inspire some good ones in support of the new values. As we mentioned earlier, having planes arrive and leave on time was vital to the turnaround. Every time Bethune boarded a Continental flight, he would stick his head in the cockpit to say hello and chat for a few minutes. One day, as he was talking with the crew, he heard someone say, "Excuse me, sir, you'll have to sit down. The plane has to leave." A flight attendant hurriedly whispered to the gate agent to let him know whom

he was ordering around. The agent responded, "That's nice, but we gotta go. Tell him to sit down." Bethune sat down. Message: on-time performance applies to everyone, even the CEO.

The turnaround in Continental Airlines' performance is one of the business successes of the 1990s. It is doubly remarkable because the turnaround was accomplished by using culture—specifically, the building of a new culture—as the key instrument of change. The lesson of the Continental about-face should be clear to business leaders elsewhere: No matter what the state of your culture today, it can be revived. But only if you put employees back into the center of the frame.

## The Reality for Most Other Companies

Not every company has been as successful as BT and Continental Airlines in responding to the trauma of the 1980s and 1990s in business. Eastman Kodak has undergone wave after wave of downsizing as it tries to adapt to the intense competitive pressure from its main competitor, Fuji. Despite successes along the way that involved the turnaround of its black-and-white film operations, the company has lurched from crisis to crisis in its drive to regain its competitive edge. Once a paragon of strong-culture companies everywhere, it may not survive intact.

At the other end of the spectrum, Boeing, a company enjoying almost unprecedented business volume, seems to be buckling under the pressure of its huge backlog of aircraft orders. Management announces a downsizing to enable Boeing to compete with Airbus Industries; days later it announces delays in shipping schedules because of its inability to meet production requirements for its popular 747 and 737 airliners. People we know in Boeing are confused and distressed; the once proud culture of this great company is struggling to cope with the new reality.

How much of the problems Kodak and Boeing are having coming to grips with the demands of the current business environment are the result of mismanagement rather than cultural misalignment? It's hard to judge. What is clear is that the solution to the business problems they face will involve a mixture of management and cultural steps if they are to regain their positions as greatly admired companies.

Boeing and Kodak are not alone, however. As we have pointed out, corporate cultures in most companies today display a number of characteristics not present in the early 1980s: fear and insecurity (employees are afraid for their jobs); cynicism (people no longer believe the boss is always right; more important, they aren't sure management is acting in the best interests of the company); distrust (employees have learned not to trust); self-interest (people are realizing that their most important job is looking out for number one); confusion (employees everywhere are suffering from a deep-seated confusion about what is expected of them and what their role in the company will be); anomie (getting by at a job has replaced work that makes a real difference); fragmentation (today there is little glue to bond people in a common quest). Although variations exist by company and country, changes occurring in the business environment are so universal that they have left a permanent stain on the psyches and souls of corporations around the world.

These cultural undercurrents hardly reflect the cohesive institutions corporate leaders of old sought to build. They do not define the kind of workplace contemporary managers would aspire to—if they had a choice. These troubling patterns have risen from assault and default. The assault has often come from outside as the business environment creates new demands. The default comes from executives and managers who have either forgotten or ignore what makes a well-run enterprise tick. They fail to pay attention to the real cultural bonding people need to function effectively at work. These tendencies can be changed, but only by concerted, sincere efforts on the part of committed managers who recall some enduring lessons about what really matters.

As the BT and Continental cases exemplify, anything is possible. Even under the most horrific conditions, good things can happen when people pull together. But nothing positive will happen when people are pulled apart or pulling in opposite directions. This is where we need a revolution in management thinking. There's a lot that can be done to reverse the disturbing trends and revitalize corporate cultures. How to go about it is the subject of Part 3.

# PART THREE

# Rebuilding Cohesive Cultures

# CHAPTER 9

# Exercising Cultural Leadership

# The Personal Challenge

In 1973 the New York Mets clinched their second National League pennant. The baseball team, an expansion franchise that had joined the league only twelve years earlier, rallied from last place at the beginning of August to win twenty-nine of their final forty-three games. Their homestretch surge was spurred on by the words of their relief pitching ace, Tug McGraw. He told fans and reporters the team's secret: "Ya gotta believe." (McGraw backed up his words by his actions. He won five games and saved another twelve in his last nineteen trips to the pitcher's mound.)

The secret to building an effective corporate culture is similar: Success will not happen unless you believe in what you're doing. Cultural leadership begins when managers search their hearts and souls for the values and beliefs that they are willing to stand behind. The process continues as others begin to accept and share these beliefs and to shape their behavior accordingly. In today's workplace, disbelief and fear too often dominate. Employees go through the motions and do the minimum required. Managers whack away at the head count to please shareholders, without a thought to what impact their actions are having on cultural cohesion. Now is the time for some Tug McGraws to step to the plate in business, to provide some highly needed cultural leadership.

## "Ya Gotta Believe"

Core beliefs are the foundation of business cultures. Beliefs tell people what is sacred, what is sanctioned, and what is taboo. Beliefs dictate implicit rules for behavior in thousands of everyday, routine events. Consistent behavior aligned with core beliefs helps a culture achieve superior performance.

Most legendary founders of business were visionaries. They saw great social enterprises whose purposes were as much to improve society as to earn a profit. They articulated these higher ideals consistently and publicly. Often these enabling purposes were codified in written credos to motivate and guide employees along the right path. Drawing on our own experiences and borrowing from Collins and Porras's *Built to Last*, we offer core ideologies of some visionary companies:

- Merck: "We are in the business of preserving and improving human life. All our actions must be measured by our success in achieving this goal."
- Nordstrom Department Stores: "A place where service is an act of faith."
- Sony: "To experience the sheer joy that comes from the advancement, application, and innovation of technology that benefits the general public."
- Johnson & Johnson: The company exists "to alleviate pain and disease."
- Southwest Airlines: "Frequency, fares, and fun."
- Anheuser-Busch: "Someone still cares about quality."
- Motorola: The company exists "to honorably serve the community by providing products and services of superior quality at a fair price."
- Marriott: "Take good care of your employees and they'll take good care of your customers. Customers are guests; make people away from home feel that they're among friends and really wanted."
- Wal-Mart: "We exist to provide value to our customers—to make their lives better via lower prices and greater selectivity; all else is secondary."

The individuals who founded and managed such exemplary companies were not only utopian visionaries, but also hardheaded businesspeople. But they were in business for more than just making money. Their "vision" articulated their raison d'être: to provide a higher service to the world, society, and their customers. Providing distinctive goods or services is their principal goal; earning profits is the consequent reward. Their compelling vision captured employees' minds and hearts in pursuit of lofty goals.

Making a profit is never far from the minds of people who build successful businesses. In 1957, with total company sales of less than $30 million, Bill Hewlett and Dave Packard organized an off-site meeting for twenty members of their senior management. The team's mission: to thrash out a statement of the company's principles. Their efforts produced what came to be known as the "HP way." To this day, these principles guide the company's management:

1.  Profit. To recognize that profit is the best single measure of our contribution to society and the ultimate source of our corporate strength. We should attempt to achieve the maximum possible profit consistent with our other objectives.

2.  Customers. To strive for continual improvement in the quality, usefulness, and value of the products and services we offer our customers.

3.  Field of Interest. To concentrate our efforts, continually seeking new opportunities for growth but limiting our involvement to fields in which we have capability and can make a contribution.

4.  Growth. To emphasize growth as a measure of strength and a requirement for survival.

5.  Employees. To provide employment opportunities for HP people that include the opportunity to share in the company's success, which they helped make possible. To provide them job security based on performance, and to provide the opportunity for personal satisfaction that comes from a sense of accomplishment in their work.

6.  Organization. To maintain an organizational environment that fosters individual motivation, initiative and creativity,

and a wide latitude of freedom in working toward established objectives and goals.

7. Citizenship. To meet the obligations of good citizenship by making contributions to the community and to the institutions in our society which generate the environment in which we operate.

Hewlett and Packard were not just social reformers. They were businessmen dedicated to profit and growth and bent on achieving financial goals and objectives. But their beliefs encompassed other worthy goals as well. They believed that employees were an integral part of the company, deserving job security and qualified to share in profits. They believed the company's work environment should offer individuals motivation, initiative, creativity, and freedom. They believed in these things for good reason: They recognized that all organizations are created to give people an opportunity to use all their skills while accepting their human foibles. They recognized that organizations work best when they accommodate people's legitimate needs and aspirations. They believed that maintaining a strong, appropriate culture helps to capture the loyalty and energies of employees. These beliefs guided Hewlett-Packard to become the exemplary company it is today.

Note that Hewlett and Packard placed profit and customers ahead of their more people-oriented beliefs. We do, too. We never argued that building and nurturing an appropriate culture was management's only mission. Instead, we highlight culture as one of the important ways to achieve financial success. Culture is an important management concern—not the sole legitimate item on the management agenda. Putting culture too far ahead of sheer functional labor—finding customers, manufacturing reasonably priced products or creating first-rate services, and making a profit—is a surefire recipe for disaster. Yet building a business without paying attention to core cultural beliefs—what is required to succeed, ground rules for acceptable behavior, sentiments employees have about their work, and pride in what they do—assures long-term stagnation and, ultimately, mediocrity or failure.

Achieving a balance between hard management—designing a good product, setting the right price, and pursuing the right strategy—and soft management—ensuring that employees are connected and motivated to give their best—is a true art. Hard-nosed, numbers-oriented managers fail to recognize that the softer, people-oriented aspect requires equal attention. Otherwise only a fraction of what makes a successful organization tick gets addressed. Our guess is that for many managers interested in providing more cultural leadership, the key question is: "How do I begin?"

As a start, any senior manager who agrees that culture is important should try the following experiment:

1. Write down five or so key beliefs you hope members of your organization share.
2. Get away from the home office, put aside your usual trappings of power, and chat informally with employees.
3. Mix with rank-and-file employees you do not know and who probably don't know you either.
4. Find out what your employees really believe is at the heart of the business. Be prepared for some shocking input and don't overreact; employees are unlikely to see the same world you experience from your corner office. Listen carefully: Not all of what you hear will be valid, but as themes emerge and are repeated again and again, you are probably getting close to cultural truth.
5. Try to get an understanding of why your employees believe what they believe. More often than not, you will find their views have real merit.
6. Once you are able to see your company through employees' eyes, compare their views to what you first wrote down. If there are significant differences in their views and yours, it will highlight the challenges that lie ahead in knitting together a more cohesive culture.

In addition to this walking-the-halls exercise, conduct a series of informal meetings with employees who have been on board for only a few months. These individuals are still cultural novices who have not yet had time to fully grasp how things work. Their views reveal how early acculturation is working, what the informal ropes are, and how well they are learning important cultural lessons. Ask them what the place stands for. They will probably feed you the party line initially. But if you persevere, you may find out what they really believe. If this is at odds with your view of what's right, then you're getting real insight into existing cultural realities. Another version of this exercise is to conduct some straightforward exit interviews with people leaving the company. Whether they quit or got fired, they'll probably tell you the truth. Their seasoned insights paired with the first impressions of new arrivals will give you a good window on what life is like for employees.

These exercises are designed to build your feel for what's really going on culturally, not to determine the next steps to take. Don't do anything right away; just let it all sink in. Managers too often leap to action before they really know what's going on or what to do. Although this gives them an elusive feeling of being in control, it usually results in their doing what they usually do—even if it's not working. (We'll have some specific suggestions for shaping culture later in the book.) If you stumble onto some obvious glitches and have a clear sense of what's needed, give it a shot. But it usually makes more sense to wait for opportunities that emerge in the days or months ahead.

Once you have an idea about the cultural lay of the land in your company, you need to exercise some personal leadership to begin the process of building into the company the kind of culture you want. The cultures that characterize so many great companies today and in the past didn't just happen. They were put into place by individuals who exercised personal leadership to instill the kind of culture—or perhaps better put, the kind of belief system—they thought was needed for their companies to survive and prosper. Instilling such a belief system is not a task you can delegate to your human resource department, nor is it a task ever to be assigned to outside consultants, however convincing their spiel may be. It is something you have to do yourself.

How should you go about taking on this daunting challenge? First a disclaimer about what it doesn't require: You don't have to turn yourself into a clone of a Tom Watson or Dave Packard in order to have a lasting impact on the culture of the company you run. What you do have to do is stand up and be counted on for what you believe in and why you consider it essential that others in your company share these beliefs. With this mindset in place, concentrate on getting a few basics right. As discussed in the sections that follow, we suggest you focus on three areas: (1) eliminating fear, (2) creating an umbrella of beliefs, and (3) converting a subset of these beliefs into an ethical code of conduct. Whether or not you buy into our suggestions, make sure you put management of the culture on your daily agenda. Spend time every day reflecting on how you might influence a cultural renaissance, always reminding yourself of a central cultural mantra: "Ya gotta believe."

## Eliminating Fear

Downsizing and other contemporary belt-tightening initiatives have left their legacy of fear in the workplace. In most places, workers are terrified of losing their jobs and being left unable to support their families. Surprise job loss creates personal stress. Self-doubt is one of the worst: What is wrong with me? Why did I lose this job? Will I be able to find another one soon? Will a new job be as good as the one I had? Will I be able to find only short-term employment? On their own these pressures are tough enough. But they are amplified by other worries, such as paying the mortgage and putting food on the table. Think about how it feels when deciding whether to search for work elsewhere. Think about selling a home and finding another. Should the family be uprooted or separated temporarily until you find work? Should the kids be taken out of school? These are some of the gut-wrenching considerations ordinary workers face when they lose their jobs. It's a series of fears that overshadows everything else. How many senior managers really understand how it feels? If they want to create a focused, cohesive workplace, they need first to understand and deal with the pervasive fear that lingers in the wake of widespread job losses.

People are afraid of losing their jobs because millions of others already have. Each day people pick up the local newspaper and read about another company laying off thousands of workers. More often than not, the story concludes on an upbeat note for shareholders: The stock price has taken a sizable jump as a result. With developing world economies soaring (until the late 1990s), new jobs opening at record rates, and unemployment at near record lows, why are the threats of further job loss casting such a pall?

The answer is simple and distasteful: The downsizings of the 1990s have carved a breach of trust between employers and employees. Employees no longer know where to turn to alleviate their anxieties. Millions of employees worked for companies who either explicitly or implicitly promised workers jobs for life if they worked hard. When companies such as IBM and Eastman Kodak, to pick just two of the former giants, suddenly announce significant down-sizings, employees are shocked. After a period of predictable disbelief, employees reluctantly accept their termination as inevitable for the company's long-term health. Buoyed also by generous severance terms, they conclude that although the company's commitment may have changed, it still was looking out for employees' welfare. Subsequent downsizing announcements forced abandonment of such rationalizations: Promises of lifetime employment and a caring employer are history. In their place fear rules the roost.

What does the word "fear" conjure up? It summons images of panic, withdrawal, uncommunicativeness, and ultimately, mistakes. To succeed, people need assurances of trust and security. Creativity and innovation are closely allied with risk-taking. But people take risks only when they feel secure. Many companies recognize this need for security that allows employees to function at their optimum. As a result, management works hard to create a trusting work environment.

Consider again Southwest Airlines. The company has grown in twenty-five years to over $3 billion in annual revenues. Its secret: emphasizing a family relationship with its employees. Southwest creates a trusting, secure work environment in addition to concentrating fiercely on its mission as a low-cost, frequent-service airline. Southwest's credo emphasizes a number of successful points:

- Profitability: The company has made a profit every year since 1973.
- Low cost: The company's raison d'être is to be the low-cost U.S. carrier.
- Family: The company insists on treating employees as family members.
- Fun: More than a catchy marketing slogan, the company goes out of its way to make both traveling with and working for them fun.
- Love: The core of the company's ethic is universal caring— for employees, customers, and the communities in which they operate.

- Hard work: Southwest is almost twice as productive as any other airline.
- Individuality: Southwest cultivates mavericks who are not afraid to express themselves in pursuit of the company's objectives.
- Ownership: Not only through offering extensive employee stock ownership plans, the company strives to treat all its employees like owners. It expects them to function like owners in return. Employee ownership and pride are one of the keys to the company's maintenance of a top-tier cost and service position.
- Legendary service: One of the pioneers of no-frills service (no meals on its flights), Southwest has distinguished itself by the "positively outrageous service" it provides customers. It's able to do so because of the extraordinarily positive attitude of its employees.
- Egalitarianism: From senior management on down, formal hierarchy is a cultural no-no. Face-to-face communications is Southwest's norm.
- Common sense/good judgment: In place of written policy and procedure manuals, Southwest relies on the judgment of its "family member" to see that its mission is carried out.
- Simplicity: To maintain its position as the most cost-effective airline, the company insists on simplicity.
- Altruism: Southwest believes it must earn the respect and loyalty of communities it serves. It bends over backward to add back something of value.

With over 25,000 employees, Southwest has never had a layoff (except for three employees furloughed early in the airline's history and then promptly rehired). How has Southwest succeeded in building such a successful enterprise in the highly competitive airline industry? By placing an enormous amount of trust in employees. Employees also trust the company. This mutual trust has paid huge dividends. But Southwest is not the only example of a people-friendly workplace. The Saturn Corporation also prides itself on being "a different kind of company." Its employees are trusted to do the right thing and are given ample opportunities to figure out how to work smarter. All employees are authorized to pull "the rope"—

handles on ropes placed along the assembly line to stop the entire line—if they see anything short of Saturn's high-quality standards. An employee told us: "Given the opportunity, everyone would like to produce a perfect product or service. At Saturn they've given us the rope; they've given us that chance."

Consider an example from another industry: the highly volatile semiconductor business. Motorola, an industry leader and much-admired employer, speaks directly to its trust in people in its credo:

> People: To treat each employee with dignity, as an individual; to maintain an open atmosphere where direct communication with employees affords the opportunity to contribute to the maximum of their potential and fosters unity of purpose with Motorola; to provide personal opportunities for training and development to ensure the most capable and most effective work force; to respect senior service; to compensate fairly by salary, benefits and, where possible, incentives; to promote on the basis of capability; and to practice the commonly accepted policies of equal opportunity and affirmative action.

Because Motorola is one of the semiconductor industry's major players, it has not been immune from periodic adjustments in its staffing levels. The most recent is an early 1998 elimination of 4,000 jobs in the company's U.S. manufacturing facilities. In keeping with its credo, however, Motorola champions a quasi-tenure employment system. New hires are initially placed on probation. After successfully passing their probationary period, they are moved to a second category. These are employees whose jobs are guaranteed for as long as they last, as long as the individuals maintain satisfactory records. Employees who have performed well and been with Motorola for ten years are then moved to a third job category—the "service club." They are guaranteed lifetime access to some job with the company even if their current jobs are eliminated. Individuals in this job category cannot be terminated without the approval of Motorola's chair. Forty-seven thousand Motorola employees, about half the company's workforce, enjoy this limited form of tenure. Although short of a job-for-life guarantee, it gives employees security to approach work with enthusiasm and confidence. It also makes them real believers. The company means what it says: Its credo places a high value on people, and its actions back it up.

Motorola is of course not alone in its people-friendly beliefs. It is joined by companies like Hewlett-Packard and Intel. Unfortunately, too many companies pay lip service to people-oriented principles while engaging in contrary practices. Of these actions, downsizings were among the most severe in spreading fear throughout the workplace.

In order for a company to rebuild a constructive culture, it must remove the fear of arbitrary job loss. Does this mean companies should recommit to lifetime employment? Such a blanket commitment would be neither believable nor possible in today's rapidly changing world economy. But companies can learn to be totally honest with their workforces. Employees have a right to know what the future holds for the company and what changes might mean for their future employment status. If further cost cutting is foreseen, companies should design and publish fair criteria for deciding which jobs or people go or are retained. Although cutting jobs is always painful, a transparent process can go a long way to alleviate workers' fears.

Along with transparency, companies should think long and hard about the issue of tenure. Motorola spent decades designing a system that works for the company, but their system may not work for others. All companies have employees who are absolutely essential to success, though, and these valuable workers deserve some form of tenure. Job security, like today's pervasive job insecurity, is infectious; it affects more than those whose longevity has been secured. If tenure cannot be guaranteed, that should also be stated up front. Instituting transparent policies and procedures and granting even a limited form of security reassures employees. So does the guarantee that they will be treated fairly if, to keep the company afloat, cuts absolutely have to be made. Fair treatment builds trust. Trust helps breed a supportive culture.

There are no easy answers in finding a balance between job security and the demands of an increasingly competitive marketplace. Managers must retain the controlling right to cut costs—even if such short-term reductions are destructive to cultural cohesion. Moreover, because company situations and the circumstances of competition are so varied, there is no simple formula to determine when costs have been reduced enough to declare a moratorium on further cuts. The tension between further cost cutting and workforce needs will remain as a fact of corporate life for some time. And the costs of the cuts will also linger, as threats to job security undermine employee confidence and dampen their short- to medium-term productivity.

The dilemma creates a unique possibility for senior managers: Put your own job on the line. Senior managers could send a powerful cultural signal by promising to resign if their economic predictions do not materialize. Odds are their jobs would be in jeopardy in any case. But by casting their lots with employees, senior managers might regain some credibility lost by previous selfish actions. This alone would begin the process of restoring cohesion in fragmented work cultures. Whether it is too scary and dramatic a step is something individual managers must decide on their own. Whatever they do, managers who want to instill a culture in their companies must find a way to drive fear out of their workplaces.

## Creating an Umbrella of Beliefs

Cultures of modern corporations are often fragmented into highly autonomous subcultures. Too often this creates watertight compartments among groups whose cooperation is essential for success. For instance, R&D takes its time to make sure a new product or service is sound and reliable. This frustrates the marketing group, which sees an immediate, maybe fleeting opportunity. The sales force keeps making promises, thinking, "Just give us the damn thing and we'll push it. But right now, we're worried about losing our credibility with customers." The financial people are too worried about costs and head count to focus on the possible creation of new revenue.

As if this were not enough, other subcultures based on longevity, race, or gender pursue their respective interests irrespective of overall company concerns or agenda. All this pulling and tugging in different directions unravels the cultural fabric that holds diverse groups together, focuses efforts on a central mission, and yields top performance. In any workplace, subcultures are inevitable and should be encouraged rather than beaten down (more about this in the next chapter). The key management challenge is to articulate core beliefs or a higher cause as a source of glue to hold separate or working subcultures together and to keep their disparate efforts focused on a common purpose. For subcultures to work together, there must be informal rules or guidelines for how these independent entities are supposed to relate to one another or link to the corporate whole. These rules best derive from a historically anchored set of beliefs about what the corporation stands for.

Umbrella beliefs to unite disparate subcultures of a company into a coherent and cohesive whole are not easy to find or define. It is not a search to be undertaken lightly. But if a company lacks a central core, where can employees look to find guidance and leadership? They of course look to their subculture or profession.

In searching for umbrella values to unite today's fragmented business cultures, simplicity is the key. Most subcultures are quite content to go their own ways. Under no circumstances will people sit still for long-winded proclamations of a new and glorious era—especially if the new direction diverges from the recent or distant past. But people still want to belong. They yearn for something that elevates their work from routine drudgery to a higher purpose. They will listen to what seems thoughtful, authentic, and comes from the heart. Top management bears a responsibility to determine what the company is going to stand for. Exercising this responsibility takes leadership and a willingness to live by and practice what you preach.

What should these central beliefs be? Some form of disciplined process is required if the right set of beliefs is to be articulated and pursued. Depending on individual leadership style, some managers pursue the process on their own. Others seek the counsel of colleagues to formulate their thoughts. Whatever the approach, a series of sensible steps should guide the process of establishing values:

### Examining the Issue of Ethics

Running a large enterprise can be risky. Those at the top are ultimately responsible for the actions of anyone who represents the corporation. In conducting business with customers and suppliers, it is important to establish a set of cultural virtues and taboos for what kind of behavior will be tolerated or punished. An ethics statement is often embedded in a company's statement of values. Values help people know what to do—the enduring rules for "right" behavior. Ethics specify what not to do—the prevailing cultural taboos.

Hammering out a code of ethics is not easy. Nor is it a decision to be taken lightly. For example, many companies insist on honesty in dealings with others. However, some highly successful companies (Microsoft and Oracle are examples) are infamous for making promises to customers and then not delivering on time—or at all. Their failure to live by the simple value of honesty in all transactions negates this as a shared value the company can claim or stand behind.

In the realm of ethics, there are many possible values that a company can consider—some for self-defense. Prohibitions on kickbacks and bribery are necessary to keep senior managers out of jail. Prohibitions against discrimination of any kind, especially where prohibited by local or national statutes, are clearly appropriate. But at the end of each day, it is up to an individual executive to decide what standards are acceptable or not. Having precisely stated ethical principles goes a long way in assuring that everyone in the company will abide by a code of appropriate conduct.

### Reviewing Relationships with Important Constituencies

With the ascendancy of the premium on shareholder value, needs of other corporate constituencies have been neglected. But these other constituencies—suppliers, employees, customers, and society—are crucial to an enterprise's long-term health. Without reliable suppliers, few companies can produce goods or services. Without employees, nothing would get done. Without customers, a company would go out of business. Without communities, companies would be homeless.

All companies depend on multiple constituents to succeed. However, a slogan like "Our customers' interests always come first" is rarely true and may be extremely difficult to live up to. Successful companies like Southwest Airlines instead make it known that employees come first. The company believes that through the actions of highly motivated, positive employees, customers will be well served. It's a value the company stands behind.

It is important to distinguish between fundamental beliefs articulating how a company will relate to its constituencies and its overall strategy. Strategies lay out steps to achieve competitive advantage. Strategies change as conditions shift in a company's market. Strategies come and go. Fundamental beliefs, in contrast, speak to sustaining, nonnegotiable values that shape life inside the workplace. Fundamental beliefs cannot be altered easily without unraveling the cultural fabric—a company's enduring ethos. Fundamental beliefs persist, whereas strategies change. This subtle distinction is crucial to determining the right equation in relating to various audiences.

## Examining Competitive Realities and Deciding How You Will Compete

A third major source of potential beliefs lies in a company's competitive realities. Some companies thrive on innovation; others seek preeminence through service. Still others try to be the low-cost suppliers in their markets. No specific way is right or wrong for all companies. To be successful, *each* company must understand as a core element of its strategy how it will compete and gain competitive superiority. Encapsulating the core of a strategy in company beliefs is a good way of creating a rallying point for employees.

For example, one company's strategy might focus on dominating carefully selected niche markets (rather than competing for share in mass markets). Another company might choose to produce improved me-too goods or services rather than being known as an innovator. A company with either of these strategies could articulate a fundamental belief that the interests of its customers always come first. Given this, they might adopt a policy of no-questions-asked refunds. Nordstrom department stores adhere to this rule as a way to make visible its value of unparalleled customer service. Or a company could espouse a value that its products and services always should add value for customers (as Hewlett-Packard does). Adhering to either one of these values does not address important questions about which markets to go after, how to position products, or any of the other things a well-run company's strategy should specify. Values may put constraints on strategies, but values do not and should not dictate a strategy per se.

## Examining the Approaches of Admired Companies

Many companies profess a set of core beliefs. Some companies adhere to them with tenacious consistency. Many companies publish what they stand for in public statements, recruiting brochures, and other publications. Examining the beliefs of other companies can offer useful clues regarding how to articulate your own values. Imitation may be a form of flattery; it can also be a source of inspiration.

Beware of adopting—or even adapting—another company's beliefs without considering whether they make sense in the context of your company's traditions and ways. Some long-established, highly regarded companies have spent decades honing their cherished values and beliefs. Many have incorporated their beliefs into the core of their strategies. Or they have extracted from their successful strategies beliefs that seem to work. Adopting beliefs just because they work elsewhere or sound nice is a sure recipe for disaster. But looking for clues from venerable companies is something many thoughtful managers do. Comparison can sharpen your vision.

### Mining Your Company's History

Most companies—especially those that have been around for some time—have a rich history. Histories include old mission statements, documents outlining corporate beliefs, oral history about the "good old days," and past traditions that have contributed to the company's success. Although it is fashionable to ignore history—especially when so much of history has been discarded to achieve global competitiveness—the past can offer valuable lessons for the future. The history of a company and how it came to embrace certain values and beliefs is potential inspiration for shaping the future. Here is an ideal place for senior managers to enlist the help of the informal cultural network described in the Introduction (and our previous book). Priests or priestesses and storytellers are particularly useful in bringing historical precedents and tales to the table for current consideration. Commissioning a group of cultural players to revisit the past for cultural lessons and value commitments can be extremely helpful in hammering out what a company should stand behind today.

If certain slogans from past eras have shown staying power, what was the source of their longevity? Could it be that the slogan represented what customers might expect from dealings with the company (the legendary Avis slogan of "We try harder" immediately comes to mind)? Or could it be that the values represented in a long-standing slogan resonated with the company's employees ("IBM means service" best personifies such a core value)? Loyal customers become sentimentally attached to historically rooted slogans or values. As a result, long-standing values should be discarded only after very careful thought.

A company's values also attract new recruits. Most companies have recruitment patterns that persist for long periods. Some are regionally based. Long-term employees tend to respond to values that hold sway in a particular part of the country. Friendly Midwesterners fill the ranks of many of America's rust belt companies. Similarly, some companies have historically recruited from well-defined socioeconomic classes. Employees carry values of their social class into the workplace. Thus the middle-class, professional profile of companies like IBM stands in sharp contrast to the upwardly mobile, yuppie image of Xerox. Companies employing regionally or socially similar groups of employees should think about which values will appeal or which will turn off the very people they want to attract.

The trick in welding history and future is not to become mesmerized by the past. We have argued that the world of business has changed dramatically. What worked in the past, no matter how popular among customers or employees, may not work in the future. It would be equal folly for most companies to try to reinvent their pasts when things have changed dramatically. Instead, they should try to understand why historical practices worked and learn lessons about beliefs that might sustain a robust future. History can be a great teacher, but it seldom forecasts the future perfectly. It can, however, be a rich source of ideas of what that future should look like.

## Examining Your Own Values

Finally, you should examine your own values. What kind of a company do you want to work for? How do you want to be remembered? What do you stand for when all else is said and done? A careful look inside, painful as it can be, is a major source of input and inspiration for the beliefs you might find useful as shared guidelines for behavior. Once again, the reality test must be applied: Don't adopt as company values or beliefs anything you could not live up to yourself.

## Turning Beliefs into Behaviors:
## An Ethical Code of Conduct

Mapping out a set of beliefs is only the first step in a long journey toward a culture that influences the behavior of employees. This journey is and will remain uncharted, since individual employees have their individual beliefs and decide how to behave based on their interpretation of values the company articulates. To be meaningful, shared beliefs should influence behavior informally and consistently. It is the job of senior managers to reinforce desired behaviors and spell out what the consequences will be if individuals' behavior fails to adhere to company-wide values. Most often transgressions arise in relation to a company's code of ethics.

Ethical standards are different from other basic values or beliefs a company may hold. Ethical standards demand strict adherence if the company is truly serious about maintaining them. Other values and beliefs serve more as guidelines for preferred behavior; very rarely do they constitute the "thou shalt not cross this line" mandate reserved for ethical standards. Having pronounced a set of ethics, it is top management's responsibility to see that these standards become woven into the cultural fabric.

Generally speaking, we oppose highly specific and prescriptive codification of corporate values and beliefs because such rigid renditions stifle creative human interpretation. Abstract values that invite multiple interpretation within culturally prescribed limits are at the heart of a strong company culture. On questions of ethics, our position changes. Violation of an ethical standard should be grounds for immediate termination. Accordingly, senior managers owe it to employees to spell out explicitly what is acceptable ethical behavior and what is not. Linking ethical standards to behavioral expectations is one of senior managers' key responsibilities. Translating ethical standards into an explicit corporate code of conduct is a useful way to communicate that the corporation stands for something.

There are other practical reasons for promulgating a code of ethics. Recent U.S. court cases, especially those related to sex discrimination, have found corporations liable if they do not take overt action—like employee training programs—to prevent violations of federal or state law. Other parts of the world may be less litigious, but still the consequences of unethical behavior can be severe (as

IBM recently found when accused of bribery in relation to a major outsourcing project in Argentina). It makes good, practical business sense to be sure that employees are fully aware of ethical standards and the consequences of violating them. Even if the standards involve no more than adhering to relevant laws, being explicit about ethical boundaries can pay direct dividends.

There are also significant cultural benefits to be gained from constructing and enforcing a uniform code of conduct—especially when a company still exhibits significant stresses as a result of downsizings, mergers, or restructurings. People yearn to believe in something that brings meaning to their lives at work. Recent years have assaulted traditional beliefs employees have held dear. Survey after survey documents the alienation of workers from managers and top management. In such a moral vacuum, publishing a corporate code of (ethical) conduct may seem a very small step. But it will begin to fill a human need to have something worthwhile to hang on to and will prepare the ground for other important cultural initiatives.

Managers in companies where cultural ties have been weakened or severed by short-term actions should tread cautiously. Employees are cynical. They distrust management, and they are tired of the hypocrisy they see so often as words and deeds fail to match up. Many employees today are not willing to sign off on initiatives that ignored the past and set objectives seemingly impossible to achieve. Until people know management really means it, their own support of a broader statement of values will be limited to words rather than deeds. Building trust takes a long time and is accomplished through consistent, transparent behavior. Companies in trouble today should learn to walk before they run, lest they stumble and fall flat. Instituting a corporate code of ethical conduct is a small step that might begin a meaningful cultural journey.

## Walking the Walk and Talking the Talk

Values and beliefs become real only when they are lived every day. No amount of corporate rhetoric or promotion can substitute for direct evidence of management's sincere and meaningful dedication to a consistent set of values. Senior managers beware: You have to walk the walk as well as talk the talk if you want your employees to believe you.

When Lou Gerstner screamed at his American Express colleagues, "That's the stupidest thing I've ever heard! You're an idiot. Get out of my office," as is reported in the book *Big Blues,* he established a reputation as an irascible manager, unconcerned about his impact on his colleagues. This reputation (along with that of being a good financial manager) will stay with him most if not all of his professional life. The event will be embellished in the retelling: Storytellers exaggerate their stories to get across their points. But worse, such behavior will be mimicked by those who aspire to senior positions in the companies he manages.

Andy Grove, who more than any other individual built Intel into the powerhouse it has become, ordered his general counsel, Roger Borovoy, to launch two lawsuits a quarter to help protect Intel's proprietary technology. In doing so, he should not have been surprised that his paranoia would influence other cultural practices: hiring private investigators to look into activities of current employees or coercing local police to search the homes of former workers. His paranoia, as demonstrated by visible actions, communicated more clearly than words his beliefs about the honesty of other people. To get ahead in Grove's Intel, employees had to adopt an appropriately paranoid attitude. Grove's favorite statement was: "Only the paranoid survive." The value thus became a virtue.

Business history is full of stories about larger-than-life individuals who shaped the enterprises of their era. Their companies are even fuller of lore about "the old man" and how his actions spelled out what was required for success. That's the nature of culture: Employees observe and copy behavior seen to indicate what is required to get ahead. A manager wishing to influence culture must recognize that his or her actions will speak louder than words in conveying company values—either to its employees or to the outside world.

Does this mean superhuman managers are needed to change cultural patterns? Certainly not. What is required, however, is a heartfelt commitment to workable, deep-seated values and beliefs that translate into routine behavior. It is too simplistic to think a company's interests will be served best by a simple commitment to putting customers (or any others) first. The most difficult challenge in shaping a company's culture is recognizing that you have to put yourself and your beliefs on display all the time; otherwise you have little hope of influencing others. The dilemma is that without deeply held and consistently reinforced convictions, not much will exist at the core of a culture for others to identify with and emulate. There will be nothing to elevate the humdrum of work to a higher level where it captures people's hearts and minds and inspires them to perform far beyond their wildest dreams—or yours.

This chapter opened with the motto "Ya gotta believe," the rallying cry of a successful relief pitcher on a struggling professional baseball team. We can turn it into a crucial cry for today's managers to step to the plate and provide some much-needed cultural leadership. As a first step, managers must look inward to find their personal beliefs and values. The next step is to find out what other managers and employees believe in and stand behind. If there is a discrepancy—and in today's fear-ridden, fragmented workplace there usually is—the third step is to engage in a process of collective soul-searching to pinpoint or hammer out a shared set of core values and business ethics. Culture is about embracing deeply held beliefs about what it takes to succeed and to excel. Strongly held and consistently practiced beliefs give culture its power to raise human expectations and performance to truly extraordinary levels. Without such values and beliefs, any attempts at manipulating culture will fail. Managers who seek to rebuild the weakened cultures of their companies and to recapture superior performance must hold strong beliefs themselves and be willing to stand up for cherished values. It takes leadership to believe in something passionately enough to inspire others. It's going to take a lot of it to revitalize today's weakened business cultures.

## CHAPTER 10

# Putting Fragmented Cultures Back Together

## Building from the Ground Up

Today's corporate cultures are often a patchwork of autonomous subcultures. These groups are typically separated from the parent corporation and one another as a result of abrupt and far-reaching changes in the business environment. Local business units and divisions are cut from different cloth. Specific functions—manufacturing, purchasing, distribution, accounting, marketing, and sales—create their own separate worlds. At times these groups come together to defend against arbitrary corporate dictums to downsize, rightsize, reengineer—you name it. Subcultures also form when clusters of employees acquired from other firms are forced to operate in a context they find hostile and threatening.

To have subcultures flourish within a larger cultural fabric is not a new development. Even in companies with tightly knit cultures, people find meaning in distinct subculture units. What is new is the proliferation of pockets of meaning almost independent of a larger context. They have either shed their collective attachments or been isolated or severed from their parent companies. In an attempt to forge a meaningful work situation, subcultures preserve their own norms and values as a defense against unwanted intrusion. They live in fear of being subsumed by other subcultures. Manufacturing worries about details, not customers and costs. Administration quibbles over costs without adequate attention to quality or customer needs. Top management focuses on shareholder returns, sacrificing customer convenience, community needs, or employee rights for higher immediate margins. If this all sounds like overreaction, stop and think a minute. The traditional response to threat is withdrawal and defense. Subcultures of today are the modern equivalent of the circled wagons of America's pioneer era, anticipating attack.

Individual corporations vary in terms of the degree their cultures have become isolated pockets of subcultural identity and activity. But virtually all companies have suffered this centrifugal pressure. Many of the decentralized, loosely tied conglomerates of earlier decades remain as they were before. These cobbled-together companies were always struggling to find meaning and coherence. Other companies, particularly in rapidly growing fields such as software, remain relatively insulated from current management and economic forces. Still, many of these young enterprises struggle to define their core culture and how it should draw together values and beliefs of different subcultures. Other companies have been so battered by the economic and management trends of recent years that they are preoccupied with survival; cultural considerations are secondary in life-or-death struggles.

Suffering most from cultural fragmentation are companies such as IBM and Eastman Kodak, which once took such great pride in their cohesive and distinctive cultures. Many of these firms saw their traditional cultural values and practices—the fabric of their culture—torn apart by successive waves of downsizings, restructurings, and mergers. They now find themselves lost. Their traditional values don't work. But people resist the imposition of new values, skeptical about adopting new and unproven practices. They lack confidence and the courage of their convictions. As a consequence, cultural cohesion gives way to a cultural vacuum. Some of the household names of the corporate world of yesterday are the real victims of the modern business era. They can't return to a secure world they once knew. Nor are they sure how to forge ahead into an uncharted future.

A key challenge for modern managers is finding a way to unite fragmented subcultures into a coherent whole around a common purpose. Only by recapturing collective coherence and meaning can they bring about more robust future performance. The work required to rebuild meaning and purpose is detailed, time-consuming, and difficult. It can, however, be done, and the benefits of reviving a former spirit are substantial.

## Organizing Culture Revitalization

Launching a process to unite fragmented subcultures into a focused and vibrant enterprise requires hard work and a dedicated team of handpicked people. In the early days of culture rebuilding or revitalization, it is unrealistic to expect the CEO or even a member of the senior management team to devote the time and attention needed to assure the project's success. CEOs are busy; they are usually paid (quite well) to devise appropriate strategies, oversee operations, and represent the enterprise to shareholders, customers, and society at large. Even when cultural revitalization is at the top of their priority list, most CEOs do not have the time to do the work necessary to construct and execute an effective revitalization program. They need the support of a dedicated group of people to get the job done.

A dedicated revitalization team should be small, a core of no more than a dozen people, regardless of a company's size. It should mix people drawn from a cross-section of relevant disciplines (not a group of human resource professionals who happen to have a personal interest). It should include representatives from major subcultures. For example, if the company has been put together through mergers, the working team should have a representative from each of the acquired businesses. It is also wise to include key players in the informal network on the team. When Arthur Andersen, a leading accounting firm, conducted a worldwide audit of its culture, the team was led by Claude Rogers, one of the company's most revered priests. He was brought out of retirement to head the effort and passed away while working on its final report.

This culture team—or whatever it is called—should never see itself as acting independently. It is the eyes and ears of senior management. The team must have total access to top management. The work of the culture team must have the bosses' public blessing. Critical decisions about the team's mission are made at the top. Top management must also be kept informed about the team's progress, what team members are learning, and any cultural initiatives that are being considered or launched. After doing its work, the culture team should be dissolved, its responsibilities assumed by some adjunct of the CEO's office. In the meantime, there is a lot of detailed work to be undertaken on top management's behalf.

## Mapping Existing Subcultures

The starting point for ferreting out existing subcultures is to glance at an organization chart (organogram, in European parlance) or a corporate address book. Cultures form in an environment of trust and a common set of beliefs—a shared worldview. Trust that leads to cultural bonding is built most easily through face-to-face human contact. Especially in times of stress, a fact of corporate life since the 1980s, people tend to rely on direct contact as the acid test of whom they can really trust. As a result, corporate subcultures develop among groups of people who work in close proximity or get together on a regular basis.

History plays an important role in determining where subcultures thrive or atrophy. Companies that have undergone one or more significant mergers will be most familiar with this aspect of organizational life. Take companies with a history of mergers, for example. Once acquired, people will continue to identify with their old cultural customs and traditions. They will band together to preserve their old ways from contamination by new and foreign mores and rituals. The us-against-them mentality helps like-minded individuals cope and find meaning in an alien workplace. Beliefs of the former culture continue to have credence, even if not endorsed by the new owner. Adherence to old beliefs becomes an underground mantra.

In addition to looking at subcultures based on proximity or a shared history, subcultures arise in areas that cut across conventional functional lines. For example, people who work in well-defined specialties such as finance and management information systems (MIS) often spend more time with people within their own discipline than with other employees. Very often stronger cultural bonds develop within functions than within more geographically or historically defined affinity groups. Karen Stephenson of UCLA reported that in one company, no one could figure out why one group of very diverse individuals was so tight. It turned out that they were smokers. Since the company maintained a smoke-free environment, several times each day this group gathered outside for a smoke. Over cigarettes, they traded stories, gossip, and opinions. They had become a cohesive cultural cabal.

By using an organization chart and address book, a manager can construct a reasonable first approximation of existing subcultures by finding out where pockets of people with shared backgrounds work together. An initial "desk mapping" of potential subcultures should help identify groupings that would logically share cultural characteristics. No matter how large the company, these initial subculture mappings should not include more than one hundred such organizational units, preferably many less. Establishing a short list of subcultures is preferable to wrestling with so many disparate units that all sense of clarity and coherence is lost. Once agreement has been reached on a starter list, additional field research is needed to test the map's accuracy.

Field research is probably too fancy a label for the next steps in mapping the subcultural terrain. To verify the existence of subcultures, the culture revitalization team discussed above should conduct interviews in areas suspected of having a cohesive and unique cultural leaning. A handful of interviews should suffice to establish if a unit actually has a separate and distinct identity and to catalogue its unique characteristics. These interviews have to be conducted with considerable discretion, however. Particularly in a company undergoing change, visits from "corporate" are typically viewed with a good deal of suspicion and skepticism. Members of the review team can overcome this problem by being straightforward and candid about the interview's main purpose. The objective is not to stamp out subcultures; rather, it is to identify them so they can be strengthened and reinforced.

Face-to-face interviews are the preferred technique for identifying and categorizing the existence of robust subcultures. But, as the culture industry (spawned in part by our earlier book) has matured, it has developed other helpful methods. A number of culture surveys have been created to assess the state of culture in different parts of companies. Kilmann and Saxton's Cultural Gap Survey (1983) is a good example. It attempts to pinpoint discrepancies between what's desired and what really is happening in cultures related to such important characteristics as information sharing, being creative, socialization within groups, and self-expression. Other surveys, many of them documented in the ever expanding culture literature, are available from culture-oriented consulting firms. Quite a few culture practitioners find these standardized surveys helpful; we prefer bespoke instruments ourselves.

Karen Stephenson, the UCLA professor cited earlier, has devised a set of software tools for mapping cultural networks in organizations. These processes identify who is talking to whom and with what regularity. Since personal contact is crucial to establishing and maintaining trust, her approach can be extremely useful in documenting the existence and coherence of individual subcultures. It also helps pinpoint human linkages between subcultures. Network maps are valuable for understanding an organization's informal working, as shown in Figure 10.1.

Although Stephenson's technology requires a substantial investment in time and resources, its results can be invaluable in identifying an organization's "hubs, gatekeepers and pulse takers." Hubs are people at the center of important cultural communications networks; most important information flows through them. Gatekeepers are unique individuals at the junctures of different cultural networks and often bridge subcultures. Their role is critical in facilitating communications across cultural boundaries. Finally, pulse takers are those who regularly keep in touch with a broad cross-section of subcultural networks. In the past, these well-connected individuals were often dismissed as company gossips. Now people are recognizing the critical role they play in shaping opinions or spreading the word and thereby linking diverse subcultures together. They are cultivated for their cultural benefits and the assistance they can provide an organization undergoing change.

Whatever the approach, the end product of this fieldwork is the identification and characterization of a company's primary subcultures. In effect, it produces a map of the cultural terrain. This map can then be used to help reinforce subcultures as well as encourage independent groups to become the backbone of a more unified company enterprise.

FIGURE 10.1    The Cultural Network

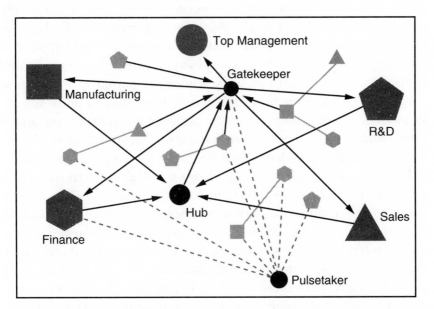

SOURCE: Authors' interpretation of a chart in the article by Tim Ferguson, "Who's Mentoring Whom?" (*Forbes*, May 19, 1997).

## Encouraging Subcultures to Flourish

Subcultures thrive today because of the chaos and confusion produced by knee-jerk management responses to changes in the business environment. In most cases, contemporary subcultures are defensive, self-protective, and extremely resistant to change. They view management's actions as a threat to their very existence. In terms of today's cultural wars, subcultures are survivors, and proud of their autonomy. Subcultures have outlasted management and continue to provide meaning for their members. These remnants of older cultures often provide the building blocks for more coherent cultures of tomorrow. But to revitalize the core culture, subcultures must be encouraged to emerge from their isolated shells. It is the responsibility of senior management to liberate these pockets of energy to play a constructive role in rebuilding a more meaningful workplace.

The first step is to legitimize subcultures. There is no better way to do this than to celebrate their existence. In some respects, this may seem unnatural. Corporations concentrate on presenting a unified face to their publics, both internal and external. For subcultures to flourish and contribute positive energy, corporations must publicly recognize and glorify the diversity they represent. If this produces temporary confusion about a company's image, it is a necessary risk. Strong subcultures always create a degree of cultural confusion. It is typically masked under the patina of order most companies cultivate to present a unified front. But to unify subcultures around a common purpose, it is better to get things out in the open. And this does not mean that subcultures need to shed their unique identities in order to become part of a greater whole.

The most direct way to acknowledge a subculture is to pay a visit and listen carefully to its history and war stories. After that, its beneficial contribution to the corporate whole can be anointed publicly. Even the most busy CEO will find occasion to visit various operations. To legitimize the way subcultures operate, CEOs should modify planned tours to include ample time for hearing the local history and listening to old-timers tell of past successes. The CEO can then recognize subculture heroes for their contributions and congratulate the unit on its unique identity as well as the energy it contributes overall. Listening and congratulating should not be gratuitous and ingratiating. It must be authentic. Few CEOs have listened themselves out of a job. Their genuine interest and heartfelt praise is one of the best ways to draw isolated subcultures into the company fold.

Once individual subcultures emerge and receive accolades, actions at the corporate level can assure on-site messages delivered by the CEO are reinforced in future words and deeds. As an example, corporate publications that extol the virtues of strength through diversity help drive home the message to still skeptical subcultural members. Beyond publications and other formal communications is a more crucial truth we stress again and again: Actions speak louder than words. Company-wide behavioral norms need to guide senior managers in their dealings with disparate subcultures. Subcultures' existence must be respected by all relevant managers, not just the messianic CEO intent on orchestrating a cultural revival. Even more critically, cultural diversity should be fostered by visibly reflecting the unique strengths of subcultures through distinctive advertising and promotion strategies. This can create discomfort in terms of potential impact on corporate strategy and image. But it can go a long way toward restoring the loyalty and confidence of embattled subcultures. Giving people of a unique subculture something to be proud of can encourage them to move more closely under the corporate tent.

Another strategy is having subcultures broadcast their unique virtues. But a word of caution: Once a company embarks on such a revival, it turns back at great peril. Subcultures that once thrived on opposing outside forces may be hypersensitive to suggestions that their existence is now officially sanctioned. They have seen fads come and go many times before. If betrayed this time, they will disappear again into the corporate underground, defying all future efforts to resurrect them. Senior management must be fully committed to cultural revitalization before asking people down the line to stand up and be counted. Management's reward for its courage, patience, and persistence will be the liberation of tremendous amounts of pent-up, isolated energy. Identifying, recognizing, and reinforcing existing pockets of identity and meaning is key to assuring across-the-board cultural revitalization.

## Reinforcing Weaker Subcultures

Not all subcultures are robust enough to take the bait in response to encouragement. Lack of robustness may result from lack of strength, will, or spirit. The failure of the L-1011 aircraft to capture a stronger share of the airline market than the DC-10 was attributed in part to the weakness of Lockheed's marketing group relative to the more powerful engineering subculture of the company. As a result, although many experts saw the L-1011 as a superior airplane, McDonnell Douglas sold far more DC-10s.

The existence of weak subcultures in a corporation poses a real dilemma for senior management. Should they be left to atrophy and eventually die out? Or should something be done to strengthen them, to fill an important niche in the informal corporate pantheon? The answer inevitably turns on hard judgments about the value they could bring to the corporate table if their health and vitality were restored.

Once a weak subculture of potential value has been identified, what actions should management consider to build its confidence and trust? For most of these walking wounded, a modest but thoughtful amount of attention is all that is needed. For example, some years ago an electronics entrepreneur succeeded in acquiring a company that manufactured a range of near commodity electronic components. The nature of its product line had subjected the acquired company's operations to repeated cost reductions. As a result, employees felt beaten down and relegated to the status of second-class citizens. On his first visit to one of the company's largest plants, the acquiring entrepreneur was appalled to find the employees' parking lot a virtual quagmire. In the interests of cost efficiency, it had not been paved, even though the plant was located in the middle of a well-known rain belt. Without hesitating, before even talking to employees, the entrepreneur ordered a contractor to pave the parking lot, landscape the grounds, and introduce a handful of other factory-wide amenities, such as a newly refurbished employee cafeteria. The total expenditure authorized on his first visit was $100,000, one-thousandth of the purchase price paid for the acquisition. The results: an immediate improvement in morale and a workforce transformed into one of the company's most loyal and reliable.

Even such modest expenditures can achieve the desired effect. The underlying issue is rekindling confidence and trust. Simply treating a beaten-down unit with respect and giving them ongoing attention is often enough to convince people that they are valued. Although this does not necessarily remove all feelings of inferiority, it represents a first step in restoring cultural buoyancy to sinking subcultures.

What of other battered groups whose contributions to the corporate whole is seriously in question? Many years ago, we worked with Waters Associates, a high-tech company near Boston. At the time, Waters had a problem: the company's R&D department, previously the source of the technical innovations on which the company depended, had lost its confidence, and its productivity had declined. Since high-tech companies live and die on their ability to invent new technology, the R&D department's situation was not a trivial problem. In response, Frank Zenie, the company's culturally attuned president, configured the R&D department into a separate enterprise called Waters Laboratories. He moved the entire operation to its own facility about a mile away from the company's head office and gave it a renewed charter. Now its mission was to innovate as it saw fit on behalf of the company. Within months the department had a new spring in its step. It soon returned to producing innovations at the caliber that had initially built the company. This cultural solution was so admired that it later was adopted by several other Boston-area high-tech companies.

The idea of setting up a separate R&D facility was not unique to Waters Associates. IBM's Thomas J. Watson Research Labs and Xerox's Research Park are comparable examples. What was notable about the Waters case was that the idea was conceived as a targeted response to a particular cultural problem. Other companies recognized Zenie's wisdom and replicated his lesson.

In some respects, the situation Waters faced is different from that of contemporary companies. Waters in those days was not fragmented into competing subcultures as a result of raging external forces and questionable management practices. It was a healthy, high-performing, and widely respected company. But what Waters did provides a precedent for managers who seek to revitalize today's business culture. If a subculture is essential (as the R&D department was for Waters) and has an important contribution to make to the corporate whole, then extraordinary measures to salvage it may well be warranted.

In responding to the needs of the weak subcultures, measures do not have to include a new physical location or a revved-up identity for a troubled unit. But strategies need to get to the root cause of the subculture's trouble—the reason it lost its confidence and identity. If the issue is inadequate and overstretched staffing, then new hires may be the way to solve the problem. If the issue is a lack of confidence fostered by repeated humiliation by stronger subcultures, then new reporting relationships or communications channels might alleviate the situation. If the issue is deep-seated cynicism caused by a series of negative events, co-opting the subculture into a leading and visible company-wide role may be the way to go. In each case, appropriate steps cost money and often disrupt ongoing corporate activities. These remedies should be launched only with the belief that something of real benefit would be lost if the subculture were to succumb. Once a commitment is made and acted upon, the effect on the subculture should be monitored and fine-tuned. If the measures are properly executed, the subculture's weakness should recede so its role in the process of knitting subcultures into a more cohesive whole can proceed.

## Knitting Subcultures Together

Once a company's subcultures have been identified and measures taken to shore up valuable subgroups, the hard work of knitting subcultures together into a unifying corporate canopy can begin. In a large corporation, this phase can last for years. It involves the discovery of common ground among subcultures and an effort to convert shared ties into a unified set of beliefs. Different from building a culture from the ground up, knitting robust subcultures back together requires acknowledging each subculture's distinctive ways and point of view. These unique differences must be accommodated in weaving the parts into a whole.

The starting point for the process of reknitting is articulating and documenting existing disparate beliefs and points of view. The best way to do this is through a series of gloves-off events facilitated by members of the revitalization team. The number of events needed will depend on several factors. For example, if a subculture's membership is very large (e.g., the remnants of a recent major acquisition), more than a few sessions will be required. If subculture members are spread across physical locations, a minimum of one session per site will probably be needed to capture the essence of what the far-flung group is all about. Whatever the number of events, each should be conducted with care, as each plays an important part in bringing subcultures back into the corporate fold.

Each event should be attended by a variety of subcultural voices. It should include old-timers, the historians of the early years. It should include some up-and-coming insiders, not hotshots imported from other parts of the company. It should also incorporate a mix of functional responsibilities so that a comprehensive group is assembled reflecting the various viewpoints that make the subculture work. No more than two members of upper management should be involved; otherwise the sessions will be seen as another corporate intrusion. As with most effective workshop sessions, active participants in any one event should be limited to ten or fewer.

Should senior leaders of the subculture be active participants in the workshop process? Or should they simply sponsor the event? In an ideal world, incorporating senior members lends legitimacy to the sessions. But if senior managers lack the time to be full-time participants, they are better off staying on the sidelines. Similarly, some senior managers are prone to dominate in public forums ("My view is the only right view"). In this case, their polite exclusion from the process makes good sense.

Agendas will vary depending on a subculture's history and the people who attend the event. Typical topics for discussion include questions such as:

- What is the history of our group? Where did it originate? How long has it been around? Who were some of its leading lights? How much has the group changed over the years? What caused the changes?
- What does this group stand for? What is unique about our group? What distinguishes us from other groups in the company? What are the common characteristics that really make us stand out?
- What are some of the stories or anecdotes from the past that best characterize what we stand for? How widely known are the stories?
- How is this part of the company different from the corporate center, sibling divisions, and units in other geographical areas?
- What half dozen or so words best capture the spirit of this group? What recent events epitomize this common spirit?
- What symbols do people in this group hold most dear? How is affection for these symbols manifest?
- What kinds of celebrations occur? What is being celebrated? How are these celebrations conducted? Are they inclusive affairs or restricted to a chosen few? Are they widely watched by others? What kind of significance is attached to these celebrations? Have long-standing celebrations been aborted? If so, why?
- Who are the acknowledged heroic figures of the subculture? Why? How are these heroes rewarded?
- How do the key aspects of this subculture contribute to the company's economic success? What are some tangible illustrations?

The obvious intent here is to capture in an intelligible way key aspects of each subculture. It can sometimes be difficult to draw people out on these "softer" topics—especially when people feel defensive about their place in the broader corporate firmament. A workshop format for these gatherings favors an informal give-and-take, helping to ease people into the subject at hand. These get-togethers need to last for at least two days (or longer). This gives participants a chance to socialize with one another and to reflect on what is being learned. Symbolic acknowledgments of the emerging group ethic or spirit—relevant mementos such as T-shirts or hats—enhance a shared sense that "what we're doing is important, and we're making a real contribution." Thoughtful thank-you notes from senior management after the event reinforce a feeling of accomplishment and recognize the event's importance.

Managers vary widely in their ability to make such a format work (that is, ensure that the sessions are seen as productive and useful and yield the kinds of information required). Some groups are more amenable to these kinds of sessions than others. Over the years, we have participated in hundreds of such cultural workshops. The vast majority have been effective in terms of building a constructive team ethic among participants. Common sense suggests there should be a reasonable tolerance for failure, especially in a session's early days when the learning curve is highest.

Once the full round of workshops has been concluded, the results need to be compiled and analyzed. This is a task for the centrally convened cultural revitalization team described earlier. It is one of the reasons a representative of this team should attend each workshop session. The analysis should be focused on identifying for each subculture:

- its core beliefs
- the origins of these core beliefs
- the effect core beliefs have on day-to-day behavior
- what the subculture celebrates and why
- who its perceived heroic figures are and why
- gaps subcultural members see between themselves and other corporate groups

Imagine a working conference room with page after page of a flipchart filled with statements in response to this list. You probably have the right image in mind. This is not high-tech work. But it requires meticulous attention to detail and judgment. The purpose of this analysis is to find areas of similarity and dissimilarity among various subcultures. Knitting begins when you find one cultural thread that runs across otherwise differing subcultures. Other threads that represent key disagreements among subcultures may well provide the color and character of the company's fabric. Differences properly acknowledged can themselves be potentially unifying. In one newly merged company, the exercise brought everyone to a revelation: "We are an odd couple, a hodgepodge of different points of view. But it can work. Like it did for Burns and Allen or Abbott and Costello."

As soon as common ground is found, a process should build on areas of agreement to help bond people more closely to the parent company without losing their existing subcultural identification. How this should be done will vary widely based on what emerges from the previous diagnostic work. For example, if it seems clear that most subcultures share strongly held values (quality, service, and respect for the individual are leading candidates), then a corporate initiative can be launched with the purpose of bringing subcultures together around a theme they agree on. Even if there isn't substantial agreement around core beliefs, common threads should be highlighted with the hope that a shared sense of a corporate ethic will eventually emerge. Any such initiative must be perceived as authentic and connected to ongoing company business. It should be action-oriented, not navelgazing. It should be reinforced with a substantial commitment of corporate resources: people, money, or time. That way, all participants can see the initiative as vital to future success. Much of today's corporate fragmentation resulted from the high level of resources committed to cost-cutting programs such as downsizing. This often had the effect of gutting the previous culture. Efforts to rebuild cohesion warrant an equally robust level of commitment.

Situations with little or no consensus about core beliefs may require a more gradualist approach. It may start with only one or two subcultures approaching common ground and working with them to expand the scope and context of their agreement. If cultural fragmentation is severe, such a piecemeal approach may take some time. But without common ground, there is no hope of building anything resembling a shared bond among competing subcultures.

Whether gradualist or a deep plunge, the process needs to concentrate on building consensus around a set of company-wide beliefs.

This process may take several years and must be reinforced continually. Corporate external publications and in-house communications should regularly refer to the emerging consensus. Corporate awards should recognize those who publicly voice their approval of a shared sense of purpose. Finally, business initiatives should be aligned with the developing set of shared values. If service is one of those values, for example, support for it can be killed quickly by activities that deny its relevance to the ongoing commercial life of the company.

Whatever the approach, top management's commitment and visibility are musts. Initial commitment needs to be voiced publicly and sincerely. Enthusiastic endorsement of a celebration to acknowledge the coming together of disparate subcultures should follow in time. Beyond commitment, top management must embrace in words and deeds the emerging consensual values and beliefs. Only through visible witness and ownership will these nascent values and beliefs thrive and form the core of the reemerging cultural bonds.

While working to build consensus around a core of shared beliefs, it is critical that independent subcultures be allowed to continue flourishing in their own ways. Any effort to build consensus around a core set of beliefs will proceed slowly on a stop-and-go basis. To prevent a loss of confidence, it is important to draw strength from existing subcultures. In addition, we are convinced that today's level of corporate fragmentation will never be replaced by a tightly woven culture characteristic of past times. We are equally convinced that such cultural uniformity and cohesion are not in the best interests of most large companies today. To succeed in the current business environment, companies need to tolerate as much diversity as possible to provide flexibility in responding to unpredictable future challenges. Maintaining subgroup strength and coherence while upholding an umbrella of shared beliefs is the formula for building a strong, competitive future enterprise. Once the total package begins to work, benefits of stronger performance will become apparent. The gains will be driven by extra efforts of individuals highly motivated because they are working for something they believe in.

## Delta Corporation's Cultural Revitalization Event

To illustrate the type of cultural revitalization we are advocating, we turn to Harrison Owen's book *Spirit,* where he describes the transformation of Delta Corporation. Years ago an entrepreneur named Harry invented a product that launched a company of 3,500 employees. The company's initial public offering was a success. But soon thereafter, soaring costs, disappointing sales, and the absence of new products arrested the company's performance. It also led to a group of dissatisfied shareholders who pressured Harry to turn over the reins of the company to a new CEO.

Harry's replacement took stock of the situation and quickly realized that she had inherited a series of independent subcultures rather than a unified company. The finance subculture consisted of a new breed of young managers brought in after Harry's departure. The R&D function was split into three different subcultures. At the executive level were those still bonded to the past who continued to look to Harry as a hero. Middle managers in the department had checked out. Behind the scenes each month, they gave a "golden fleece" award to anyone who came up with the idea with the least likely bottom-line potential. At the operational level, a similar attitude prevailed. The widely admired subcultural hero was a guy by the name of Serendipity Sam who won the lion's share of the golden fleece awards. He represented the excitement and innovative ideas of the good old days under Harry's leadership. In essence, the operational group was split into two distinct factions: newcomers who championed the bottom line and old-timers who still were used to the freewheeling days under Harry. Not surprisingly, the war between these rival subcultures was tearing the company apart and destroying its ability to perform.

Once the new CEO knew what she was up against, she convened thirty-five carefully selected people for a two-day management retreat. At the retreat, she announced her vision. She wanted a company where "engineers could fly" rather than a company "at a standstill, going downhill." As Owen recounts, she surprised everyone with her strategy:

> She opened with some stories of the early days, describing the intensity of Old Harry and the Garage Gang (now known as the Leper Colony). She even had one of the early models of Harry's machine out on a table. Most people had never seen one. It looked rather primitive, but during the coffee break, members of the Leper Colony surrounded the ancient artifact and began swapping tales of the blind alleys, the

late nights, and the breakthroughs. That dusty old machine became a magnet. Young shop floor folks went up and touched it, sort of snickering as they compared this prototype with the sleek creations they were manufacturing now. But, even as they snickered, they stopped to listen as the Leper Colony recounted tales of accomplishment. It may have been just a "prototype," but that's where it all began.

After an animated coffee break, the CEO divided the group into subgroups. Each subgroup consisted of a mix of existing subculture members. She asked the groups to share their hopes for the company. When the groups reconvened, the chairs had been arranged into a circle. Harry's first prototype was now in the circle's center. The CEO then led a discussion weaving in stories from the various subcultures. Serendipity Sam suddenly rose to his feet with an excited but almost incomprehensible idea for a new product. Then the group came together:

> The noise level was fierce, but the rest of the group was being left out. Taking Sam by the hand, the CEO led him to the center of the circle, right next to the old prototype. There it was, the old and the new—the past, present and potential. She whispered in Sam's ear that he ought to take a deep breath and start over in words of one syllable. He did so, and in ways less than elegant, the concept emerged. He guessed about applications, competitors, market shares, and before long, the old VP for finance was drawn in. No longer was he thinking about selling (tax) losses, but rather thinking out loud about how he was going to develop the capital to support the new project. The group from the shop floor . . . began to spin a likely tale as to how they might transform the assembly line to make Sam's new machine. Even the Golden Fleece crowd became excited, telling each other how they had always known Serendipity Sam could pull it off. They conveniently forgot that Sam had been the recipient of a record number of their awards, to say nothing of the fact that this new idea had emerged in spite of their rules.

In one fell swoop, the CEO got what she wanted: "a group of engineers who could fly"—in a profitable way. Existing subcultural boundaries were bridged, everyone coming together behind the shared new idea. The event succeeded because (1) the CEO had done her homework identifying the existing subcultural divisions, (2) she included all the key people in the off-site event, and (3) the event itself was well organized with a real symbolic flair. The CEO's next task was to be sure the new spirit would translate into measurable results. We cannot, of course, guarantee you similar results from cultural revitalization efforts you undertake. But the potential for meaningful change and coming together is always there.

## Measuring Progress

Common business sense says that you can't manage what you don't measure. Despite our interest in the softer side of companies, we are firm devotees of measurement. Cultural revitalization programs require a substantial commitment of corporate time, energy, and resources. It is only fitting that progress should be measured.

There are two interrelated reasons for working hard to rebuild a coherent corporate culture. First and most important is that cultural revitalization will improve financial performance over the long term. Improved performance occurs step by step along the way. It can and should be measured and monitored. One of the main responsibilities of senior management is to ensure that an appropriate monitoring system is in place. The second reason is that measuring progress is the only way to manage the evolution of the program itself, as discussed below.

What should such a measurement program look like? On the surface, it should be very conventional, measuring performance in terms familiar to the company's financial managers. The trick is in deciding what baseline to use. Performance improvement comes about because the employees are more confident in what they are doing. They are also more willing to put in the extra effort required to produce exemplary results. Because the starting point is cultural shambles, these improvements take time. But they can be anticipated and tracked. As confidence in individual units mounts, it is perfectly reasonable to expect performance levels to improve over baseline budgets. Thus a monitoring unit can be targeted to look for upside performance surprises where cultural revitalization is beginning to take off. When the revitalization program extends throughout the entire corporation, overall performance should begin to show upside surprises. This progress can be tracked and monitored—if for no other reason than to justify continued investment in rebuilding a shattered culture. Attention to the cultural side of company life should soon yield improved performance increments of pleasingly large dimensions.

To track financial performance meaningfully, the progress of the revival effort also must be tracked. This is more complicated technically since there are few valid or agreed-on measures of cultural strength or coherence. Unfortunately, the state of the art remains highly judgmental: You know it when you see it. Yet cultural revitalization can be tracked—even if measures are somewhat suspect and subject to frequent fine-tuning. For example, employee attitude surveys have long been used to gauge overall workplace climate. Most are useless because they try to be all things to all people. As a result, attitude surveys usually end up with results so homogenized as to defy interpretation or action. But the idea remains sound, even if past execution is questionable. Survey instruments can be designed to measure specific changes in attitude—changes the revitalization team anticipates. By tailoring surveys to individual situations and modifying them as the program progresses, these can become valuable tools for tracking success. Coupled with a hard-nosed look at performance numbers, surveys can provide oversight necessary to manage cultural revitalization effectively. You can manage only what you measure. But if you do it right, the measurements you take should quickly convince you of the merits of addressing cultural needs. The gains should be particularly obvious in the aftermath of the cultural damage throughout the 1980s and 1990s. The potential payoff is twofold: the well-being of employees and the financial performance of the company.

•    •    •

Revitalizing wounded cultures is not an easy undertaking. Efforts of the type we advocate are daunting. But they provide the only hope for rebuilding corporate unity severely damaged by the business developments of recent decades. Companies that have had the good fortune to survive relatively unscathed should be able to pick and choose elements without committing to a full-blown effort. Others may well have to start virtually from scratch. Whatever it takes, the journey is well worth the effort.

## CHAPTER 11

# Building Momentum

## The Fun Part

Management, by definition, means taking purposeful action. Suppose your company is experiencing a cultural crisis. If you are a top dog and care enough about the human and performance implications, you have no real choice but to act. The only question is how. To some managers this may loom as a burdensome chore far outside their comfort zone, but it doesn't have to be. Managing culture can be fun. And the fun can yield even greater performance benefits from a turned-on workforce. The fun parts of the job come once the basics are under control. What are the tools you can use to turn cultural crisis into an opportunity for having fun at work? They are limited only by your creativity and imagination. We scratch the surface here.

### Work and the "F" Word—"Fun"

"Fun and work don't belong on the same combo plate," a participant in a Kodak Park meeting once remarked to Stephen Frangos. "Besides—it just doesn't sound dignified. I don't think anyone is going to take us seriously if they heard about 'fun,'" he went on to add. As reported in his book *Team Zebra,* Frangos was bothered by this comment. But he bit his tongue and agreed to use the word "enjoyable" as a substitution for the "f" word. Later in the book he observed, "Every culture can accommodate some level of enjoyment, and when people loosen up, their creativity reaches new heights." Unfortunately, the last couple of decades of work have replaced fun with fear. W. Edward Deming, the quality guru, saw fear as a major predator of creativity at work. We agree.

A leading postwar British politician, it was reported, never permitted himself to urinate before giving a public speech. His reasoning: tension brought on by discomfort kept him on edge. Although modern managers might think his reasoning specious, many approach their managerial tasks assuming that high stress is key to inducing top employee performance. "The beatings will continue until we improve," a popular poster proclaims. The evidence to the contrary is simply overwhelming. People produce their best results when they are relaxed and comfortable in their work environments. Nothing relaxes people more than a touch of humor. And an atmosphere that is fun is conducive to laughter. Putting the fun back into work is one of the key steps managers can take to revitalize a fear-bound and overly tense workforce.

Of course work has its serious side. People at all levels work to do a job, to accomplish goals both for themselves and for the company, and to get paid a decent wage for their labor. These are the rational, serious aspects of work. But people work for other reasons. They go to work to meet other people and to share experiences with them. They work to feel good about themselves and to experience a sense of satisfaction. These are some of the social reasons people work, and they are at least as important as work's serious side.

Because of its social context, life at work is more than just doing a job. It is a way of life where people spend lots of time. If work is fulfilling, people will perform to their optimum. If work is enjoyable, they will be more willing to commit themselves. If work is even more, read "fun," people will pour their hearts and souls into what they do. That's why putting fun into work is such an important topic for managers: It produces better results for everyone concerned—employers, employees, and society at large.

## Making Meetings—Planned and Unplanned—Memorable

Within large organizations, a good deal of face-to-face contact takes place in meetings. Oddly enough, the actual agenda, however important, is less material than the informal chitchat occurring around a meeting's periphery. It is in such informal exchanges that crucial information is exchanged, big deals are consummated, and relationships among attendees are cemented. Informal communication dominates the formal agenda of virtually all corporate meetings. Memories of bons mots uttered during the meeting become the "minutes" participants recall and become part of a company's legend and lore.

Take, for example, this meeting: Senior managers of a large and respected capital goods manufacturer were meeting to plan an international strategy for the business. At the end of a long presentation arguing that an investment of $150 million might be needed to "lock up" the business in a major Latin American market, the head guy leaned back in his chair and remarked, "This business has the appetite of an elephant and the asshole of a bird." Later in the meeting, when asked to comment on the overall thrust of the presentations outlining the proposed business strategy, the same leader commented: "The graphics were dazzling." This individual, one of the most beloved and respected businesspeople of his time, left an immortal legacy. He is remembered as much for his remarks as he is for thirty years of accomplishment in an illustrious career.

The single most important communications channel in any organization is word of mouth. This is true because people place a premium on trust in their communications. The business world has yet to invent a means of establishing trust to compete with close, face-to-face contact. For those who have established a personal bond, e-mail has provided a means to keep the relationship alive when direct contact is not feasible. But only for the small number of computer geeks haunting chat rooms on the Internet can electronic handshakes compete with the old-fashioned physical kind. There is just no substitute for flesh-to-flesh, eyeball-to-eyeball contact.

What do people talk about when they bump into one another? Whether it's in the hall, around the watercooler, on the telephone—even over the Internet—they talk about human issues. They compare notes on their families and social lives. They share anecdotes about mutual acquaintances. When this list of topics is exhausted, they tell the latest joke they have heard. Such interactions are valuable because they affirm people's humanity. Informal comings and goings provide a context in which relationships are formed and renewed.

Companies invest enormous time and energy in planning meetings. They want their forums to be efficient uses of executive time. They want participants focused on specific issues at hand and attuned to actionable results. But most companies don't realize that just getting people together is probably the most important aspect of meetings. All of us have suffered through bad meetings—a poorly formulated agenda and a discussion run amuck. We tend to forget that even poorly conceived meetings serve other purposes, sometimes just providing grist for gossip mills in months to come.

Some time ago we sat through a series of meetings when frontline employees of a large multinational corporation were paraded before their bosses and peers. They reported on significant problems they were having in delivering routine services to customers. The theory behind the meetings was that time spent by senior management listening to problems of frontline service staff would send strong signals about the cultural importance of customers. The actual signals received were somewhat different. In the course of one meeting, a senior executive reacted negatively when one of "his people" described a service problem unique to "his organization." At the first available break, he rushed to a pay phone in the hotel lobby where the meeting was being held. He placed a call to the headquarters of his operation. A passerby overheard him telling the person on the other end: "Fix the f——ing problem or find some other way to make a living in the future." Anyone who participated in the meeting remembers only the string of expletives the senior executive poured into the pay phone. The message was clear: "This is an organization that operates along strong hierarchical lines. Don't ever do anything again to embarrass your boss in front of his peers." The signal received was obviously not the one intended by the meeting's organizers.

Informal communication plays a major role in influencing the culture of companies. The informal network resounds with stories about what is going on, who is doing what, and how people are reacting to events. Stories fill people in on who seems to be getting ahead or left behind in recent corporate changes and how the mission is changing. Not all stories passed along in the informal network are true. They are truer than true. They are perceived to be true because of their source, another human being. Even if greeted with skepticism, stories are believed to convey important metaphorical messages. The informal network of communications has a life of its own and creates a unique reality that has real meaning for most people.

If informal communications are so important, how can managers make use of this channel to revitalize a company's culture? The answer is obvious: They need to get out and about. Actions of the "big boss" are the most closely scrutinized actions in any corporate hierarchy. Relatively insignificant events and comments are rapidly transcribed into the daily-changing cultural mythology. If the boss appears concerned, rumors go forth that the company is in trouble. If the boss appears to be happy, stories are created to explain the origin of his or her happiness and what it means for the company's priorities. If the boss chastises someone in the course of making rounds, rumors fly as to whose career is on the upswing or whose star is fading. The behavior of the "big boss" is always watched and interpreted. Like it or not, senior managers are living logos. Their words and deeds send strong cultural signals.

Many years ago, Joe Wilson, the legendary chief executive of then fledgling Xerox, was walking through the company's main factory in Webster, New York (just outside Rochester). He spied a copier being packaged for shipment and objected to the bright orange panels on the machine. The people within earshot immediately interpreted his objection as an order to remove the offensive panels. From that day forward, Xerox has never manufactured a machine with orange panels.

Steve Case, CEO of Internet highflyer America Online, has a reputation as an introvert and a loner. He was reported in *Aol.com*, Kara Swisher's 1998 book, as spending more time in chat-line conversations at his computer terminal than meeting with employees— all this during the company's turbulent growth years. This did not prevent the employees from determining that the stone-faced Case was an island of calm in the surrounding turmoil. His perceived steadiness is cited as a key factor in holding the company together as it stumbled from one apparent disaster to another.

Case's experience at America Online offers valuable insights for other senior managers. To assume a leadership role does not require a person to be a performer on stage. Although some CEOs are natural-born showpeople, some aren't. Case was not. But he was deeply devoted to the company. His influence was far broader than his actual role because of his sincere concern for the company and its progress. CEOs should take the example of Case (and legions of others like him) to heart. What's most important is what you stand for, not how well you play the game.

Hewlett-Packard popularized the phrase "management by walking around." It was based on its founders' penchant for informality and close contact with employees. We see walking around as an activity very well suited for communicating openly and visibly what you really stand for. The characters in informal cultural networks need fodder for doing their work of interpreting the culture. Having the boss observed demonstrating values on a day-to-day basis gives them great material. Although it is not a complete antidote for a sick culture, failure to use the most powerful communications tool available makes the rest of the job harder.

Besides, getting out and about is fun. Walking around lets you meet a lot of interesting people. You become privy to information that's otherwise unavailable. You have a chance to share in the workplace banter and laughter. If you listen very carefully, you can pick up on people's real concerns. Getting out there may help you feel more human. Even more important, it will help others see you as a real person—living out important values.

## When Formal and Informal Communications Interact

Every company has an array of formal internal communications media—company magazines (known mostly by their informal name as house organs), company newsletters, press releases, and summaries of press coverage. These are distributed widely so employees know what images are being communicated to the outside world. They also keep employees up-to-date on breaking news and the latest developments. Most of these documents are extremely well done and rival the glossiest consumer publications in quality of artwork and design. Unfortunately, they often fall behind market-oriented publications in conveying meaningful information to the internal target audience. Despite this, they are among the best-read print publications in the world. Employees devour internal media for signals and clues about what's really going on.

Why do most formal employee-oriented publications fail so miserably in their attempts to communicate? The answer is because production of these documents is delegated to a specialized unit often known as the corporate communications department. Its members are often ill equipped to shoulder the crucial responsibility they are given. Corporate communications people are almost always journalists or journalism majors. They know little about business and spend most of their time in awe of the fact that they are earning so much doing a real corporate job. They should not be blamed for failure to do a better job. They often receive inadequate support from senior management and sit outside the loop of important information. They hear little of substance. As a consequence, they focus on form rather than function. A corporate communicator we know once complained to his CEO about the weight of the paper available for the company's newsletter. The CEO asked him in return: "What's that got to do with either your job or our business?"

Have you ever wondered why personality-oriented magazines such as *People* in the United States or *L'Express* in Europe enjoy such huge readerships? It is because they satisfy a natural curiosity we all have about the comings and goings of other people. Corporate magazines could up their levels of popularity if they satisfied the same curiosity, if they addressed important everyday comings and goings and featured real people doing their jobs. Typically, they do not. What is lost is an opportunity to convey cultural messages to the corporate community.

The managing director of a major professional services firm was determined to put his stamp on the firm during his tenure. One of his pet peeves was the firm's laid-back nature. The firm had become so successful that people waited for the phone to ring to alert them to new business opportunities (rather than actively searching for potential new clients). To counteract this lethargy, he published a feature in the monthly staff publication called "Notes from the Managing Director's Calendar." His column was crammed with examples of his regular and vigorous effort to beat the bushes for new business. His notes became required reading among the staff about what the boss was up to.

Shortly after the column appeared, the managing director was dealing with two of the firm's major clients, an automobile manufacturer and a major consumer products company. In a perhaps apocryphal story, one day he found himself in a meeting at the latter firm, an appointment he rushed to after a hurried visit to operations in Europe. The topic of the meeting was a debate over a major policy in the consumer products field. Fatigued from his travels, the manager arose from a temporary reverie to ask, "What kind of a car company do you want to be?" His colleagues quickly jumped in to smooth over the noticeable gaffe and managed to get the meeting back on track. From that time on, "Notes from the Managing Director's Calendar" always seemed to have a subtitle: "And What Kind of Car Company Do You Want to Be?" This humorous error even spiked employee interest in the column.

Interviews with the press are another underexploited means of reinforcing cultural themes. But many if not most senior managers are afraid of the news media. They feel little or nothing positive comes from publicity not controlled by the company. What they should realize is that the most interested readers of their public pronouncements are their own employees (and a few financiers hoping to make a profit on the company's stock). Public interviews are superb ways to communicate to the public as well as to employees that the company stands for more than its current roster of products and reported financial performance. Few senior managers take appropriate advantage of them (with some notable exceptions, like the remarkable Percy Barnevik of Asea Brown Boveri, who enlisted the world's press in his campaign to reorient his company).

In most corporations, advertisements are seen as the province of marketing people as they try to gain market share for goods and services. Occasionally, an ad might catch the eye of the public because of its obvious appeal to employees as well as the consuming public. Advertisements by Avis, Saturn, and Southwest Airlines are good examples. Unfortunately, most advertisements offer banal messages, as though human beings aren't producing the product or service. As a result, opportunities for reinforcing cultural messages and themes are lost.

Similarly, companies engage in a variety of promotions to project their identity into public view. Often this is done in the context of supporting a worthy charity. In recent years, a favorite target of sponsorship is sports events, especially professional golf tournaments. What exactly do the sponsors of such events hope to convey to the public? The intended messages fall prey to other interpretations, such as, "Our senior executives are fat cats with nothing better to do than swan around golf courses with overpaid golf professionals." Or, "If you work your behind off as an employee, you, too, can take time off to play golf in the middle of the workweek." Surely thoughtful corporate executives can do better than this. Quite modest adjustments in ongoing communications programs can capture lost opportunities to reinforce what the company believes in and stands for.

## Heroic Figures

Every day, employees carry out thousands of company activities. Many activities are boring and routine. Others are selfishly motivated and self-serving. Still others represent extraordinary efforts to further the interests of the company. Looking across all employee activities in a typical business day, it should be clear that hundreds of extraordinary feats are performed routinely by nearly anonymous employees. Ordinary people doing extraordinary things are cultural heroes. But how often are they recognized or rewarded for their heroic behavior?

Heroic figures are important because they represent the larger-than-life characters others aspire to become. They are the subjects of endless stories celebrating their exploits. Over time, if their heroic exploits continue, they will be elevated into a cultural hall of fame reserved for those who do so much and seem incapable of doing wrong. People often invent heroes to fill gaps in their own experiences.

Most good companies seek out role models and play an active part in singling out special people for attention. For example, British Telecom has been on a virtual crusade to instill quality thinking as part of its culture. One of the devices used is a quality awards dinner. Individuals or groups of employees who have performed above and beyond normal expectations receive awards and recognition. Following the dinner, the company publishes a glossy booklet summarizing the history of the quality program and describing the exploits of the contemporary figures who exemplify what the program is trying to accomplish. Although the celebration is somewhat mechanistic (perhaps in keeping with the ethos of a British business institution), the company showcases the making of heroes at its finest. Few employees of BT are left in doubt about what the company values or why.

Other companies make an even bigger splash in singling out employees who have performed above and beyond the call of duty. For example, Southwest Airlines, renowned for its people orientation, honors ten to twelve employees every month for actions that exemplify the company's values. Candidates for "winning spirit" awards, as they are called, are nominated by fellow employees or customers. A central committee decides who warrants the awards each month. Those chosen are invited to headquarters and receive special pins, plaques, and free travel passes. Their stories are then published in the regular employee newsletter, "Luv Lines." This monthly process is augmented with an annual awards banquet. Long-standing employees are rewarded for their tenure with the company. Extraordinary individuals are singled out for their contributions to the company's values. Not stopping at regularly scheduled occasions, the company is quick to sponsor a spontaneous, on-the-spot celebration when something special occurs. Examples include the "sense of humor" award, the "most spirited in-law" award, the "heart and soul" award, the "creativity and guts" award, an award for training excellence, a "tell it like it is" award, and a "hairdresser of the year" award. Remember Southwest has the highest employee productivity of any airline in the world. By all reports, it is also a fun place to work.

Face-to-face events present opportunities for recognition. But they also enrich management with a wealth of anecdotes about what is going right. When recounted, such anecdotes help spread cultural messages and priorities. There is nothing more satisfying and gratifying than congratulating people for special efforts made on behalf of the company. There are rarely long faces associated with sincere efforts to recognize exemplary performance. The manual of corporate behavior does not specify that senior managers are not allowed to enjoy themselves, or even have fun, as they perform their duties. Anointing heroic figures is one of management's most fun activities.

## Celebrating Victories

At one time or another, virtually every corporation puts on a special event to acknowledge the extra performance of some group of its

employees. Classic among these corporate celebrations are retirement ceremonies in which loyal employees of thirty, forty, and fifty
years' tenure are awarded their proverbial gold watch in recognition
of faithful service. With the advent of downsizing, many older employees are being encouraged (actually forced) to make their futures
elsewhere. As a result, retirement celebrations have diminished as a
fixture on corporate calendars. But they continue as an informal aspect of corporate life, often as occasions for employees to denigrate
the company for its heartless policies.

What's wrong with this picture? What is missing from the current
batch of corporate events that once made them the most anticipated
occasions on employees' calendars? We believe the answer is soul—
a sincere belief in the importance of what is being celebrated. Issues
of scale also inhibit many corporations from continuing long-standing traditions of celebration. Thus many corporate environments are
denuded of trappings that once had broad appeal for employees and
customers alike.

Where do authentic celebrations come from? They arise from attempts by people to embellish the milestones in their lives. In our
personal lives, birthdays, weddings, anniversaries, births—even
deaths—provide occasions for celebration. These, of course, differ
depending on the focus of the event. Larger social groupings also
celebrate the passing of great events. Anniversaries of historical moments provide occasions for national holidays. In most parts of the
world, these are events of great joy. Even events as seemingly trivial
as winning a sports competition give rise to deeply held emotions of
pride. People enjoy being part of something bigger (such as the over-
the-top celebrations of France's unexpected triumph in the World
Cup soccer tournament).

Why do modern corporations eschew such natural human responses to the passing of significant milestones? Part of the reason is
that many corporations have fewer and fewer things to celebrate—
at least in public. Other than the family of the beneficiary, who
would gather to celebrate the cashing in of yet another stock option
by an overpaid CEO (particularly when it comes on the heels of continuing announcements of belt-tightening)? Who even among stock-
owning employees would rally to a meeting commemorating new
stock price highs? Who, other than a team of investment bankers,
would celebrate the announcement of yet another merger (especially

when another 10,000 jobs are about to be eliminated)? This is the kind of news that has commanded attention in the corporate world during the 1990s. It is no surprise that traditions of celebration have atrophied or have died out altogether.

Not all corporations are deprived. As noted above, Southwest Airlines, admittedly buoyed by a string of corporate successes, holds celebratory events at the drop of a hat. Despite all the changes the institution has undergone over the years, Citicorp has kept alive a tradition of lavish staff Christmas parties that celebrate being part of the Citibank family. One wonders whether this will continue under the cost-conscious scrutiny of Sandy Weill and his Travelers colleagues now that the world's largest mooted merger has gone through. America Online celebrated the entry of Microsoft into the online services market. The entry of an established company like Microsoft legitimized the online services arena for all participants, including AOL. The event they threw to commemorate the occasion was one of AOL's most memorable festivities: Its central motif was a picture of a dinosaur, Microsoft, about to be slain.

The truth is that celebrations are good for the soul. The failure of modern corporations to continue such spirited traditions is a huge mistake. Celebrations, in their purest form, are occasions to applaud belonging to something worthwhile. We're all social animals. We want to belong to a community of other people. There is no excuse for not encouraging celebrations to bring people together around things that they are proud of. In companies intent on revitalizing a fragmented culture, rediscovering celebrations is a significant step in the recovery process.

## Play

Ordinary people play at work—not all of the time and usually not in a way that prevents them or others from carrying out their work. People play to relax from the tensions of the normal workday. They play because it helps them get their minds off whatever work (or personal) subject they are preoccupied with. They play because it offers an innocent opportunity to bond with their work colleagues. Finally, people play because it is just nice to let your hair down and relax sometimes. By playing, employees are just being human. They are returning to a simpler time in their lives when they were younger and play was expected of them. As a result, they became a lot more creative.

Microsoft programmers involved in writing and debugging code for the operating system that became the standard for IBM-compatible PCs around the world used to have water fights in the corridors outside their offices. These same programmers often worked through the night to make sure they met their deadlines. Nevertheless, their behavior was said to shock their more disciplined colleagues from IBM. They were not used to such antics on the job (or would not admit to it, even if they were). These same IBMers likely spent time during the day arranging their golf dates for the coming weekend (when most of the water-fighting Microsoft programmers were still toiling away). IBM, after all, was and still is a golfing culture.

Staffers at America Online are accustomed to holding Friday afternoon beer blasts in their offices in Virginia. They are not alone in adopting this practice. Hundreds of other companies, especially those in high-tech industries, are devotees of beer blasts. The late Robert Miner, responsible for developing the database technology that propelled Oracle to its leading market position, took a break most afternoons to play a quiet game of chess. His boss, Larry Ellison (now a billionaire), used to interrupt his own and colleagues' work for impromptu games of tennis or basketball. Actuaries at John Hancock Insurance put almost as much energy into intramural softball games as they put into their work for the company. Many years ago, two trainee actuaries spent their spare time using the insurance company's computers to analyze patterns at the nearby Wonderland dog-racing track. Consultants at McKinsey & Company traditionally reserved their most competitive tendencies, if that can be believed, for challenging their peers in a weekly pro football pool. In recent years, the season has extended into the summer, where a particularly virulent game of rotisserie baseball is the focus of their competitive drive. People at work do play, and do so at the drop of a hat. No malice toward employers is intended.

If play is such an important part of work, why isn't it part of the managerial agenda? It can't be because managers are afraid to interfere in the personal lives of their employees: Cost-reduction initiatives of the 1990s have thrown millions of lives into disarray. Perhaps it is simply because managers, especially senior managers, feel it is beneath them to participate in the playful side of work. Whatever the reason, managers are missing a lot by standing on the sidelines rather than being active participants.

Play at work relaxes tensions. It acts as a leveler between different hierarchical ranks. It creates innumerable, informal opportunities for the exchange of views. Because it is so much fun, play becomes a major focus for informal conversations that help define what any company is about. Play is the dance of culture, the most expressive and creative act that occurs to bring people together and make them feel that they belong. Play bonds people together as human beings who can laugh together, strive together, and compete against one another without rancor.

Are we suggesting that a CEO of a major corporation should put on his running shoes and try out for one of the softball teams competing in a company league? We are not at all opposed to such an idea: Direct involvement in the company's play may well pay dividends far beyond anything else a CEO may undertake to try to pull a workforce together into a closely knit team. CEOs make more time for golf games with fellow CEOs and with close cronies. Perhaps they should consider making time for informal participation in other, more broadly based examples of play as well. Short of this, CEOs and senior managers can signal their genuine involvement in the life of the company by taking the playful side of company life more seriously. Showing up at an intramural softball game may not have the same impact as actually playing in it, but it can make the manager appear more human. Participating in a corporate-sponsored golf tournament offers few opportunities for informal, face-to-face interactions with employees because of the way the game of golf is played. Still, it may signal a willingness to get down in the sand trap with everyone else if that's what it takes. Being an enthusiastic member of the office betting pool may not win friends and influence the rank and file, especially if the manager has either good judgment or good luck, but it gives employees someone they can relate to. Maybe the next time a communication comes down from the executive suite, people will pay attention.

There are many different styles of leadership senior managers can adopt. They should always adopt a style that is real and makes them feel comfortable. Any senior manager interested in revitalizing the culture of his or her company cannot afford to ignore major opportunities to exercise influence and to demonstrate a commitment to company-wide values. Participating in play is one such major opportunity to be exploited.

## Humor

Ernest Hemingway was once quoted as having said, "Humor is like a layer of good manure: It makes things grow." So it is with humor in the workplace. It loosens people up. It helps people keep the inevitable challenges of the job in context and attack work-related problems with fresh vigor and perspective. It helps people take themselves less seriously than they might otherwise. As a result, it clears their minds to take seriously what others around them have to say. It defuses tense situations and makes it easier to get on with the tasks at hand. It energizes people to put forward their best efforts because it helps prevent them from becoming embittered and discouraged in the heat of battle. It is not that work itself is not deadly serious. It is, but it is done best when people are feeling good. Humor makes people feel good about themselves and their work environment.

No matter how grim the situation, humor is pervasive in the workplace. Most often it manifests itself in the indomitable desire of people to tell one another jokes, however banal. In the best of places and among the best of people, many of the jokes are turned inward: People make fun of themselves and by doing so convince others around them that they are people to be reckoned with. Anything that leads to laughter is fair game in the world of jokesters. The work environment always has one or more of them around all the time. Without humor, going to work day in and day out would be dull and oppressive.

Modern computer technology, surprisingly, has given a new impetus to humor at work through the widespread use of intranets and electronic mail. In the early days of the Internet, many said that its main use was to carry pornographic material around the world. No more: electronic mail is the ultimate comedy club, particularly at work. More time is likely spent sharing jokes around company networks and across company boundaries than is spent in routine correspondence. That's how important jokes are to people at work.

The funny thing about humor at work is that it is often turned off in the presence of the boss. For whatever reason (prior experience, in most cases), people at work tend to assume that the boss has no sense of humor. They also assume that the boss will be upset if they are seen joking at work. Bosses reinforce this perception by being overly serious and walking around with the sort of grim demeanor that would discourage even the liveliest of pranksters. What a lost opportunity this is. Southwest Airlines actively encourages its employees to joke at work by offering awards to those who do the best job of it in the eyes of their colleagues. Cynics would argue that Southwest's encouragement of humor is designed to appeal in an offbeat way to the customers who choose it because it is a low-fare airline. Although there may be some truth in this, we doubt it is all of the explanation for Southwest's policy. We believe that Southwest encourages humor in the workplace because it recognizes that a happy workforce works harder and better than a workforce turned in on itself. Why others haven't realized this is one of the mysteries of modern worklife.

Aside from getting more work out of a happy workforce, why should managers encourage their workers to see the lighter side of life? We believe that the answer lies deep in the heart of the cultural life of companies and societies everywhere. People who live in tight-knit societies and people who work in strong corporate cultures continually celebrate the fact that they are members of an elite. Although celebrations can have their serious side, they would not be celebrations if they were not shot through with laughter (implicitly, laughter on the part of individuals who feel happy and privileged to belong to the society or culture that embraces them). Thus laughter is the clue or trigger that brings back fond memories of belonging to something worthwhile. Put in this context, managers who want to revitalize the cultural lives of their corporations should applaud every time they hear laughter around them. Laughter is a visible sign and reminder that people are happy doing what they are doing. They appreciate belonging to something they value and are glad to be part of something special. An increase in the level of day-to-day humor is the surest sign that progress is being made toward rebuilding a cohesive culture.

## Managing the Fun Quotient

Max Gould, a senior vice president of Citibank, was famous not only for his effectiveness as a manager but also for "Max's maxims." These pithy little sayings encapsulated Gould's managerial view of the world and much wisdom about the art of management itself. Two of the more notable of the maxims are "You can't manage what you don't measure" and "Inspect, don't expect." If as a manager you want to put some fun into your workplace, we suggest you take Max's maxims to heart.

To enter the paradoxical world of managing fun, you must decide whether you are having any fun at work yourself. We suggest you go about this in a slightly more structured way than you might otherwise. Start keeping a "fun diary." In this daily commentary, start keeping cryptic notes about everything fun you come across in the workplace. If you had fun at a meeting, note it; if someone told you a story or a joke that made you laugh, write it down; if a situation strikes you as so absurd that it makes you laugh, make an entry. At the end of the month, check back to see how much fun you have had.

You might even want to keep a little measure of fun; for the sake of argument, we'll call it the fun quotient (FQ). This FQ could measure how many times you had fun each day and whether the trend was up or down during the month—nothing fancy, just a simple little metric of whether or not you are enjoying yourself at work. As you look at this metric, ask yourself the question, "What can I do to make going to work more fun?" No matter how uncomfortable the answer is, go for it.

Having more fun yourself is only the first baby step in managing fun into the workplace. Really advanced fun management comes when you try to make sure that everyone around you is having fun, too. Your diary and its fun quotient may come in handy here. When you observe people having fun, note it. Try wherever possible to understand and note why they are gleeful. Is it because of who is running the meeting? Is it because of the kind of agenda that was set? Is it a function of the mix of people who are assembled? Did you play any role yourself in making sure the event was a fun experience for the people involved? Remember not to philosophize too much about your observations or read too much into them as you write them down. If you take the exercise too seriously, you may kill the fun. Keep a record so you can go back and think about it at your leisure.

Once you have enough observations, step back and look at who is having fun and why. Look into your heart and try to make a judgment about whether the overall fun quotient is where you want it to be. If it is not, think what you can do to change it—you, personally: God forbid appointing a committee to the task. Take some personal responsibility for making a difference along this simple dimension of the organization you run. You may surprise yourself at the amount of influence you can have and the speed with which it is manifest.

The trick, of course, is balance. Work is not meant to be fun all the time. But neither is it meant always to be drudgery. If you truly believe, as we do, that people enjoying themselves will be more committed and more productive, give it a try. What have you got to lose? Besides, it's fun.

# CHAPTER 12

# Ensuring High Performance

## The Tough Part

W hy work to rebuild a strong corporate culture? Among the many reasons, a good one stands out: because you want the company to achieve sustained, superior financial performance. Playing the culture card is one way to pursue such an objective. A strong and revitalized business culture, attuned to the prevailing environment, should be capable of producing extraordinary results. But no organization has ever raised the performance bar without having both the management and leadership to achieve higher standards. Moreover, no organization meets extraordinary standards for very long without continually monitoring performance. To succeed, individuals and groups need feedback on what they are doing right and where they can do better.

Achieving performance gains is not an automatic by-product of building a cohesive and confident culture. It also takes purposeful management. It makes no sense to invest significant time and energy into revitalizing culture without seeking bottom-line benefits that should begin to accrue. Since every business is a people business, creating a high-performing culture puts managing people center stage.

251

## Hiring the Right People

Randall Stross, in *The Microsoft Way*, cites the coherence and consistency of the company's long-standing hiring practices as a primary reason behind its phenomenal success. Microsoft hires only the very brightest people. Management, from Bill Gates on down, is heavily involved in all aspects of the hiring process. Aggressive interviewing techniques used with candidates suggest that verbal quickness is also essential for getting a job offer. Microsoft eschews experience and academic credentials in looking for new hires. It believes that smart people will figure out what to do, and really smart people will be far more productive than their more average counterparts. Although smart and verbally aggressive people may not always make for a pleasant working environment, Microsoft's hiring practices guarantee it a degree of cultural cohesion that few companies can match.

In an industry entirely different, though just as dependent on intellectual prowess, a similar emphasis on hiring the right people is evident. McKinsey & Company, the world's leading management consulting firm, invests incredible amounts of senior management time in recruitment. In addition to intelligence, McKinsey looks for evidence of leadership in its candidates, expressed in either conventional or unconventional ways. Verbal facility and superior performance earlier in their lives are musts. Consistency of recruitment policies over the years has guaranteed McKinsey a cohesive and aggressive culture. It is a major factor in the company's lengthy reign at the top of the management consulting industry.

Both Microsoft and McKinsey recognize a reality of life in business: People want to be surrounded by others just like them. It is no real surprise that casual observers can spot members of strong-identity companies in otherwise casual meetings. IBMers of old looked and thought alike. Old-line GE engineers were distinguishable from other engineers because of the technical and business savvy they exuded. McKinsey consultants stood out from consultants in other top-line firms because of their total presentation, an integral and consistent part of a uniquely confident self-image. P&G marketeers were identifiable as they trolled supermarket aisles checking on shelf-space allocations for theirs versus competitors' products. Digital Equipment's field personnel could be spotted because of the collegiate aura of their personal presentations. Most were recruited or trained in Boston, the ultimate American college town.

To build a culture with a consistent set of values and beliefs, rigid standards must define a profile for recruits. A cultural mold is needed that is close enough to qualify recruits for inclusion but flexible enough that new behaviors will emerge as circumstances shift. Recruiting people too different from the prevailing norm is a guaranteed recipe for disaster. By the same token, recruiting only clones will produce an organization without real vitality. Finding the right balance is the key. To do this, an explicit set of hiring policies and standards is needed, and these are essential in building or changing any culture.

In recent years, more attention has been focused on firings and layoffs than on recruiting people to fill job slots. But the same cultural rules apply in "reverse hiring"—choosing who should go—as in finding new hires. Unfortunately few downsizing efforts even consider important cultural undertones in separation decisions. Good companies hire and fire according to cultural models of what an ideal member should be. They invest enormous resources—mainly the time and attention of key members of management—in assuring these important decisions are sound. Weak or diffuse company cultures treat hiring (and firing) as routine matters, and pay the piper later on.

Aside from mass hirings and mass layoffs, the most critical company-wide decisions focus on filling top managerial posts. Searching for a new senior management post, those responsible often look for new blood and new skills, candidates who epitomize qualities lacking in the existing culture. Thus America Online recruits the executive vice president of Federal Express because the buttoned-down and seasoned Razzouk represents everything the chaotic and entrepreneurial AOL is not. He lasted four months, not because he did not have the know-how to solve the company's pressing problems but because his style was too foreign to AOL's free-form culture. By contrast, Chrysler went outside its own ranks—but stayed within the auto industry—when it recruited Lee Iacocca from Ford to be its new president. Controversial as his tenure was, at times, this outside hiring was a great success. The trick in looking for new blood, therefore, is finding the right balance between the old and the new.

## Rewarding the Right People

At any point in time, a company has hundreds of ways to reward people who perform above and beyond expectations. These range from an informal pat on the back to bonuses, unexpected "sabbaticals," or tuition for special career-enhancing training programs. Rewards also include special assignments and grants of trust—giving a person more responsibility. The only thing limiting the scope of rewards is the creativity of management.

For the most part, rewards provide recognition short of promotions. Offering job advancement is complicated, as promotions can seldom be reclaimed without a severe downside. Promotions therefore are limited to those projected to play a future leadership role. In contrast, other rewards are available to anyone who has done something that merits acknowledgment. They can be large or small depending on the contribution. Because their purpose is to convey recognition, they should almost always be celebrated outside the day-to-day grind.

In cultural terms, recognition should be reserved for behavior that exemplifies core values and beliefs. Other areas of performance warrant recognition as well, but many of these are of less cultural significance. For example, it is customary (and appropriate) to reward outstanding sales performance, whether or not selling is considered a core value. Even when effective selling is not a major cultural priority, it is still appropriate to reward superior salespeople. What is, sadly, often overlooked is reward for culturally important activities. For example, actions that serve simply to maintain cultural vitality should be recognized and rewarded. Employees who exemplify core values deserve such rewards if these values are to be reinforced. People whose actions signal possible new areas of cultural growth and expansion also warrant recognition. When risk-takers step outside of existing cultural boundaries and accomplish something that can serve as a model for others, they should be recognized. If they are not, the opposite signal is sent: Avoid this kind of behavior at all costs; it is not valued.

A third reason for rewarding unusual behavior is when it negates a particularly troublesome existing cultural norm. For example, some cultures have become competitive to a fault. Often this value is cherished as a universal modus operandi. But overt competitiveness, especially when focused inward, can be dysfunctional. To preserve the value of competition while blunting its potentially disruptive aspects, recognizing someone who chooses to serve the interests of a larger objective can send a moderating message to others, fostering cooperation and competition alike.

Recognition and rewards are meaningless unless widely publicized. Managers who use rewards to reinforce cultural values and beliefs must pay as much attention to how these rewards are communicated to others as to who receives the rewards. Rewards are strongly motivational to individuals. They are even more effective in signaling cultural priorities.

## Promoting the Right People

Of all the workplace rewards, promotions are most closely watched for the cultural messages they send. Deciding on which people to promote is one of the most difficult jobs for management. When cultural concerns are added to other important criteria, the decision becomes nearly impossible. But cultural considerations are always present, whether acknowledged or not, irrespective of whether the promotion is to a top management position or to a new clerical grade.

Think for a minute about the managerial considerations brought to bear on any given promotion. First, if the job is supervisory, the candidate should have reasonable qualifications suggesting he or she can supervise effectively. Of course the promotion decision is more complicated than just finding the best-qualified candidate. There may be others less qualified whose long-term future with the company looks very bright. Alternatively, the promotion may jump-start a fast-track career. Maybe a candidate with greater credentials seems right, but someone else deserves a chance to prove what he or she can do. Or consider another candidate who needs exposure to a broader set of work and managerial experiences. And what about the employee near the limits of his or her potential but who knows the ins and outs of a job as a result of years of faithful tenure? The mind boggles at the complexity of the issue.

Promoting the right way is a major managerial priority. Even though such decisions are made day in and day out, more often than not they are made poorly. Favoritism often decides which candidate will win the job. Arbitrary interventions are often made by people at the top who know nothing about relative merits of various candidates. Promotions are often allocated to someone viewed as having a future rather than someone who has immediate qualifications. Such issues and what they mean quickly become fodder for informal discussions and gossip.

Cultural criteria add a whole new set of dimensions to the problem of picking the right person for a particular job. Does candidate A fit with the existing culture, or would the appointment of candidate B send signals about desired changes? Would the appointment of an outside candidate signal an entirely new direction? If an outsider is appointed, would he or she receive the cold shoulder from others? Anyone charged with making promotion decisions can go mad weighing all the relevant issues.

In considering a promotion, finding a qualified candidate is a must. Promoting someone not qualified constitutes disaster for the promoted person and for those who will fall under the person's supervision. However, when cultural revitalization or change is a major consideration, the qualified person most likely to send the right cultural signals should always get the nod. Promotions are too important in the cultural life of a company to be made without taking into account the cultural agenda.

## Providing the Right (Monetary) Incentives

People everywhere go to work to earn money. Although they may work for other reasons, these pale in the face of an acceptable level of monetary rewards. There is a human resource expression describing compensation as the three Ms: me, mine, and more. Many otherwise thoughtful managers share the view that the IQ of an employee drops substantially when the issue of money comes up. Money counts, and it counts as much for the lowest-paid employee as it does for the outrageously overpaid CEO.

Deciding how to compensate people fairly is an extremely complex subject well beyond the scope of a book on corporate cultures. Some privileged companies riding the crest of superior stock market performance simplify the problem by being generous in distributing stock options. As stock market valuations soar, compensation ceases to be an immediate concern as large numbers of employees end up rich beyond their wildest expectations. The legion of Microsoft millionaires is strong testimony to the efficacy of being in the right place at the right time. For most other companies not so favored by the stock market boom of the 1990s, compensation remains an ongoing matter of concern.

The key cultural rule about compensation is fairness. Differences in compensation levels for people performing comparable kinds of work are divisive. Such differences may arise from setting pay according to education levels before taking into account previous work experience, age, or tenure in a given job. To anyone doing the same job, these discrepancies are hard to defend. Differences arising out of variable incentive terms like executive bonus and stock option plans are even more difficult for individuals to justify. Unless the compensation scheme's objective is to promote an ethic of "to the winner belongs the spoils," such plans are inevitably disruptive to cultural cohesion.

If differences in compensation levels are such a subversive factor at work, is there such a thing as a culturally sound method of distributing pay? The only culturally sound scheme is one in which all members of a fairly defined peer group are paid exactly the same. Of course the question of what constitutes a fairly defined peer group must be addressed. In some companies, it will be all people working at a particular grade level with the same performance rating. In others a peer group will be defined in terms of the people striving to achieve promotion to the next level. For example, McKinsey & Company has for years paid its associates and junior partners exactly the same amount depending on how many years the company thinks it will take them to reach the next rung on the firm's up-or-out ladder (which means the level of junior partner for all associates and senior partner for junior partners). The system works: There are complaints about overall compensation levels but no disputes about relative compensation levels within a group of peers. This arrangement is a significant factor in preserving the firm's strong culture.

Despite the continuing popularity of incentive compensation schemes to "motivate" people, differences between pay levels erect barriers between people. As such they are anathema to requirements for building a strong culture. Keep that in mind the next time you sit around a table trying to decide who gets how much for what.

## Organizing to Get the Most from People

Companies organize themselves structurally to accomplish different and often competing objectives. At the top, it is impossible for even the most energetic CEOs to "supervise," much less manage, all of an enterprise's diverse activities. Consequently, the enterprise is broken into logical parts; work responsibilities are assigned to various functions reporting to the CEO. The CEO is then free to focus on overall corporate policy and priorities. Is this arrangement proper? Whether or not, it's essential.

In deciding which groups of executives should report to the CEO, companies have applied a number of rationales. Far back in history, the predominant mode of organization was functional, grouping together under one person particular parts of the operation such as manufacturing, marketing and sales, research and development. The theory was to fill the function's top job with someone with substantial technical knowledge of the function. He or she could then best decide how the function should operate, thus ensuring functional excellence. Since lower levels of many companies are often organized along these lines, there is reason to believe this organizing rationale has some credibility. Unfortunately, a functional organization—especially in a large enterprise—makes it difficult to facilitate cross-functional communications and coordination. Important decisions have to flow to the top of the pyramid in order to be resolved. However useful functional organizational schema have been, they are being replaced with more decentralized models of organizations designed to speed necessary communications across functional boundaries.

The most common form of decentralized organization was the divisional structure first proposed by the legendary Alfred Sloan of General Motors. In this form, all functions needed to support a particular line of products were grouped together as though the divisional product lines were stand-alone businesses. At higher levels, various company businesses were brought together. Certain functions, finance and/or human resource management, were centralized at the corporate level. This allowed them to provide oversight and central policy guidance to activities spanning business units. This form of organization worked quite well for the most part. It is still one of the major structural forms in large organizations.

Problems arise in a decentralized structure when there are insufficient resources available in any particular division to do anything out of the ordinary, such as take products into markets outside of the company's home base. These problems were typically solved by applying Band-Aids—temporary solutions intended to address a particular shortcoming. The classic example was the creation of international departments or divisions to group foreign activities under one umbrella. Even when international operations were at their most powerful, these organizational arrangements were widely known as short-term solutions. For as soon as domestic divisions grew large enough, it made more sense for them to run their own international operations because of their superior product knowledge.

The importance of temporary organizations such as international divisions has been seriously underestimated in the literature on organization. In our view, temporary organizations are a major factor responsible for producing superior performance in companies with strong corporate cultures. No one is smart enough to figure out the absolutely optimum organizational structure for an organization at any point in time. Even if someone were, as time moved on circumstances would change and the once optimum structure would be obsolete. To overcome this inherent difficulty in organizing companies, smart companies have turned to temporary organizations.

A temporary organization by definition has a very well defined purpose; when it has served this purpose, it has no need or charter to hang around, and hence it disappears. Creating temporary structures to solve specific problems as they arise is far preferable to continually reorganizing to achieve the same goal.

Enterprises are organized to bring coherence to diverse activities. Whatever form is used, rules spring up around who can talk to whom under what circumstances, how activities are reported (or not reported) to higher levels, and what the limits of freedom are. Rules are necessary in running large enterprises; rigid, formal rules, however, stifle creativity and initiative. In a strong culture, there are rules as well, but these are typically softer and less explicit. Procedural manuals become unnecessary because the unwritten rules are sufficient to channel behavior in the right direction. As a result, strong cultures facilitate the launching of unfettered entrepreneurial ventures through temporary organizations. These are simply not available to companies with less cultural coherence in the ranks. This is one reason strong cultures have been able to produce demonstrably superior performance over the long term.

Let's look at one case. IBM in the early days of the personal computer revolution stood on the sidelines. When it decided to jump in, the company set up a temporary organization headed by a longtime IBM stalwart, Don Estridge. He reported to another long-term IBMer, Bill Lowe, in Boca Raton, Florida. Twelve months later, IBM entered the market with the IBM PC, which soon became the worldwide industry standard. Getting a new product to market in twelve months was unthinkable in the heavily bureaucratic and slow-moving environment of 1980s IBM. This group of dedicated IBMers was able to accomplish a miracle because at the end of the day they belonged to the wider culture (both subsequently held other high-ranking jobs in the company, which is exactly what they expected to do). Although IBM later made a hash of the PC business, it was able to accomplish the impossible because of the company's ability to create subunits within the IBM family.

In strong-culture companies, people are able to move across functional boundaries with relative ease. Shifting from one organizational unit to another within the company may involve a physical move on the part of the employee. It may even occasion considerable stress as the individual seeks to prove him- or herself to his or her new colleagues. But it seldom causes a great deal of spiritual disruption. In a strong-culture environment, these moves are all made under the same cultural canopy. In an organization, a not uncommon orientation ritual for a new transferee is a friendly grilling about the comings and goings of former members who moved on to other parts of the company. By establishing links with mutual friends and acquaintances, those receiving transferees welcome them to their new homes and make them comfortable with their new surroundings. The collective history and values of the culture ease such moves and help keep the organization functioning.

Today's battered company cultures are rarely in a position to facilitate the cross-organizational transfers that were once such a feature of life in strong-culture companies. (IBM used to be known humorously as the "I've Been Moved" Corporation.) At the extreme, a transfer from one unit to another that has been grafted onto the company by acquisition is like a transfer across cultural battle lines, a virtual exchange of prisoners of war. Both newcomers (from the acquiring culture) and old-timers (survivors from the acquired culture) are likely to feel isolated and ostracized. The natural human response is to transfer even more familiar faces from the acquiring company to help ease the burden of isolation acquirers feel in their new situations. This aggravates the cultural schism by further emphasizing the takeover's winners and losers. When this is accompanied by seemingly arbitrary layoffs to meet the merger's financial targets, the takeover pathology becomes complete and chances for cultural reconciliation are put on hold.

A manager seeking to rebuild cultural coherence should see transfers as a mechanism to achieve understanding between competing cultural groupings. Selecting to transfer people who may blend in and make friends is clearly a better path to rapprochement than sending in a combative employee with another worldview. Finding ways to offer career-enhancing transfers to members of an alienated subculture is way of both rebuilding confidence and building bridges across cultural lines. Unfortunately, in the rush for short-term results, such considerations are often lost. They are lessons a manager who wishes to revitalize a culture should rediscover.

Once a revitalized culture begins to show signs of coherence, vast new opportunities for exploration arise. The ability to form and dissolve organizational units quickly without recrimination is one of the healthiest features of a strong-culture company.

## Setting Performance Standards

Strong cultures tend to be more psychologically supportive to employees who fit and thus makes them happier in their jobs. But in the bottom-line-oriented business culture of today, is there anyone who really cares whether employees are happy or not? Not many who have made it to the ranks of senior management and want to stay there. Achieving truly superior performance over the long term is another thing altogether. Companies do whatever they can to inspire superior performance. Why not focus on culture? The question is how to achieve superior performance once a culture is robust enough to deliver it. One answer is to set tougher performance standards.

By "performance standards," we do not mean the usual financial targets companies establish to spur performance and monitor results. These are set by budgeting and planning processes and tend to have lives of their own. In strong-culture companies, these targets may well be higher and may be achieved with more regularity than in the run-of-the-mill corporations. People in cohesive cultures tend to be proud of their institutions and are more likely to treat goals as givens rather than the current wish list of senior management. Setting and attaining such goals is the stuff of day-to-day management. In our view, the key to achieving truly outstanding performance is asking, even insisting, that managers and employees take on challenges over and above their normal work responsibilities (which already include meeting high performance standards).

People who work in strong-culture environments feel part of an elite group. One characteristic of such an environment is that it does not admit new members without subjecting them to some sort of rite of passage. Once members earn their stripes, they feel proud of belonging. They therefore have every reason to want to maintain their status as members in good standing. When asked to take on special duties, they will almost always accept the challenge. And more often than not, they will rise to meet it.

Why should challenges not just be part of an employee's normal job? There are two reasons. The first is that they are probably already doing about all they can to maintain the high standards. If they are not, there is probably something very wrong with a company's normal target-setting processes. The second reason is more subtle: People who belong to elite cultures tend to have a high self-worth (probably higher than is realistically warranted). This high self-worth is there because the culture reminds them that there are few limits to what they can achieve. Strong cultures thrive on the accomplishments of members. They reinforce peoples' strength in the face of hostile external challenges. Feats of strong cultures are widely celebrated and shared as part of the sustaining mythology. Surrounded by so much positive reinforcement, someone confronted with a new challenge, however daunting, finds it hard to refuse the call. Although they don't always succeed, they do a high proportion of the time. The aggregate of these successes results in higher company performance. As a manager, if you don't ask, you will not receive. It is management's responsibility to set targets for employees that motivate them as a group to exceed all normal expectations.

Generally speaking, challenges that are most motivational to high-performance individuals who work in strong-culture environments are inspirational but lacking in detail. "Find us a way to make us the leader in ——" are words that stimulate highly motivated people. The notion of teamwork is even more motivating to members of strong cultural groupings. So "Set up a team to . . ." kindles even more energy than any set of individual assignments. People stand in line to become part of teams because they want to be an integral part of cultural success. They want to stand in the pantheon of well-remembered cultural heroes of prior generations.

People thrive on challenge. The attractiveness of most strong-culture environments is that they challenge members to reach for the stars. They also provide a safety net when people fail. The biggest tragedy of the modern era is the limited amount of time true human capability is used. Obviously, management should be alert to signs of burnout to protect individuals from their overenthusiasm. Equally, it is management's job to make sure that adequate levels of resources are allocated to special tasks. But aside from ensuring the health and welfare of workers, we believe it is the responsibility of management to challenge workers to produce the best they can.

This raises the question of how much extra effort management can realistically expect from a workforce in a cultural environment that is less than robust. The answer is not much, without incurring the wrath and ridicule of the employees. Employees in a culturally threatened environment have to spend time and energy on simple survival. They have little time and even less energy for the grandiose, out-of-touch plans of management. We watched the new CEO of a very large and at the time quite troubled company use his first major opportunity to speak to employees to extol the virtues and rewards of "high-wire performance" (the phrase was so odd in the context of this company at that time that it really stuck in our minds). That CEO, brought in because of his exemplary performance elsewhere, lasted less than a year. His demands were not believable in the context of everything else going on in the company. He was, in effect, laughed out. So beware: Only issue challenges appropriate to the circumstances at the time. This means being closely attuned to the health and coherence of the culture. But if you keep improving the culture and keep issuing challenges, in due course superior performance will result.

## Tracking Performance

Issuing a challenge and forgetting it is worse than not having the challenge at all. What is the point of being on a winning team if no one is keeping score? Employees in high-performance environments expect to be held to commitments they make. More to the point, they count on recognition for the extra effort they put out.

The best way to set performance challenges and monitor progress against their achievement is to do it face to face. A manager who expects employees to overachieve must be so visibly interested in their efforts that he or she is willing to commit whatever time it takes to track progress. This does not mean a manager must actually oversee the details of how a project is carried out. Quite the contrary: Too much hands-on management will get in the way of the assignment being carried through to successful completion. The manager must be sufficiently interested in progress to keep employees on task and on their toes.

Managers who take a personal interest in tracking progress can also play a material role in assuring success. By being intimately familiar with the progress of an impossible mission, the manager can identify resource constraints and take immediate steps to remove them. Such familiarity and attention can facilitate progress in other ways, such as putting teams at work on an assignment in touch with other groups working on similar problems. Visible interest confirms the importance of the assignment in the eyes of those working on it and encourages them to redouble their efforts.

The final responsibility of a manager who wants to create a high-performance company is to make sure that extra efforts are recognized. In the evolution of any difficult project, there are times when no publicity is desirable. There are other times when visible encouragement from peers can make the difference between success and failure. This can happen only if others know what is going on. The manager commissioning the assignment must ensure that recognition takes place at the right time. If a high performance ethic is to be sustained, it is very important that team members receive congratulations and rewards for their extraordinary efforts, during and after. If an assignment fails despite superhuman efforts, team members must be remotivated to accept challenging new responsibilities even though they previously fell short of the mark.

Citicorp was known for assigning individuals to the "penalty box" when they failed, then reassigning them to tough new roles within the organization. The key point is this: You get to leave the penalty box and rejoin the game once you've served your time. "Failure" ceases to be part of the lexicon when the consequence of failure despite best efforts to succeed is a smooth transition to new responsibilities.

High-performance organizations are fun to be part of. They are a joy to manage. They produce superior results time and time again. Being associated with a continuing stream of success brings out the best in people. They challenge themselves to their utmost to contribute to success. High-performance people in high-performance organizations gravitate to each other, producing unimaginable synergies by pooling their energies and talents. Creating a high-performance organization requires building a strong and cohesive culture supportive in every way of efforts required to produce exceptional results. Being part of a strong culture that yields superior performance is the best reward available to anyone who works.

## How Do Your People Policies Stack up Culturally?

If managing the people side of the equation is so important to building a strong culture into a company, assessing the effectiveness of people policies is one way to get a quick handle on how well you and your company stack up. For example,

- Can you write down on a sheet of paper in twenty words or less the unique characteristics of people who "belong" in your company's culture? If not, why not?
- How explicit are your recruiting standards? Are they always applied?
- How much senior management time goes into recruiting new members of your culture?
- When you are promoting people, do you apply the same standards you use in recruiting new people? If not, why not?
- How many promotions and rewards doled out in your company really reinforce cultural standards?
- How well do your pay policies work in reinforcing a common culture?

- Are your executive compensation plans consistent with what is required to build a shared sense of purpose in the company?
- How often do you move people around in the company? How easy do you find it to make such moves?
- Do you orchestrate career moves to achieve cultural objectives, such as binding different parts of the company closer together?
- How often do you really challenge your people to excel? How well do they respond?
- Do you have hands-on involvement in special projects?
- Do people who take on special projects receive appropriate rewards, short and long term?
- Do you keep score? Do your people know you do? How well do they respond?

No one company is going to bat 1.000 all the time against challenging questions like these. Equally, no truly high-performance company will be afraid to ask itself such hard questions. If you want to achieve truly superior performance, take the test yourself. And then do something about it.

# CHAPTER 13

# Rebuilding the Social Context of Work

Since the early 1980s, the average workplace has been stripped of most vestiges of cultural cohesion. Ordinary people once went to work happily. Work fulfilled their need to make a living. But it offered more: companionship, stimulation, and a few laughs. It provided a chance to participate in something bigger, to achieve, and to get ahead. It allowed people to feel good about being able to contribute.

Now work often offers no more than a routine job, and not a very secure one at that. Instead of finding companionship, community, and meaning, people compete for a diminishing number of secure positions. Instead of stimulation, today's jobs provide insurmountable challenges that remind people of their potential to fail and eventually to be discarded. Laughter has been replaced with intense, pessimistic conversations about unpleasant options. Rather than making people feel they belong, today's jobs are often exploitative. They seem designed to make the boss richer while extracting the maximum from individual workers, who break their backs for puny rewards. Survival has replaced achievement as a worthy goal in a perilous job marketplace. Instead of hopes for advancement, today's work environment offers cold calculations about who wins and who loses when promotions are announced. Feelings of contribution fall victim to demands for greater efforts just to retain a job. A paycheck is cherished since the next one may not come. All this sucks the joy and meaning from life at work.

Gordon Bethune, the chairman of Continental Airlines responsible for its remarkable turnaround, asserts:

> I could see Continental's biggest problem the second I walked in the door in February of 1994: This was a crummy place to work. The culture of Continental, after years of layoffs and wage freezes and wage cuts and broken promises, was one of backbiting, mistrust, fear and loathing. People, to put it mildly, were not happy to come to work. They were surly with customers, surly to each other, and ashamed of their company. And you can't have a good product without people who like coming to work. It just can't be done.

Yet Continental Airlines was not alone in creating such a defeatist work environment. Hundreds of companies around the world, most eagerly adopting the latest management fad or championing short-term results, have succeeded in reproducing the same toxic atmosphere. In the pursuit of shareholder value and wealth accrued from a steadily rising stock market, managers everywhere have forgotten a fundamental lesson: Nothing gets done without people. People in any organization create culture to give meaning to what they do, something bigger they can relate to and be proud of. Is it any wonder that cultures of most organizations today have crumbled into self-protective pockets, people held together in opposition to hostile surroundings? There's only one way out of this impasse. Go back to basics and rebuild a social environment that meets employees' needs and encourages them to reach out to reembrace a greater purpose.

We advocate the rehumanization of the workplace. The steps we outline may help, but they are incidental to the larger challenge: returning meaningful work to people. Only then will a sense of enabling purpose return, reinforcing the feeling that it's worthwhile to put in extra effort to achieve a shared goal. Our approach emphasizes paying more attention to culture, the softer side of business.

## Making People Want to Go to Work

Let's start with the basics: Why do people go to work in the first place?

## Pay

People work for a paycheck. The most compelling reason for working is to be able to maintain a comfortable life. Making people want to go to work begins, therefore, with providing a decent wage. But there's more to it. No matter what their level of responsibility in a company, employees bring their brains to work. They are smart about what is going on around them, especially those aspects of work that impinge on them directly. If people are paid less than others who carry out similar duties with no satisfactory explanation for the differences, they resent it. If they are paid less than people in other companies, they know it. If bonuses and raises are dispensed in an arbitrary and capricious way, it makes people angry. "Fair pay for a fair day's work" may sound like a union organizing slogan, but it also captures how people feel.

Just as people are smart about pay, they are also not stupid about conditions affecting their paychecks. If a company is performing poorly for reasons outside its control (e.g., old technology that needs an upgrade, low-cost imports undercutting market prices), people will understand why their wages are depressed. They may become impatient if nothing is being done to correct the situation, but they will usually go along with less-than-satisfactory wages while the company works its way through an understandable problem. But if a company is earning record profits and wages are not improving, people will be justifiably angry and resentful. And if soaring profits are producing record levels of executive compensation through stock options, employees can become downright hostile.

The only way a company can remove pay as a demotivating factor is to pay fair wages. If a company can afford high levels of total compensation (as has been the case with high-tech, start-up companies), other things being equal, employees will be ecstatic to come to work. Unfortunately, most companies today are not in such a favorable position, so they have to fall back on equity as the operating ethic behind their compensation programs. There is no avoiding the issue of fair pay. But a good wage is only the tip of the iceberg in reinforcing happy people who are highly motivated about their work: It is a necessary but not sufficient condition.

## Reasonable Levels of Job Security

The era of lifetime employment guarantees is a thing of the past. People today don't expect such guarantees. Few today would find any company that offered such guarantees credible. This shift in the business environment, however, does not mean job security is no longer an issue of concern to employees. Evidence of repeated downsizings aside, an employment system founded on total unpredictability is not a viable option.

People need some degree of job security because they plan their lives around assumptions related to continuing incomes. Mortgage commitments are made. Sons and daughters enroll in colleges expecting tuition to be covered as long as they make the grades. Family vacations are planned and tickets booked in advance. Medical checkups are scheduled as required to maintain good health. All of these personal commitments have to be paid for, one way or another. A sudden loss of income, unexpected and often undeserved, throws all these normal family arrangements into disarray.

Most people today would concede, however grudgingly, that the world is a more competitive place. Competitors enter markets with products at lower prices and other businesses suffer. Everyone who works for a struggling company likely acknowledges that something has to be done to stay afloat. If this involves layoffs, so be it: That is the business world of today. When layoffs follow layoffs, some carried out at periods when record profits are being earned, initial acceptance turns to resentment and feelings of being victimized. Such a reaction is normal. It is also a real human reaction as an atmosphere of continuing cutbacks creates turmoil in life outside work.

Most employers recognize this. The pressure for ever increasing quarterly earnings, however, assigns human concerns a far lower priority. This is simply bad management. It results in demoralized workforces. It impedes real efforts to improve productivity. And it destroys the social fabric of the lives of affected workers. Over enough time, it will destroy the very fabric and competitiveness of a company that employs such impersonal practices as a matter of course. All of that is common sense. The question is what can be done to change the situation.

There are no easy answers. But there are steps any employer can take to improve the situation. First, if downsizings are required because of changes in the firm's economic environment, do them right. Be open about the threat and the needed response. Be fair, scrupulously fair, in how the burden of the downsizing falls on individuals. And be as generous as the economic circumstances permit in easing the transition to new jobs and lives for displaced workers. Moreover, do it once and do it right. If necessary, cut more costs than are apparently needed immediately in order to guarantee survivors as much job security as possible.

For those remaining after such a onetime layoff, work hard to restore a sense of trust and maintain loyalty and commitment. At the extreme, if there are no workers left, there is no company either. For the workers unlikely to be let go, then, there is little downside risk to offering them a guarantee of employment for as long as the company survives. Realistically, in most large companies, this limited form of job tenure can apply to a large percentage of employees. But it doesn't apply unless an employer thinks it through and lets them know. If an employer has done the necessary homework, even junior employees, who should be the most likely to go if another downturn occurs, can be told the truth about exactly where they stand. Although the promise of a job for, say, two years is hardly enough to allow workers to feel secure, even such a limited guarantee can make a massive difference. All it takes on the part of an employer is a little foresight and a willingness to be fair to employees. Employers have created the problem of rampant job insecurity by their own actions; is it too much to ask that they now take steps to try to alleviate it?

## Job Content and Job Satisfaction

A third major factor motivating people at work is the satisfaction they derive from doing their jobs. Interview people who do not have enough to keep them busy during working hours and your eyes will be opened to the effect this has on satisfaction and motivation. Some people like routine and are uncomfortable if the status quo varies too much. Others prefer variety and get bored easily if they face the same situation day after day. Getting people into jobs to fit their personalities and preferences is one of the major challenges facing managers everywhere. But it is not the crux of producing job satisfaction.

The heart of the matter is putting people in jobs that use their talents to the fullest. Over the years, much ado has been made of job enrichment (and other popular phrases that mean roughly the same thing). But nothing enriches work more than asking people to bring all their faculties to the job and use the full range of their abilities in carrying out their assignments. The managerial dilemma is that there are only a given number of tasks that need to be done, and not all the people can be deployed in the most interesting ones. But any task can be made interesting if it is flexible enough so that individuals can exercise judgment and discretion. People find it hardest to accept having work dumbed down so they cannot use their skills to do it as best they can.

It amazes us that people seem astonished when productivity improves when people are asked to take on more responsibility. Take a production worker off the line where duties are limited to being another cog in the assembly line, assign him or her to production teams performing a variety of tasks, and watch productivity go up. Alternatively, take the same worker off the line and assign him or her to a quality team, and see how many ideas the team generates to improve the production process. There is no magic here; it's not rocket science. People perform better when asked to use their talents, including their brains.

Taylorism, so widely practiced around the world, reduces work to the simplest tasks and ignores the potential of individuals to do more. It virtually guarantees a lower level of productivity than what is possible if people are asked to utilize their full sets of skills. Think about installing a complex and capable machine tool in a factory and restricting it to performing the same repetitive chore again and again. We would never think of underutilizing an expensive tool; we do it all the time with human capital.

We are not advocating the redesign of every work task. There are much simpler ways to accomplish the same objective. The most powerful is decentralization of responsibility to a level as close as possible to people who do the work. This requires trusting employees and tolerating occasional failure. But it works: It makes jobs more interesting and motivates people to do their best. Of course decentralization works only if measurement systems are in place to assure that things are running smoothly. But these measurement systems need to measure outputs, rather than how "hard" an employee is working at a mind-numbing task.

True decentralization with appropriate monitoring not only increases productivity and effectiveness but also makes people happier. It allows people to take satisfaction from achieving success without always having someone looking over their shoulders. It helps engender the feeling that it's worthwhile to go to work. A happy workforce makes managers happier to come to work as well. When both managers and their employees enjoy coming to work, the likelihood of raising productivity levels goes up enormously.

## A Socially Rewarding Environment

People also go to work to have a good time—which is not meant to imply partying, laughing and joking, or having a universally pleasant experience. What constitutes a good time for some will not for others. A "good time" on the job is best defined by its opposite: No one wants to go home from work with the feeling of having had a miserable time unredeemed by anything positive.

People spend an enormous amount of their waking moments at work. Although family occupies a higher rung in a personal hierarchy, work enables families to thrive. Work takes precedence over family life because it intrudes on time employees spend at home. In fact the demands of work tend to define family time. Of even more importance, work tends to define the nonfamily personality of individuals because of the amount of time people are on the job. Many friends and acquaintances are made at work, and afterwork interaction with them can consume a large proportion of people's lives. If work is so important, how can the social environment be tailored to meet human expectations?

The first crucial element is respect: No normal person can find work to be socially rewarding if he or she is not valued. Respect in the workplace can be summed up as treating everyone as an intelligent human being. Different jobs command different degrees of status, the greatest deference afforded to those in the most senior positions. But no matter what their jobs, the people who fill them deserve respect. Receiving respect does not rule out getting critical input. People expect to be told when they do something wrong—or rewarded when they do something special. How else would they learn what was expected? Criticism and supervision need not imply a lack of respect.

Building respect is central to creating a work environment that fosters happy and productive employees. Good corporations place respect for individuals high on the list of corporate values. Articulating respect as a value is not enough; it must be confirmed in all aspects of daily behavior. This is the cornerstone of a socially attractive workplace.

Beyond respect, other social dimensions make a workplace attractive. Of these, the most important is a sense of fun and adventure. Countless studies have shown that people perform better when they have fun. When interactions with others are upbeat, people's sense of well-being is enhanced. This feeling encourages people to work harder and accept larger challenges. They leave work eager to return. Flying in the face of a desire to have fun at work is the widespread assumption that work is supposed to be serious. As Gary Geresi, senior vice president of an important division of Citibank, once said to one of us, "If they meant it to be fun, they would have spelled it *f-u-n*. They didn't. Instead, they spelled it *w-o-r-k*." We might have responded, "But, Gary, that's where the adventure comes in." But everyone was convulsed with laughter in this supposedly serious environment of work.

At work people expect to be challenged. If challenges are adequate, work becomes an adventure. Overcoming challenges begets personal satisfaction and becomes a cause for celebration. In Chapter 11, we spoke about the role management can play in bringing a sense of fun to the workplace. Paradoxically, one of the most important ways managers can encourage fun is to challenge individuals to do more than they think they can. Challenge without reward will not work. But work without challenge is spirit deadening. Managers who do not challenge employees to perform to their limits lose out in two ways: They miss the benefits of having the challenges surmounted, and they lose the chance to make the workplace engaging for employees.

One final aspect of life at work contributes to making it a socially rewarding environment. It has to do with fellowship at work. Most successful corporations look for distinctive traits in people they hire.

Although the result is often homogeneity, it helps make the workplace attractive to compatible people. As we have mentioned, Microsoft is renowned for hiring bright people. It is convinced that the corporation will win by having a disproportionate share of bright people on its payroll. In contrast, McDonald's used to hire compulsive individuals. Their natures led them to set and enforce high standards in an emerging fast food industry. Southwest Airlines insists on hiring people for attitude. Herb Kelleher, the airline's founder, is quoted as saying: "We look for attitudes; people with a sense of humor who don't take themselves too seriously. We'll train you on what it is you have to do, but the one thing Southwest cannot change in people is inherent attitudes." The result is that Southwest is a fun airline to fly and has one of the highest service ratings of any in the business.

Why are stringent hiring practices such an important part of building a socially attractive environment? People tend to get along better with people they can identify with. They tend to make friends more easily with like-minded people. They find it easier to resolve disputes, even when like-mindedness extends to a shared confrontational attitude (as it does in companies like Intel). They feel better being part of a team of people with similar values. Homogeneous hiring practices can be a two-edged sword. Too much homogeneity severs any company from the diversity of experience and perspective needed to succeed in a complex and competitive marketplace. But too little is a recipe for social awkwardness, making the workplace uncomfortable. Finding the right balance between similarity and incongruity is key.

### A Physically Comfortable Environment

The final important aspect of a workplace is that it be comfortable. Standards for what constitutes comfort can and do vary enormously. Companies like Intel and Hewlett-Packard espouse values that place a large premium on open-plan offices. Companies like Microsoft are so conscious of the thoughtful nature of their work that they insist on closable individual offices. Many manufacturing-oriented companies cultivate a style that makes workers feel close to the assembly-line activities (e.g., spartan office furnishings, linoleum-tiled halls). Despite what architects and design consultants say, there is no one right answer: What's right is what works for people in the particular context in which they operate.

If there is no one right answer, there are any number of practices that can make a workplace inviting. Most important is cleanliness, mundane as that might seem. No one wants to work in a pigsty. Routine cleaning of work areas is essential for creating an inviting atmosphere. Standards should extend from removing grease and spills from factory floors to removing used coffee cups from coffee stations and waste paper from copying and shredding machines. Physical upkeep of buildings, parking lots, employee cafeterias, and toilet facilities all contribute a sense of comfort. Failure to maintain housekeeping standards signals a degree of sloppiness likely to intrude into work practices.

Beyond simple sanitary criteria, providing space for informal interactions helps foster a socially friendly working environment. The real work of companies gets done around watercoolers, in kitchens equipped with coffee machines, in informal meeting rooms, or in locker rooms. Managers score big points when they make the common gathering places appealing. Nice spots encourage staff to congregate, exchange views informally, and form work-related friendships. Facilities for positive informal interaction will not transform a bad culture into a good one overnight. But attractive gathering places help create a working environment that makes people happy to come to work—a step in the right direction.

## Preparing to Live in a Globalized World

Modern communications and travel technology enable us, at the drop of a hat, to place calls around the globe at any time or arrange meetings anywhere. Millions of people have thereby had their world expanded and communicate regularly with colleagues and business partners around the globe. Some colleagues work in factories outsourced to lower-wage-cost countries; others work for suppliers located in the world's far-flung corners. Still others work for firms assembled from a variety of joint ventures and shared ownership schemes. With the liberalization of world capital markets and consequent international flow of investment funds, still others may well be your bosses. Since the 1970s, the business world has gone global to an extent never witnessed in recent recorded history. Failure to come to grips with this phenomenon will condemn any effort to rebuild the social context of work to the junkyard of outdated methods.

As discussed in Chapter 7, a more global economy has caused severe strains in company cultures. Despite increases in cross-border travel and communications, rapid globalization has caught people unprepared for confusing cross-cultural business dealings. Too often people fall back on prejudices and stereotypes about others. When people engage in stereotypical behavior, they typecast others in prewritten scripts: "I'm okay; you're weird." The result is poor communication, inadequate cooperation, and alienation. All of this dehumanizes the workplace, making it a place people want to avoid. Still, the movement toward global markets increases in both pace and scope. What can be done to better prepare people to cope in a world without borders?

The obvious answer is to learn more about foreign cultures and practices. Many countries around the world are already well advanced in such preparations. Young Europeans, for example, spurred by prospects of ever increasing integration across the Continent, are studying different languages and actively seeking out work experiences in foreign countries. Increasing numbers of young Asians are learning English as a second language. Young and old Asians are traveling to other parts of the world whenever possible. Although it is common for the Western world to make light of organized tour groups shepherding Asians from one destination to another, their interest in learning about the rest of the world should be admired. Only in the United States does parochialism still reign supreme. The vast majority of Americans are insular, even though globalization is forcing a reevaluation of their basic precepts. As a result, cross-cultural confrontation and misunderstanding dominate.

Why? Many U.S. corporations leading the globalization movement have failed to prepare their workforces for life in a boundaryless world. Some companies such as Gillette have clearly excelled, but most companies become aware of the need for a truly global presence too late. The result is tension, inadequate communications, and a breakdown in cooperation across cultural divides. This makes it nearly impossible to do business across national borders. Without successful commerce, there is little potential for a strong culture to emerge. Lack of preparation for global business activities also ignores potential synergies to be gained from understanding and using others' values, knowledge, or experience.

How should managers prepare companies for living in a global economy? It is incomprehensible that many companies still hire and promote young people without requiring them to learn foreign languages. It is even more nonsensical that young employees are not routinely given assignments in foreign countries. Living and working in another country is the best way to develop a sensitivity to cultural differences. Yet early rotation of staff into foreign assignments is the exception, not the rule. Too often companies wait until employees have proven themselves in a series of domestic assignments before shipping them to posts of relative responsibility in foreign settings.

Despite the literature on global management, the issue is not one of "controlling" foreign operations by making sure a domestic employee is in charge. Nor is the issue developing foreign staff and assimilating them into domestic operations. Both actions may be required on a short-term basis to overcome past failures. But these are only temporary measures to a long-term solution of building a global staff comfortable with working with people anywhere.

Given the gap that exists between this long-term ideal and the short-term reality, it is unrealistic to expect any company to transform its workforce overnight. But companies with a commitment to a sustained role in a global economy should start preparing young staff for what lies ahead twenty years and more.

Companies can do a lot to bridge the shortfall in universal understanding with their current workforces. Companies everywhere invest in training. How much is now devoted to understanding foreign cultures? Very little. Most companies reward employees with tuition reimbursement and direct pay supplements when they go to school, but how many companies reimburse employees for language courses when proficiency is not a current job requirement? How many companies staff temporary projects with a mix of international people as a way to help team members learn to deal with different cultures? There are hundreds of low-cost ways companies can advance the cause of globalization if they just have the will and foresight. Few companies today invest in such programs.

For a company truly to globalize operations, it must develop cosmopolitan attitudes. In doing so, a company can take strides toward making its work environment more human. Instead of rejecting foreign intrusions, a global staff welcomes other cultural influences because of the differing perspectives people bring. Instead of making foreign colleagues the butt of jokes, a globalized workforce views them as a source of learning and stimulation. Instead of isolating cultural strangers, a global workforce welcomes people and looks for new friendships as opportunities to expand limited horizons. Most companies have global aspirations. To realize potential benefits, they must make strides to prepare the way. With a concerted and long-term effort, a truly global culture can be instilled in a company. But the time to start is now.

## Building a Learning Environment at Work

In 1969, in the first edition of his landmark book, *The Age of Discontinuity*, Peter Drucker coined the phrase "the knowledge society." He set off a revolution in management thinking. It's an idea just now starting to bear fruit. As one indicator, in July 1998 Amazon.com, the online bookseller, listed ninety-five separate book titles that included the phrase "knowledge management" and 345 book titles with the phrase "information age," the more modern equivalent of "knowledge society."

Exactly what changes do these popular labels imply for a modern business? Does the dawn of the information age signal a new era in business practices? How will these changes affect the nature of work? Drucker's explanation suggests that in this new era "knowledge has become the central economic asset" determining business success or failure. As knowledge becomes increasingly important, can the role of people, as the carriers of knowledge, lag far behind? Again, according to Drucker, the new business knowledge will be more codified, anchored more solidly on scientific discoveries and less dependent on the experience of individuals. As a result, mechanisms designed to capture knowledge and systems to bring knowledge to bear on business problems will focus less on the role of individuals as carriers of this knowledge. Thus many companies are investing significant resources in developing systems to capture knowledge. We see this as the final attempt at Taylorism in the modern world: a last-gasp effort to put individuals in their places as cogs of an industrial machine.

The *Concise Oxford Dictionary* defines knowledge as "the sum of what is known to mankind." If this definition is taken at face value, knowledge management must be viewed as the mobilization of people to access and exploit the sum total of what they know. Accepting such a definition represents one of management's most liberating trends ever. People go to work thirsting for ways to use their full range of skills, including their intelligence and knowledge. People have always used time at work to learn since it is central to their self-image as thinking human beings. The disciples of Taylor, the guru whose ideas were so important to organizing twentieth-century industrial life, have struggled to sterilize business, eliminating messy human inputs. Could the dawn of the information era once and for all move people back to center stage as keepers of knowledge—the primary asset of business?

Any company that values employee knowledge will place a premium on people with good teamwork and communications skills. Protecting people for what they bring to the table will become a core value of forward-looking enterprises. Seeking people with a burning desire to learn will become the main goal for those who do the hiring. Encouraging people to share knowledge in a productive way will become a primary requirement for membership in a knowledge-based culture. Creating a stimulating learning environment where people can grow and thrive will become an overriding task of managers. Requirements of the information age to acquire, retain, and share knowledge can change the face of modern business. It can make the work environment particularly attractive because it values employees and capitalizes on their skills in the shared pursuit of business success.

Creating a knowledge-based business environment can also serve the selfish interests of twentieth-century employees. Whereas work was once seen as a source of security, with expectation of lifetime employment in return for diligent effort, modern employees have no such guarantees. Actions of management since the mid-1980s have removed job security as a credible promise. In response, most employees now look out for their personal welfare. Part of this selfish priority relishes any opportunity to acquire new skills and knowledge. The search is motivated less by company interests and more by how useful such skills will be in pursuing future job opportunities. Most modern employees are eager for knowledge that can aid them in pursuit of personal career goals. A corporation that sincerely values and supports the pursuit of knowledge is likely to be the most attractive employer for this generation of suspicious but self-motivated people.

True learning occurs when an individual is eager to explore. It occurs most readily in an environment that supports learning as a basic value. The needs of modern employees thus fit perfectly with the interests of a company pursuing the acquisition and exploitation of knowledge as a key to long-term business success. Many progressive companies have made the most of this overlap in needs and interests and have constructed a work environment allowing mutual interests to flourish. Microsoft seeks to hire only the brightest people available in the job market then works hard to make them feel at home. Companies as diverse as Motorola, Citicorp, and Procter & Gamble have adopted employment policies that guarantee employees access to training intended to develop a full range of capabilities. This guarantee is a fallback from traditional guarantees of job security but one in keeping with the uncertain business world of today. Few companies we know, however, make the acquisition and sharing of knowledge a core value of their cultural identity. Therein lies an unexploited potential of the information age.

A company that embraced knowledge as its main corporate asset would create a work environment that cherished people eager to acquire knowledge. Such a company would encourage people to learn and support them in the hard work and sometimes high risk of pursuing knowledge as an end. Such a company would encourage sharing—what good would the knowledge be if it were not shared with fellow employees? Such a company would reward individuals for developing their knowledge and expanding their capabilities. Such a company would encourage employees at all levels to express themselves and contribute ideas for the improvement of the prospects of the company. Such a company would work very hard to retain its core asset, its knowledgeable people, because it would see embodied in these people the basis of its future business success. Such a company would be a wonderful place to work, the kind of place every employee would be eager to return to day after day.

•    •    •

Business inevitably moves in cycles. We are optimistic enough to think that we may be nearing the end of a cycle emphasizing the short term over the long term and shareholders over all other valid claimants for their share of the corporate pie. As this troublesome cycle abates, management decisions will show more balance, shaking off some of the recent excesses. This rebalancing of business interests is needed to help restore some semblance of sanity to the workplace. Without a revival of the social side of work, long-term corporate and economic performance will suffer.

The developments in business since the mid-1980s have seriously undermined the human or social attractiveness of work. Actions carried to extremes by managers obsessed with improving stock market performance have alienated employees and driven them into protective pockets of self-interest unprecedented in modern times. In the most extreme cases, employees are left so disillusioned that they go to work reluctantly and only because they need a livelihood. Short-term-driven actions have fragmented traditionally strong corporate cultures and weakened their long-term performance potential.

The advent of the information age and the recognition that knowledge is a key corporate asset has created the potential for a workplace revival much more appealing to employees. Managers who recognize the potential of the new business culture can reverse the trends of the 1980s and 1990s. These managers can begin the process of redefining the workplace as a meaningful human environment with high potential for top productivity. They can help to make work an attractive place to be. They can recapture the spirit of employees and channel this energy into furthering the goals of the business. But they can do so only if they recognize the mutual dependencies of employees and employers and the need to create a cultural milieu that benefits all. Managers who accept this challenge will become the business leaders of tomorrow. The prize is there for the taking if anyone is bold enough to grab it.

# Notes

## Introduction

1   Much of the material contained in the Introduction is covered in greater depth in our first book, *Corporate Cultures: The Rites and Rituals of Corporate Life* (Addison-Wesley, 1982). We encourage readers interested in the subject to refresh their memories by returning to the earlier book.

1   The quote from Edgar Schein is taken from *Organizational Culture and Leadership* (Jossey-Bass, 1992), p. 5.

4   The quote from Collins and Porras's book *Built to Last* (HarperBusiness, 1994) appears on p. 16.

7   The quote about storytelling comes from Richard Stone's fine book *The Healing Art of Storytelling* (Hyperion Press, 1996), p. 4.

8   Southwest Airlines' various modes of celebration are covered in Kevin Freiberg and Jackie Freiberg, *Nuts!* (Bard Press, 1996).

## Chapter 1

21   To begin this chapter, we extracted some information from our previous book, *Corporate Cultures* (Addison-Wesley, 1982).

22   The quotes from Starbucks CEO Howard Schultz are from his book with Dori Jones Yang, *Put Your Heart into It: How Starbucks Built a Company One Cup at a Time* (Hyperion Press, 1997), pp. 7–8.

22   Gordon Bethune's remark about the people aspects of running a business is from his book with Scott Huler, *From Worst to First* (John Wiley & Sons, 1998), pp. 128–129.

22   The quote from Herb Kelleher and Colleen Barrett was taken from the Kevin Freiberg and Jackie Freiberg, *Nuts!* (Bard Press, 1996), p. 145. The subsequent quote from the Freibergs appears on p. 144 of their book.

22   The quote about the Marine Corps comes from Thomas E. Ricks, *Making the Corps* (Scribner, 1997), p. 161.
24   One of the two major books published since 1982 that looks at the issue of culture and performance is John Kotter and James Heskett's *Corporate Culture and Performance* (Free Press, 1992). We drew extensively from Kotter and Heskett's findings in putting together this chapter.
25   The second major book on culture and performance is James Collins and Jerry Porras's *Built to Last* (HarperBusiness, 1994). We relied heavily on Collins and Porras's volume in writing this chapter.

## Chapter 2

43   The background material on Jamie Uys's remarkable film *The Gods Must Be Crazy,* which we first saw in the mid-1980s, was taken from a review of the movie written by Daniel Leary, downloaded from the Website http://www.infonet.runet.edu/. There are over 700 Websites that comment on some aspect of this film; for those who haven't seen it, we urge them to rent the video.
44   There is a vast literature on the theory and practice of shareholder value. The book considered the bible on the subject is Alfred Rappaport, *Creating Shareholder Value* (Free Press, 1986). Rappaport was a prolific publisher of articles as well as books. Two we referenced in preparing this text are "Strategic Analysis for More Profitable Acquisitions" *(Harvard Business Review,* July-August 1979) and "Executive Incentives vs. Corporate Growth" *(Harvard Business Review,* July-August 1978). Rappaport also reprinted one of the landmark articles in the field, Ezra Solomon's "Return on Investment: The Relation of Book-Yield to True Yield," originally published in *Research in Accounting Measurement* (1966) and reprinted in Rappaport's book *Information for Decision Making* (Prentice Hall, 1979). Although we confess we weren't following the relevant literature back in the 1960s, if Rappaport is currently regarded as the guru of shareholder value thinking, Solomon must surely be viewed as its father.
44   Throughout this book we quote from the written legacy of Peter Drucker, the most respected and prolific writer on management topics of all time. Aside from having clear ideas well before others latch onto them, Drucker is marvelous in his ability to retain and subsequently use relevant quotes from times gone by. In this chapter, we borrow from Drucker a quote by Ralph Cordiner of GE. This particular quote was contained in Drucker's article "Reckoning with the Pension Fund Revolution" *(Harvard Business Review,* March-April

1991). Later in the chapter, in our section on the dominance of equity markets by institutional investors, we mention that Drucker had anticipated this trend in his book *The Unseen Revolution* (Harper-Collins, 1976).

44     Another book we refer to several times is David Packard's landmark *The HP Way* (HarperBusiness, 1995). In this chapter, our reference is to Packard's amazement that his view that corporations serve multiple constituencies was not shared by other managers at a conference he attended in the late 1940s; this quote is taken from p. 166 of the book.

46     Marvin Bower, the man who built McKinsey into the institution it became, has written two books on management that deserve a wider reading than they appear to have received. The first of these is *The Will to Manage* (McGraw-Hill, 1966); the second book is *The Will to Lead* (Harvard Business School Press, 1997).

46     Most of the background material on LBOs and the rise of KKR was taken from Sarah Bartlett's fine (but hard-to-find) book *Money Machine* (Warner Books, 1991). We also reviewed a number of press clippings from the *Wall Street Journal* associated with some of KKR's more famous deals.

49     The quote about managers who want protection in their jobs was taken from Michael Jensen's article "Takeovers: Folklore and Science" *(Harvard Business Review,* November-December 1984), which won the McKinsey Award as the best *Harvard Business Review* article of 1984.

49     Our exploration of the origins of executive compensation practices began with an article by Malcolm Salter, "Tailor Incentive Compensation to Strategy" *(Harvard Business Review,* March-April 1973). As the momentum shifted more toward shareholder value, we studied Rappaport's "Executive Incentives vs. Corporate Growth," cited above. After critics began to question the wisdom of these shifts, our attention turned to a piece by Alfie Kohn, "Why Incentive Plans Cannot Work" *(Harvard Business Review,* September-October 1993).

50     To get behind the executive pay debate, we focused first on an article by Kevin Murphy, "Top Executives Are Worth Every Nickel They Get" *(Harvard Business Review,* March-April 1986). Updating the data beyond the mid-1980s proved to be more difficult than we had imagined. Eventually we went to that most dependable of sources, *Business Week,* whose annual survey of executive pay trends, published around April or May of each year, proved invaluable. Many of the key articles in this series have been written by John Byrnes, a business journalist for whom our regard grows year after year. Some of

his most important articles on the subject include "Executive Pay: The Party Ain't Over Yet" *(Business Week,* April 26, 1993) and "How CEO Paychecks Got So Unreal" *(Business Week,* November 18, 1991). To get a picture of Wall Street pay levels, we turned to an article by Steven Taub, David Carey, and Joseph Epstein, "The Wall Street 100: Compensation Way Down in 1994 for Wall Street's Highest Earners" *(Financial World,* July 4, 1995).

50    Stock market quotes throughout the book were taken from the Dow Jones stock quotation service.

50    The data we presented about the well-documented increase in institutional ownership of equities and mutual fund churn was first displayed to us in Michael Useem's fine book *Investor Capitalism* (Basic Books, 1996). The information about the flow of new money into equity funds we downloaded from the Investment Company Institute's Website, http://www.ici.org/. The quote from Boone Pickens was taken from his article "Professions of a Short-Termer" *(Harvard Business Review,* May-June 1986). The long quote from *Business Week* is from an article by Edson Spencer, "The U.S. Should Stop Playing Poker with Its Future" (November 17, 1986).

55    Our comment on overall pay levels was downloaded from the AFL-CIO Website, http://www.aflcio.org/.

55    The takeover bid for Gillette is beautifully chronicled in Gordon McKibben's Cutting Edge (Harvard Business School Press, 1998). This book is an excellent chronicle of the building of a multinational enterprise and is must reading for any student in this field.

60    We adapted the material about IBM's ill-fated attempts to wrest control of PC operating system technology from Microsoft from Paul Carroll's *Big Blues* (Crown Publishers, 1993).

## Chapter 3

63    The section describing the evolution of cost-cutting practices is based on firsthand experience with and use of most of the techniques chronicled. For details on any particular approach, please refer to the sources mentioned in the text. The main books cited on various of the techniques are Harvey M. Wagner, *The Principles of Operations Research, with Applications to Managerial Decisions* (Prentice Hall, 1969); John Neuman, "Overhead Value Analysis" *(Harvard Business Review,* May-June 1975); Joe Juran and Frank Gryna, *Quality Planning and Analysis: From Product Development Through Usage* (McGraw-Hill, 1970); Philip B. Crosby, *Quality Is Free: The Art of Making Quality Certain* (McGraw-Hill, 1978); W. Edward Deming,

*Quality, Productivity and Competitive Position* (Massachusetts Institute of Technology Center for Advanced Engineering Study, 1982); Wickham Skinner, "The Productivity Paradox" (*Harvard Business Review,* July-August 1986); Bob Tomasko, *Downsizing: Reshaping the Corporation for the Future* (AMACOM, 1990); Thomas Davenport and James Short, "The New Industrial Engineering: Information Technology and Business Process Redesign" (*Sloan Management Review,* Summer 1990); Mike Hammer and James Champy, "Re-engineer Work: Don't Automate, Obliterate" (*Harvard Business Review,* July-August 1990); and Mike Hammer and James Champy, *Reengineering the Corporation* (HarperBusiness, 1994). Most followers of modern business practices will already be familiar with these classics.

66    We gathered most of the data on corporate layoffs from reports in the business press, including the *Wall Street Journal, Business Week, Forbes,* and the *Financial Times.* Data on executive pay levels in relation to major announced downsizing programs are from the business press as well. Specific dates for each particular are included in the text. In this section we also used excerpts from the American Management Association's surveys on downsizing trends, which have been conducted yearly since 1988.

66    In the section assessing reengineering, we drew some material from James Champy's book *Reengineering Management* (HarperCollins, 1994). But the bulk of the material in this section came from our own experience on the periphery of a number of major reengineering projects. The analysis of the effectiveness of reengineering projects in achieving their goals was taken from an unpublished working paper by Nitin Nohria and Geoffrey Love, "Adaptive or Disruptive: When Does Downsizing Pay in Large Industrial Corporations?" (Harvard Business School, Division of Research, 1996) and an interview with Geoffrey Love.

69    Data on the statistical impact of job reductions were taken from various reports widely available from the Bureau of Labor Statistics. We also used some data from the Economic Policy Institute's report by Jared Bernstein, John Schmitt, and Lawrence Mishel, *The State of Working America, 1996–97* (Economic Policy Institute, 1997).

78    Our look at the qualitative effects of downsizing on individuals was helped immeasurably by a superb article by Bruce Butterfield in the *Boston Globe* (October 10, 1993). We also used the article "Downward Mobility" by Bruce Nussbaum, Ann Therese Palmer, and Alice Z. Cuneo (*Business Week,* March 23, 1992). Finally, we included a brief excerpt from Juliet Brudney and Hilda Scott's *Forced Out* (Simon & Schuster, 1987); pp. 130 and 170.

80    The quotes from people laid off by AT&T appeared in Barbara Rudolph's book *Disconnected* (Free Press, 1998), pp. 40–41 and 123.

85    We quoted James Challenger of Challenger, Gray & Christmas on the loss of corporate memory resulting from corporate downsizings; see his "Risk of Corporate Alzheimer's" (Bank Personnel News, April 1996). The quotes from Karen Stephenson on a related topic are from Zurich Insurance Group, Internal Communications Focus, no. 36 (1995); the articles were downloaded from the web site www.net form-stephenson.com/html/articles_icf.html.

## Chapter 4

89    Our copy of Adam Smith's much-read classic *The Wealth of Nations* is the University of Chicago Press paperback edition published in 1976. The pin-manufacturing example is in chapter 1, p. 8.

90    The quotation from the *New York Times* columnist was taken from Mike Johnson, *Outsourcing . . . in Brief* (Butterworth-Heinemann, 1997).

90    The material on the background of the ADP company is derived from conversations we had with executives of the company.

91    We employed some data on the extent to which individual firms, ranging from Apple Computer to Chrysler Corporation, relied on outside suppliers for component parts of their products. These data were taken from several sources, including James Brian Quinn and Fred Hilmer, "Strategic Outsourcing" (*Sloan Management Review,* Fall 1994) and Cara Trager, "Takeout Health Care: Hospital Food Service Takes Corporate Turn" (*Crain's New York Business,* October 27, 1997).

92    The rationale for outsourcing based on a concentration of core competencies was launched by two articles. The first of these was James Brian Quinn, Thomas L. Doorley, and Penny C. Paquette, "Beyond Products: Services-Based Strategy" (*Harvard Business Review,* March-April 1990). The second was the classic by C. Prahalad and Gary K. Hamel, "The Core Competence of the Corporation" (*Harvard Business Review,* May-June 1990).

93    We cited a number of journalistic sources for information on how companies had taken the lessons of Hamel and others to heart. Chief among these were the *Economist* (September 20, 1997, p. 69), *Business Week* (May 13, 1996, p. 24; July 17, 1995, p. 60; September 25, 1995, p. 130; and June 10, 1996, p. 42), and the *Financial Times* (January 6, 1995). The reference to the outsourcing of strategic plan-

ning activities was taken from Hugh Courtney, Jane Kirkland, and Patrick Viguerie, "Strategy Under Uncertainty" (*Harvard Business Review,* November-December 1997).

94    As noted in the text, it is extremely hard to pin down with any accuracy the size and scope of the outsourcing "industry" today. As best we could, we relied on a variety of sources for bits and pieces of the relevant data. These included the *Conference Board,* which publishes any number of surveys related to the topic; *Outsourcing Institute,* which should be the definitive source but whose secrets we had difficulty penetrating; and the *Journal of Commerce,* which supplies a lot of good data on a variety of subjects. Detailed references are included in the text passages. We also consulted the regular business press, of which *Business Week* once again proved to be the most fruitful source.

95    The *Monthly Labor Review* of the U.S. Department of Commerce published a major report in October 1996 titled, "Workers in Alternative Employment Arrangements." We made extensive use of the data in this report in our exposition of the effects of outsourcing on the labor market.

96    Joseph Sponholz, the outspoken executive vice president of Chase Bank put it all into perspective in his comments reported in Frederick Gabriel's article "Chemical Chase Looks to Farm Out Operations; Mega-banks Weigh Savings" (*Crain's New York Business,* February 12, 1996).

97    The quotation related to Wall Street's reaction to focus was taken from "Separate and Lift" (*Economist,* September 20, 1997).

98    Our description of the serendipity for IT workers whose companies want to downsize them but immediately hire them back was based on a series of confidential conversations we had with friends directly involved in the situation described.

99    The situations in the pulp mill in Canada that resulted from wholesale outsourcing were described to a colleague of ours, on a confidential basis, by someone who worked in the mill.

100   The material for the case study of outsourcing in the UK public sector was drawn mostly from firsthand experience with the program. We supplemented this knowledge with data from the report *Competing for Quality Policy Review* (Her Majesty's Stationery Office, 1996).

104   The material we used describing the life of a temp was extracted from a superb article by Jackie Krasas Rogers, "Just a Temp: Experience and Structure of Alienation in Temporary Clerical Employment" (*Human Resource Management Journal,* May 1995).

## Chapter 5

115    We took the reference to Michael Porter's analysis of acquisitions from Dwight L. Gertz and João P. A. Baptista, *Grow To Be Great* (Free Press, 1995), p. 35; we were unable to find the original Porter analysis cited in this book, however. The closest approximation we could find was a class note, "Note on Diversification as a Strategy," written in 1982 by Porter and Malcolm S. Salter and available from HBS Case Services of the Harvard Business School; this note, at a minimum, summarizes the available literature at that time on the performance of diversified companies.

115    The comments about the failure of many acquisition deals to earn back their cost of capital were taken from Leslie Norton, "Merger Mayhem" (*Barron's,* April 20, 1998, p. 33). The McKinsey study referred to in this article was published in Tom Copeland, Tim Koller, and Jack Marvin, *Valuation: Measuring and Managing the Value of Companies* (John Wiley & Sons, 1994).

119    The increase in the market valuation of Travelers and Citicorp and the value of the stock holdings of Sandy Weill and John Reed were broadcast by CNBC on April 9, 1998, and reported widely by various members of the business press.

120    The comments by Weill and Reed and others in relation to their planned merger were part of a press release about the planned merger we downloaded from Citicorp's corporate Website (http://www.citibank.com). Similarly, the comments about the planned Nations Bank–BankAmerica merger were taken from their press release about the deal, downloaded from BankAmerica's Website (http://www.bankamerica.com).

122    The quotations about the effect of mergers on individuals were taken from the Louis Uchitelle and N. R. Kleinfield article reprinted in *The Downsizing of America* (Times Books, 1996), p. 28. This book was also the source of some of the information we used in describing the Chemical Bank–Chase Manhattan merger, supplemented by conversations with managers personally involved in the process.

125    We downloaded details about the SBC takeover of PacTel from http://www.amcity.com/sanfrancisco/stories/040698/story4/ (and related sites). The material was taken from a series of stories written by Steve Ginsberg and Lorna Fernandes for the *San Francisco Business Times* (April 1998).

126    Several quotations in the chapter are about particulars of deals. The ones about the Dean Witter–Morgan Stanley combination came from Allan Sloan, "Will Morgan Stanley's Merger Work? The Praying

Mantis May Hold a Clue," *Washington Post* (February 11, 1997). The James Barksdale quote was taken from Marcia Ludwig, "McCaw's Culture Predicted to Survive AT&T Takeover," *Valley Daily News* (September 20, 1994). The material about Lotus and IBM was taken from Stephanie Armour, "Merger Melting Pot," *USA Today* (March 26, 1998).

## Chapter 6

131  We downloaded information about the history of the development of the microcomputer from the site http://www.mcsi.memphis.edu/~ryburnp/comp1200/history/microhist.html/ to refresh our memories about the timing of key events.

132  Data on the use of computers were taken from a part of the U.S. Bureau of the Census "Current Population Survey" that was discontinued in the mid-1990s. The relative use of computers by age, education level, and race was taken from the U.S. Department of Education, National Center for Education Statistics, *Digest of Education Statistics* (National Center for Education Statistics, 1994); these data are available online at http://www.nces.ed.gov/pubs/. The information about the penetration of home computers by income level was downloaded from the *Computer Intelligence* site, http://www.ci.infobeads.com/, which contained a March 10, 1998, article "Home PC Penetration Soars in the U.S."

137  The background and quotes related to the evolution of blue-collar work practices were taken from Harry Braverman's classic *Labor and Monopoly Capital* (Monthly Review Press, 1974). The specific quotes from Frederick Taylor were taken from pp. 112–120; according to Braverman, the original quotes were extracted from a one-volume compilation of Taylor's ideas published in 1947 under the title *Scientific Management*. We also used Braverman's book for statistics on the early evolution of white-collar work (pp. 295 and 296).

139  The data used in our analysis of capital investment and productivity trends in the banking industry come from Richard H. Franke, "Technological Revolution and Productivity Decline: Computer Introduction in the Financial Industry" (*Technological Forecasting and Social Change* 31 [1987]).

141  We drew heavily from Shoshana Zuboff's book *In the Age of the Smart Machine: The Future of Work and Power* (Basic Books, 1988). The specific quotations were taken from pp. 136 and 215.

143  The material about the insurance company workers in Canada comes from Heather Menzies, *Whose Brave New World? The Information*

*Highway and the New Economy* (Between the Lines Press, 1996), pp. 63 and 64.

144    The survey on the relative uses of computers by clerical workers and managers was reported in Rob Kling, Suzanne Iacono, and Joey George, "Occupational Power, Patterns of Desktop Computer Use and Quality of Worklife," in K. M. Kaiser and H. J. Oppelland, eds., *Desktop Information Technology* (Elsevier Science, 1990).

144    We extracted data on the relative use of e-mail technology by clerical workers and managers from Ronald E. Rice and Douglas E. Shook, "Relationship of Job Categories and Organizational Levels to Use of Communications Channels, Including Electronic Mail: A Meta-Analysis and Extension" (*Journal of Management Studies* 27, 2 [March 1990]).

## Chapter 7

149    The two quotations we used at the start of this chapter, by Angell and Friedman, were brought together in a wonderful article by Peter Beinart, "An Illusion for Our Time" (*New Republic*, October 20, 1997).

150    The data on trade as a percentage of GDP are from Dani Rodrik, *Has Globalization Gone Too Far?* (Institute for International Economics, 1997), p. 7. Rodrik took the original information from a discussion paper, "Globalization Myths: Some Historical Reflections on Integration, Industrialization, and Growth in the World Economy," prepared by Paul Bairoch and Richard Kozul-Wright for a United Nations conference on trade and development in 1996.

152    The hardships of life in Nigeria during a revolution were recounted to the authors directly by the protagonist.

152    Data on phone calls and overseas trips were downloaded from the online version of the U.S. Statistical Abstract at http://www.blue.census.gov/prod/www/abs/.

152    The information on the decline in the real cost of international travel was taken from William B. Johnston's article "Global Workforce 2000: The Globalization of Labor" (*Harvard Business Review*, March-April 1991).

155    The data on the shift in makeup of Motorola's workforce was taken from William Greider, *One World Ready or Not* (Touchstone, 1997), p. 91. Wage rates for making toys in China appear on p. 345 of Greider's book.

155    General Electric's employment status in Singapore was taken from Robert B. Reich's article "Who Is Us?" (*Harvard Business Review*,

January-February 1990). We also used this article as the source for information on the makeup of the U.S.-Taiwan trade gap.

155    The information on AT&T's transfer of jobs to factories in Mexico was taken from Aaron Bernstein's article with Wally Konrad and Lois Therrien, "The Global Economy: Who Gets Hurt" *(Business Week,* August 10, 1992). This article also contained the information we quoted on declining wage rates of high school dropouts in the United States.

155    We found information on the wage rates earned by Indonesian workers at Nike factories, originally published in a survey by *Indonesia Today,* in Richard Barnet and John Cavanagh, *Global Dreams* (Touchstone, 1994), p. 326. Information on the percentages of various U.S. industries owned by foreign investors appeared on p. 54. We also took the story about cultural miscommunication in Bertelsmann from this book.

156    The information on investment flows into and out of the United States is from U.S. Department of Commerce, Bureau of Economic Analysis, *Survey of Current Business* (September 1996).

158    The wonderful quote on the multinational diversity of day-to-day life was taken from Norman Glickman and Douglas Woodward, *The New Competitors: How Foreign Investors Are Changing the U.S. Economy* (Basic Books, 1989). This book was also the source of a number of statistics on relative wage rates and illustrations of labor strife attendant on foreign ownership of U.S. plants.

159    The astounding figure of 73 million workers who are employed by foreign bosses occurs in Robert Z. Lawrence, *Single World, Divided Nations?* (Brookings Institute Press, OECD Development Centre, 1996), p. 91.

159    The survey of executive attitudes and beliefs was taken from Rosabeth Moss Kanter's article "Transcending Business Boundaries: How 12,000 World Managers View Change" *(Harvard Business Review,* May-June 1991).

161    The two quotes from the American managers in Germany are from Andrew Martinez, "Corporate Cultures Can Be Shocking," *(Pittsburgh Post Gazette,* September 3, 1995).

163    The two classics about American business overseas are William J. Lederer and Eugene Burdick, *The Ugly American* (Norton, 1958) and Jean Jacques Servan Schreiber, *The American Challenge* (Avon, 1968).

167    The material on Gillette's executive development activities was taken from Gordon McKibben's *Cutting Edge* (Harvard Business School Press, 1998).

168 The quotation at the end of the chapter was taken from one of the best articles we have read on global business in a long time: C. K. Prahalad and Kenneth Lieberthal, "The End of Corporate Imperialism" (*Harvard Business Review,* July-August 1998).

## Chapter 8

175 Background material for the example of British Telecom's transformation was drawn primarily from firsthand experience with the company. This was supplemented by data from a research report of the Communications Workers Union, "British Telecom: Staffing Problems and Processes" (August 12, 1997). We also referred to the British Telecom publication "BT Awards for Quality: Award Winners 1997."

182 The case material and quotations about the turnaround of Continental Airlines appeared in Gordon Bethune's *From Worst to First* (John Wiley & Sons, 1998). This is one of the best and most honest books on management we have read in the 1990s.

186 The Eastman Kodak story is chronicled in Stephen J. Frangos, *Team Zebra* (John Wiley & Sons, 1993).

## Chapter 9

191 Historical information on the New York Mets was downloaded from the Mets' Website, http://www.icu.com/mets/HISTORY/1973.html/, to supplement our own fond memories of that memorable baseball season.

192 The material on the core ideologies of companies was taken with some license from James Collins and Jerry Porras, *Built to Last* (HarperBusiness, 1994).

193 The description and articulation of the "HP way" was drawn from the book of that name by David Packard (HarperBusiness, 1995).

198 The material about Southwest Airlines was taken from Kevin Freiberg and Jackie Freiberg, *Nuts!* (Bard Press, 1996).

200 Motorola's credo and personnel practices are described in the company's Website, http://www.mot.com/; we also interviewed former managers in the company.

210 The historical material on IBM, including the quote about Gerstner's behavior as CEO of American Express before he moved to IBM, was taken from Paul Carroll's *Big Blues* (Crown Publishers, 1993).

210 For material on Intel, we turned to Tim Jackson, *Inside Intel* (Dutton Books, 1997).

# Chapter 10

217 Kilmann and Saxton's survey is described in R. H. Kilmann and M. J. Saxton, *The Kilmann Saxton Culture Gap Survey* (Organizational Design Consultants, 1983).

218 The material about the techniques Karen Stephenson has developed for mapping cultural communications patterns is contained in Tim Ferguson's article "Who's Mentoring Whom?" (*Forbes,* May 19, 1997).

222 We observed firsthand Frank Zenie's culturally correct solution to the problem with Waters Associates R&D activities.

227 The "odd couple" quote we overheard in the course of a confidential consulting assignment for a major telecommunications company.

228 The Delta Corporation example was taken from Harrison Owen's *Spirit: Transformation and Development in Organizations* (Abbott Publishing, 1987). Specific material quoted was taken from pp. 172–174.

# Chapter 11

233 The quotation about fun with which we begin the chapter was taken from Stephen J. Frangos, *Team Zebra* (John Wiley & Sons, 1993).

235 The anecdotes about the nature of capital goods companies and the story about the comments made in meetings were taken from our own experience in confidential consulting assignments.

237 A longtime employee of the Xerox Corporation told us the story about Joe Wilson.

237 The material about America Online was taken from the book by Kara Swisher, *Aol.com* (Random House, 1998).

239 The anecdotes about the professional services firm were derived from firsthand experience in confidential assignments with the company.

244 The information about Citibank's traditional Christmas parties was derived from consulting assignments with that fine institution.

244 The material on play in large companies was derived from a long-standing playful and participative relationship on the part of the authors.

# Chapter 12

252 The material on Microsoft's approach to recruitment was taken from Randall Stross, *The Microsoft Way* (Addison-Wesley, 1996).

253   The experience of Bill Razzouk at America Online was described in Kara Swisher, *Aol.com* (Random House, 1998).

260   The background on IBM's entry into the personal computer business was drawn from Paul Carroll's *Big Blues* (Crown Publishers, 1993).

263   Useful perspective on coaxing high performance out of teams can be gained from Jon Katzenbach and Douglas Smith, *The Wisdom of Teams* (Harvard Business School Press, 1993).

## Chapter 13

268   Quotations from Gordon Bethune were taken from his book with Scott Huler, *From Worst to First* (John Wiley & Sons, 1998).

274   The quotation from Gary Geresi was taken from firsthand experience consulting with Citibank.

275   Herb Kelleher's remark appears in Kevin Freiberg and Jackie Freiberg, *Nuts!* (Bard Press, 1996), p. 67.

279   The material from Peter Drucker was taken from his book *The Age of Discontinuity* (Transaction Publishers, 1994; originally published in 1983).

# Permissions
# Acknowledgments

# Index